What People Are Say[ing]
Human Moment[s]

"Ned Hallowell has written a breakthrough approach to how to deal with the pressures and complexities of life by identifying and learning from the special 'human moments' that we experience in our daily lives. *Human Moments*' moving stories, including the author's own account of his troubled childhood, is a unique 'how-to' for a life of friendship and fulfillment."

—Jack Canfield
coauthor, *Chicken Soup for the Soul* series

"It is impossible to read *Human Moments* and not be touched over and over by the power of these stories.

"Dr. Edward Hallowell believes that love and connection are what make us truly human.

"In his moving book, we are invited to share in those sacred moments when people rediscover love in hospital waiting rooms, while playing the drums with an autistic child, or while handing leaflets to strangers on the street.

"Dr. Hallowell has collected some amazing and touching stories from a variety of 'ordinary' people, but he does not hide behind his anonymous authors. He puts his own autobiographical cards on the table and shares the moments in his life when he has found love and connection.

"This book will help you remember and focus on the love to be found in the everyday moments of your life."

—Michael Thompson
coauthor, *Raising Cain; Speaking of Boys;* and
Best Friends, Worst Enemies

"In this unique and heartwarming book, Ned Hallowell opens up his heart, and the hearts of many others, by telling true stories of crucial moments of close connection. The wonderfully poignant stories in *Human Moments* will make you laugh and cry, and above all, feel good about life. They will also show you how to make changes in your life so that you will connect more closely to all that matters to you the most. I loved this book and I am sure you will, too!"

—**Harriet Lerner, Ph.D.**
author, *The Dance of Anger*

Human Moments ™

How to find meaning and
love in your everyday life

*Happy Birthday
and all my love,
Ricky x*

DR EDWARD HALLOWELL

Thorsons

Thorsons
An Imprint of HarperCollins*Publishers*
77-85 Fulham Palace Road
Hammersmith, London, W6 8JB

The Thorsons website address is www.thorsons.com

and *Thorsons*
are trademarks of HarperCollins*Publishers* Ltd

First published in the USA by Health Communications, Inc 2001
This edition published by Thorsons 2002

10 9 8 7 6 5 4 3

Human Moments™ is a trademark of Dr Edward Hallowell

Dr Edward Hallowell asserts the moral right to
be identified as the author of this work

A catalogue record of this book
is available from the British Library

ISBN 0 00 713008 2

Printed and bound in Great Britain by
Creative Print and Design Wales, (Ebbw Vale)

This book is dedicated
to Eileen, Louise and Robin,
three women at the Norfolk Library
in Norfolk, Connecticut, who generously
helped me with this book and
have helped me with other
books in the past.

Happiness is not having what you want,
but wanting what you have.

—Rabbi H. Schachtel
The Real Enjoyment of Living

I am certain of nothing but of
the holiness of the heart's affections
and the truth of imagination. . . .

—John Keats
Letter to Benjamin Bailey
November 22, 1817

Contents

Acknowledgments xi

INTRODUCTION:
WHERE MEANING AND LOVE ABIDE xiii

CHAPTER ONE:
THE POWER OF HUMAN MOMENTS

What Saved Me 3
Crazy Talk 16
Leaflets...26
Echoes 36
Creating Connections 55

CHAPTER TWO: CHILDHOOD

Where's My Dad? 59
Echoes 65
Creating Connections 76

CHAPTER THREE: FAMILIES

Hockey Night..81
My Brother, John Hallowell 88

My Own Mom..97
The End of an Era..103
Echoes 107
Creating Connections 135

CHAPTER FOUR: TEACHERS AND SCHOOL
I Am Here Because They Were There..................139
Echoes 148
Creating Connections 171

CHAPTER FIVE: FRIENDSHIPS
Fact: I'd Be Lost Without My Friends 177
Naked Men 185
Echoes 191
Creating Connections 202

CHAPTER SIX: FALLING IN LOVE
First Love 207
Echoes 211
Creating Connections 220

CHAPTER SEVEN: MARRIAGE AND RELATIONSHIPS
The One I Still Wake Up With........................225
Echoes 234
Creating Connections 249

CHAPTER EIGHT: OUR CHILDREN
No Greater Responsibility, No Greater Joy.........253
A Penguin-Family Story 265
Loaners 268

Echoes 271
Creating Connections 286

CHAPTER NINE:
WORK, SUCCESS AND FRUSTRATION

The Nerve to Do It 291
The Choice 302
Echoes 305
Creating Connections 316

CHAPTER TEN: SELF-DISCOVERY

Turning Fifty 321
Echoes 328
Creating Connections 353

CHAPTER ELEVEN: SPIRITUALITY

What Tucker Taught Me 359
Echoes 364
Creating Connections 387

A FINAL WORD:
HUMAN MOMENTS NEVER DIE 389

An Invitation to Readers 393

Acknowledgments

My first debt is to all the people who gave me their stories. Although the authors of these stories are not named in the text, let me thank them all here. This book would not exist were it not for them.

I also owe a huge debt to my editor at Health Communications, Lisa Drucker. Depending on what you count as a revision, the most conservative estimate is that we went through seven complete revisions of this manuscript. That she was able both to tell me to "do it over" seven times and to stave off my mental breakdown each one of those times is proof not only of her editorial standards but also her skill in providing emotional support to fragile authors. Thank you, Lisa.

And, to Tom Sand, vice president and general manager of Health Communications, I owe as much as I owe Lisa. Tom encouraged me to develop the idea for this book when it was just a pipe dream of mine. When I explained to him that I wanted to follow my book *Connect* with a book called *Human Moments*, and when I explained the unusual format I envisioned for the book, Tom immediately said, "Yes!" — even before I had laid the idea out in much detail. He then alternately prodded me and reassured me, depending on what was needed at the time. The fact that he could see the possibilities right away emboldened me to go on during the inevitable periods of writing when I got discouraged.

When I write a book, I usually plummet from immense enthusiasm at the beginning into a period of intense dissatisfaction during the long middle phase. I usually despair over the book's ever turning out right, and I brood and pace like a farmer whose crops just won't grow. During this wretched time, both Tom and Lisa always had a helpful word, for which I am deeply appreciative. Their faith in this project finally made the crop reach harvest.

In addition, there were many readers of my previous books who urged me to plunge ahead with this idea. I communicate with these people mainly by e-mail, so most of them I have never met in person. Let me say thank you, here, to all of you. Let me especially acknowledge Heidi Pastore, who helped me so very, very much.

Finally, as always, I thank my family for their love and the permission they give me to write. They give me the hours I spend up in my third-floor office, typing away on my laptop, and they never complain about it. Indeed, I am the only one who complains, as I wrestle with a book trying to get it right. If I do succeed it is only because I know that even while Sue, Lucy, Jack and Tucker are out there somewhere—downstairs, in the backyard, at work or at school, or off playing—they are with me nonetheless, and we are always with each other. Thank you, Sue. Thank you, Lucy. Thank you, Jack. Thank you, Tucker. May we relish human moments together forever.

WHERE MEANING AND LOVE ABIDE

Life is just a series of mostly forgettable events, unless we love — and love in as many different ways as we can, from loving a person, to loving a book, a spirit, a place, an idea or a dog — to loving almost anything. With love, we endow certain moments with a special power and significance. With love, and its cousin, imagination, we conjure up the richness and power that lie beneath the surface of even the most trivial second in our lives. Through the power of love and imagination, we turn ordinary, inert moments into what I call *human moments*, those moments when we feel connected to someone or something outside of ourselves and in the presence of what matters, what we call *meaning*.

The most reliable places to find human moments are in the *connections* you make. I am not referring to your business connections, of course, but to the connections of your heart. The people and the places that you love. The part of work you really care about. The children you raise and the grand-children they may give you. The friends you trust. The pets you adore. The garden (or any pastime) that you fuss over. Even the teams you fanatically root for.

All these connections lead to human moments. We hold these moments in our hearts, long after they occur, and feed on them when we are hungry for something to lift our spirits, or simply for something that we believe in and care about. I adopt as a credo what the poet, John Keats, wrote almost two centuries ago: "I am certain of nothing but of the holiness of the heart's affections." That is the subject of this book: the holiness of the heart's affections, the importance of our most heartfelt connections and the human moments they lead to every day in so many different, wonderful ways.

Heartfelt connections and the human moments they spark are what make life good. Of course, how we rank them changes over time. When I was in high school, my vision of heaven was sitting on the third-base line at Fenway Park, in the ninth inning of a never-ending game that I was guaranteed the Red Sox would ultimately win. Now, my vision of heaven is sitting at a table in some restaurant, where my wife Sue and my three kids (frozen in time at their current ages: eleven, eight and five) and all my closest relatives and friends are eating a dinner that goes on forever.

But, until we get to heaven, nothing goes on forever. So we don't have time to wait. We have to make these connections matter now—these relationships, passions and interests—if we are to draw out of them all the juice they have to give.

In this country, most of us actually have what we need to be happy. The challenge is to make what we have matter—

matter now, today—and matter *enough*.

The basic ingredients of a happy life are simple. They include friends and neighbors; relatives; some work you like; perhaps some pets; a club, or a church, or a team; a garden or other passionate pastime or hobby; maybe a good book or a movie; and some hopes and memories, too. To relish the pleasure of these connections, we have to delve deeply into them and make the most of them. We have to nourish them lovingly, so they become as strong as they possibly can be.

But how? It is one thing to say it, another to do it. I often stop and wonder if I am doing it in my own life. For example, as a parent, I give my kids a lot of my time, but someday, I will wish I had given more. Who can ever give their kids all the time they wish they could? There isn't that much time available, even to the idle rich (which I am not), because childhood is brief. And, after our children's childhoods are over, who doesn't wish for one more day—one more sunny afternoon in the park—when our kids were young?

In a piece appearing in *Newsweek*, Anna Quindlen wrote that the biggest mistake she made as a parent:

> . . . is the one most parents make. I did not live in the moment enough. This is particularly clear now that the moment is gone, captured only in photographs. There is one picture of the three of them sitting in the grass on a quilt in the shadow of the swing set on a summer day, ages six, four and one. And I wish I could remember what we ate, and what we talked about, and how they sounded, and how they looked when they slept that night. I wish I

*had not been in such a hurry to get on to the next thing:
dinner, bath, book, bed. I wish I had treasured the doing
a little bit more and the getting it done a little less.*

I want to urge you—and me—to learn from Anna
Quindlen's words. I want to urge us not to simply nod wistfully
in agreement, but to take action. I want this book to inspire us
to deepen our lives, using what we've already got, not waiting
until we have the mythical "more"—more money, more time
or more freedom.

What we've already got is with us now, aching to be
noticed.

We need to make time for all the people and places and
projects where our hearts have set a significant mooring. To
do this, we have to weed out the insignificant ones. We have
to get rid of what hurts us or wastes our precious time, if we
can, so we can involve ourselves fully in what and whom we
love. I think this is the secret to a happy life.

Our loving connections beget meaningful moments, like a
magical plant that blossoms all year 'round. The flowers of
these healthy connections are human moments. They grow
before our eyes in unique and different ways, and they blos-
som day by day.

There is an immense variety to human moments, so much
so that it is difficult to define a human moment more precisely than I already have without losing the variety in the
process. So, instead of offering further definition as you
might find in a textbook, I will *show* you, through the real-life
examples in this book, not only the meaning but also the
power of the human moment. Let me now give you some

examples of human moments taken from my own life.

My family and I had been driving in bad weather for six hours, and we had about another hour to go when my youngest child, Tucker, announced, "I can't hold it any longer."

I felt grumpy, tired and in no mood to stop. Having battled holiday traffic for ten hours the day before, spent the night at a Hampton Inn, and headed out for the second leg of our long trip from Boston to West Virginia early that morning, I was eager to arrive at my wife's sister's home, where I envisioned my body gently collapsing into an easy chair like a parachute collapses when its cargo hits land, accompanied, I hoped, by some beverage consisting mostly of alcohol. I did not want to stop for anybody to do anything. But Tucker repeated his plea: "I reeeeeally need to pee!"

Annoyed, I pulled over onto the snow-covered shoulder of the highway way up in the West Virginia hills. Tucker, age five, got out while the rest of us waited. And waited.

Finally, Tucker climbed back into the car.

"What took you so long?" I gruffly asked.

"I was writing your name in the snow with my pee!" Tucker proudly replied. "D-A-D."

In a heartbeat, my mood changed. "Thank you, Tucker," I replied with a smile, imagining my name being playfully carved into a snowbank by a little boy doing something little boys have done forever. Even though that warm-water inscription would soon disappear, it mattered more to me than any permanent inscription I could ever see in cold stone.

Human moments happen unannounced, and then they disappear, like names drawn in the snow. But, if we capture them—by noticing them and letting them matter—they can infuse our daily lives with meaning and with love forever.

This is how we cherish what we have: by not looking past it, by not saying to ourselves, *But this isn't what I really want; it isn't what I have been waiting for my whole life long.*

Was Tucker peeing my name in the snow what I had been waiting for my whole life long? Well, in a way, yes, it was. If I was ever going to be a happy man, I had to catch on to that fact. I had to relish that moment, cherish it and remember it—eat it up like the spiritual food that it was—as I drove along through the hills of West Virginia and into the rest of my life.

But what about the millions of dollars I might have wanted, the perfect marriage, perfect children, fame, power and who knows what else, maybe perfect teeth? No one has it all. Instead, we have this thing called life. Like an unnoticed child, life so wishes we would take notice. If we do that, it repays us, as that child would, with more than we ever, ever dreamed possible. It gives us the treasure of human moments, the blossoms of connection.

It is *in connection* that we are most fulfilled. The feeling of connectedness goes with us everywhere we go. It is the most comforting feeling there is.

Today's world both promotes and threatens connectedness. Thanks to technology, it is easier to be in touch with people now than ever before in human history. Technology has given us miraculous tools of connection. Yet, oddly enough, the connections people need to feed their hearts and souls are gradually breaking down in many lives. We no longer spend as much good time with each other as we need to. We risk losing the human moment if we don't take care of it, and we *need* the human moment, just as dearly as we need any vitamin. As a doctor, I think of human contact as a vitamin in its own right. It is the other Vitamin C. This one is not ascorbic acid but Vitamin Connect. We all need it, not only to feel happy and fulfilled, but for our physical health, as well.

Numerous studies have shown that connected people live longer than those who are socially isolated. Connected people have lower rates of heart disease and colds and flu. Connected people suffer fewer physical illnesses, as well as fewer mental illnesses such as depression and anxiety. Furthermore, they report much higher rates of satisfaction in life and general feelings of well-being. Connectedness and positive human contact not only feel good, they *are* good, in every measurable way. Science has *proven* that they prolong our lives, enhance our health, and deepen our enjoyment and appreciation of what we have and the people we care about.

But, in today's world, we have to hack through the bramble bush of our schedules to find time for each other. Unless we prune and cut, the bramble bush becomes a thicket. As one woman said to me, "I barely have time to go to my job, feed my kids and do the laundry. Where am I supposed to find time to *connect?*" We have to pare down our daily schedules if we intend to preserve our most important connections. We have to cut our way out of the thicket before it completely traps us. We must *make time.*

We are connected electronically—with television, the Internet, e-mail, voice mail and cell phones. If we use our electronics wisely, they can connect us heart-to-heart. But, if we let the electronics control us, rather than vice versa, we can spend our whole day watching a computer screen, answering voice mails or speaking on our cell phones, as we hurry on through time, starved for one conversation we actually care about.

Let me give you another example of a human moment from my own life. My name for my grandfather on my mother's side was Skipper. He never had much money, but he was rich in the ways that count. He was a true gentleman. I could not have had a more accomplished expert to teach me one of life's most essential skills: how to shake hands. "Look the person straight in the eye," Skipper always said, "and give their hand a strong shake, like you really mean it." We often practiced this skill. After I would make a few attempts that Skipper deemed not firm enough, I would finally squeeze his hand as hard as I possibly could. To my surprise, my tightest grip always brought a smile to his face and a sparkle to his eyes. "Atta boy!" he would exclaim. "Now *that's* a real handshake!" To this day, people sometimes wince when I shake their hands.

Skipper worked in the financial industry, and he took many trips from his home in Newton, Massachusetts, to New York, where he would win waltz contests dancing with his daughter (my Aunt Duckie) to the music of Guy Lombardo. (People said they looked just like Ginger Rogers and Fred Astaire.) He became friends with Guy Lombardo, and with practically everyone he ever met. Skipper—known to the world as John McKey—was my first model of virtue. Even his appearance was stylish and honest: White hair, tortoiseshell glasses, well-worn three-piece suits and knit ties adorned this six-foot, two-inch thin-as-a-rail Gentle Man. Skipper loved friends, he loved to dance, he loved baseball, he loved taking the train to New York and he loved his "heists," his term for the Scotch-and-water he imbibed often and to the enjoyment of all around him. In retrospect, I guess he drank more than a doctor might recommend, but no one cared. He was always one of the most kindly and dignified men I ever knew.

Skipper died slowly, and it was hard. He had emphysema, and he struggled to breathe. But he was a gentleman to the end. The last time I saw him, I was still a little boy. Skipper was lying on a couch, oxygen hooked up to his nose. I gave him a hug. But then he put out his hand, to shake one last time. I looked him squarely in the eye, as he had taught me to do. His hand trembled as he squeezed my hand, hard. As I squeezed back, hard as I could, I saw his eyes brighten for a few seconds, and the old twinkle I knew so well reappeared, as if magically charged by the handshake. In that moment, I said good-bye to Skipper for the final time.

Human moments connect us not only to what matters, but also to what gives us joy. Unless you are careful, though, you can lose your sources of true joy. Just the other day, I was talking to a man in my office who told me his life had become one-dimensional. "I am very successful," he said. "I make a lot of money, and I am happy that I do. But it seems like that's all I do. I work my tail off, then I come home, often tired and grumpy, watch TV, say a few words to my kids and my wife, and go to sleep. The next day, I do it all over again. Is this all there is?"

Even in the midst of success, you can find yourself looking for something deeper, for what's called meaning. Even though you may be well-off, you can have periods when you feel lost, tired or just not sure what your life adds up to.

Human moments can provide the answer. As you begin to look for human moments in your own life, you will find them everywhere, even when you are alone and least expect to.

For example, I was driving to work by myself the other day and that corny old song, "Climb Every Mountain," came on the radio. The next thing I knew, I had tears coming down my cheeks as I thought of my mother, dead now for more than a decade, and her many struggles in life. But she sure did try to bravely face those struggles, as the song exhorts us all to do. As I continued to cry and drive, I remembered seeing *The Sound of Music* (the movie in which that song became famous) with my mother when it first came out. Corny and silly? Sure. But my tears were real, and my feelings were true. In that moment, I revisited my mother and felt once more how much I loved her, no matter what. Suddenly, what had seemed mundane—an old song on the radio—radiated warmth, as I felt in the moment the power that was there, just waiting to be captured and taken in. All I had to do was suspend my critical, cynical side and let the human moment emerge. All I had to do was let it happen.

No one will stand next to you and tell you, "Look! This is a human moment! Cherish it! Make it last! You will be a happy person if you do!" That you have to do for yourself. This book will show you many examples, so as you read, you can start recognizing human moments more and more in your own life.

I have observed many times and in many ways that the antidote to the emptiness in the question, "Is this all there is?" isn't more money, or more fame, or more trophies, or fewer pounds, or a new lover, or a trip to Timbuktu.

The answer is learning how to value deeply what we already have. What makes life magic isn't hard to find, but it is invisible. It is the emotion found in close connections. That emotion shoots back the bolt that guards our hearts and opens us up to what matters the most.

The other night, I came home from work late. Jack, who was supposed to be asleep, called to me as I was coming up the stairs. I was tired, so I ducked into his room, quickly said good night, and left. Jack called out, "Dad, come back." I could have said, "No, go to sleep." But, thank goodness, I went back in. There, in the moonlight, I saw Jack, standing on his head in his bed. "Dad, I'm sleeping upside down!"

So what's the big deal about that? Just that if I hadn't taken the extra ten seconds it took to go back, I wouldn't have had that moment with Jack, and more poignant to me, Jack wouldn't have had the moment of pride and delight he had as he showed me his new posture for sleeping. He would have gone to sleep thinking, *Dad was too busy.* I am sure there have been nights when he did go to sleep thinking that thought, but I hope not too many, because moments like that with Jack give us both what we need the most.

The vignettes in this book are all true. They each provide doses of that other Vitamin C, the Vitamin Connect that ministers to our emotions. With enough of this kind of Vitamin C in your system, you can do what otherwise would be insurmountable.

The Format of This Book:
My Story with Other People's Stories

I have organized this book as a series of autobiographical vignettes, taking me from childhood to adulthood, from troubled child to my present (less troubled) self. I use my life as an example—and other people's lives, as well—to show the power of human moments in everyday life.

Chapter 1 begins with me looking back on what saved me from ending up the broken man my shaky start in life set me up to become, then leaps ahead to tell two stories from different points in my adult life. Following these, I bring in some stories from other people—told in their own voices—to add variety and strength. Throughout the book, I call the stories from other people, "Echoes . . .".

After chapter 1, the book moves chronologically through various stages of life. The format for each chapter is the combination of autobiographical stories from me, followed by stories and scenes from other people's lives. My idea is that, by drawing in different voices, I will create a kind of back-and-forth dialogue for the book. My autobiographical stories bring up a theme, for example, childhood. Then, another voice—another writer—comes in with a variation on, or an "echo" of, that theme. Then, a few final voices complete the dialogue with their "echoes" of the chapter's main theme.

I will provide a brief introductory comment for each of the passages written by other people, followed by my initials, "E. H.," so you will know where my words leave off and the other people's words begin.

The theme of chapter 2 is Childhood; chapter 3 is Families; chapter 4 is Teachers and School; chapter 5 is Friendships; chapter 6 is Falling in Love; chapter 7 is Marriage and Relationships; chapter 8 is Our Children; chapter 9 is Work, Success and Frustration; chapter 10 is Self-Discovery; and chapter 11 is Spirituality.

This is like no book I have written before. The format of writing an autobiographical narrative of my own, combined with autobiographical writings of other people, is a structure I have devised just for this book. I hope that my story will serve as a kind of plot and provide a voice to carry the book, while the contributions of others will provide more variety than my story could alone.

To complement the personal stories, I close each chapter with a section called "Creating Connections . . . ", in which I invite you, the reader, to pause and reflect on your own life. This is a chance, if you like, to compose your own story.

I expect that, as you read, you will feel a desire to reconnect with someone or visit some place. Rather than let the emotion fade without your acting on it, you might like to write a brief note to yourself as a reminder—like, "Call Marie," or "Reminds me of Bill"—so that later on you won't forget to follow up. The "Creating Connections . . ." section at the end of each chapter makes space for concrete, practical, how-can-I-use-this-in-my-life kind of thinking.

Each "Creating Connections . . ." section will consist of three parts.

First, I will invite you to reflect on some part of your life that relates to what has appeared in the preceding chapter.

Second, I will offer a few comments on the obstacles that often make connections in this part of life difficult.

Third, I will suggest some practical methods for overcoming these obstacles.

I made the tone of "Creating Connections . . ." personal, in the hope that I can become a companion to you as you read.

I intend for other books like this one to follow, books that pick up one kind of human moment or connection and develop it in greater detail and variety. I anticipate, for example, a book entirely devoted to marriage and relationships, another to grandparents, another to pets, another to sisters and brothers, another to work, and maybe, if I dare, one devoted to the Red Sox and other sports teams!

I remember my grandmother, whom I called Gammy, picking up the shears she used to snip her roses, the charm bracelet on her wrist jangling as she snipped. That bracelet held a charm for each of her eight grandchildren, with one of our names on each charm. In wearing that bracelet, Gammy kept her grandchildren with her, literally as well as emotionally. She has been dead for thirty-five years, but I can still hear the faint tinkle of that bracelet, as it calls me back to Gammy's garden and a part of my life long gone.

As you read this book, I hope that you will hear a tinkling of charms from your past, too.

Chapter One

THE POWER OF HUMAN MOMENTS

WHAT SAVED ME

I come from a crazy, old New England family cursed and in some ways blessed by what I call the WASP triad: alcoholism, mental illness and politeness. My parents and their parents and their parents' parents and so on all the way back up my family tree had major doses of each element of the WASP triad.

My sweet, dear, but alcoholic mother was divorced twice. My father was hospitalized many times for manic-depressive illness. My stepfather was a sadistic alcoholic. On top of this, I had (and, of course, still have) two learning disabilities: dyslexia and attention deficit disorder. Because people couldn't handle me at home, I was sent away to boarding school at the age of ten, when I was in the fifth grade. I grew up mainly in such institutions.

As you can see, my family "tradition" was not one of happiness. The Hallowells tried to be upbeat but, behind the cheerful effort, considerable trouble smoldered.

Around the tenth or eleventh grade—whenever you start to think realistically about what you will become—I figured that I probably never would be what is called a happy man. I hoped I'd find happiness, but I didn't think it was in the cards or, more precisely, in the genes, for me.

I decided my only course of action was to make the best of what I'd been dealt, to learn not to burden others with my problems, and to find a way of adapting my melancholy interior to what I perceived to be the rather noncomprehending world at large.

I remember lying on my bed at school, staring at the ceiling and wondering, *Will I ever be happy?* The odds were on the side of no.

Now, about thirty-five years later, at age fifty I can answer that question. Amazingly enough, I have found a good life for myself. (Wouldn't it be wonderful if my present self could rush back in time and whisper into the ear of my fifteen-year-old self, *"Don't worry, things will turn out okay"*? But I guess that's against the rules of life.) I am not tickled-pink happy all the time, in the sense that I know some people to be happy. I am not one of those lucky people who always seems pleased, although I do know some of those blessed souls. They are gems. I wish I were one of them, but I am not.

However, I am basically a happy man, much happier than I was when I lay on that bed in high school bleakly contemplating my fate, and hugely happier than my genetic endowment and childhood experience would have led anyone to predict I would become.

From a statistical standpoint—and people actually do research to compile these statistics—children with the many strikes against them that I had usually end up in a bad place. They end up in jail, or in and out of mental hospitals, or boozed out, or just chronically miserable.

What saved me? I will answer that question in a moment.

But first, let me give a clearer idea of what I needed to be saved from. My mom's second marriage plunged me into the worst years of my life, years from which I might not ever have recovered were it not for the help of people outside my family.

My mom and dad divorced when I was four years old. Soon after, my mother fell in love with Noble Cathcart, an older man who lived in Chatham, the small town on the elbow of Cape Cod where we lived back then. Mr. Cathcart hailed from the South originally, but he had been living in Chatham for quite a few years.

When I first met him, I was happily living with my mom and my cousins, Lyn and Jamie, and my aunt, whom I called Duckie, and my Uncle Jim. My parents had divorced, but I had accepted that fact without too much fuss. I loved my dad, but Mom's dating Noble Cathcart was fine with me. In fact, I liked Mr. Cathcart a lot. I started calling him Uncle Noble, and I looked forward to the times I would go visit him with my mom. I remember once she coaxed me to go see the dentist to get a cavity filled by telling me that, as a reward, we could go visit Uncle Noble afterward.

I was seven, in second grade in the public school in Chatham, when one day my mother asked me how I would feel if she married Uncle Noble. She went on to tell me that, if she did marry him, we would move to Charleston, South Carolina. As much as I liked Uncle Noble, the idea of leaving Chatham—and leaving my cousins, Jamie and Lyn— seemed like an awful idea. So, I told Mom I was against her marrying this guy, unless I could stay behind in Chatham.

Uncle Noble won. Mom married him, and all three of us moved to Charleston.

Then, Uncle Noble's true colors began to show. I would usually come home from school to find him drunk. School let out around two o'clock, and by the time I rode my bike home it would be two-thirty. In the custom of Charleston at the time, we would then all sit down to eat "dinner," the main meal of the day, around three o'clock.

At those meals, Uncle Noble and I waged war.

I went from loving him to hating him, not only because he moved me out of Chatham and away from my beloved cousins and aunt and uncle, but also because he mistreated my mother. For example, Uncle Noble and Mom used to play a child's game together—rock, paper, scissors—a game that is benign when played by children. But, when Uncle Noble played it, it became vicious. There is a point in the game where you can slap your opponent with two fingers (the position of the two fingers looks like a scissors). Uncle Noble developed the two-finger slap into a painful blow that would leave a bruise on my mother for days. He forced her to play the game all the time. It horrified me to see the look of glee that filled Uncle Noble's eyes when he would get to slap my mother. I don't know why she didn't leave him, then and there.

One time, when I was about eight, I tackled him around his ankles after he backhanded my mother because she lit a cigarette for him in a way he deemed incorrect. Rather than bother with me, he sat back down to his martini and kicked me away, but at least he left Mom alone. Another night, I walked into the living room and found my mother trying to fend him off as he came at her with a poker. When he saw me, he put the poker back in the rack with the other fireplace tools, and uttered one of his favorite phrases, "Shove off." This was frequently preceded by the words, "If you don't like it, why don't you just . . . shove off!"

It wasn't long before I desperately did want to shove off. My mother was joining Uncle Noble in his drinking, so the two of them were pretty much unavailable to do what parents need to do—like help kids with homework, go to games, go fishing or play ball. My life became one of school, followed by fights with Uncle Noble, followed by watching TV by myself and then going to bed.

What made it more difficult was that Uncle Noble could be nice. Life is so rarely black or white. He was good to me now and then, even after we started to wage war. For example, when I came down with measles at around age nine, I got very sick. I developed a fever of 105, and I became delirious, lapsing in and out of nightmares. I was sweating so heavily that my sheets were sopping wet, and I was scared. I remember vividly, perhaps because altered states of mind enhance memory, how Uncle Noble sat with me, waiting for the fever to break. He stayed up with me late into the night, sponging my forehead with a cool washcloth by the light of the moon, while he told me stories from his days as an under-cover agent . . . when I was alert enough to be able to listen. The stories were fabulous; to this day I don't know if they were true, but they were great to listen to in the midst of a fever. Then, in the middle of the night, the doctor appeared, gave me a suppository, and my fever soon broke. The next day, Uncle Noble was back to his old—drunken—self.

I wrestled with him, and he with me. We sparred with

words, and we sparred physically. He spanked me now and then, but he never beat me up or did me any physical harm, as he did to my mother. I wanted to love him, and I do believe he wanted to love me, but we ended up tormenting each other. I was sticking up for my mother, and I was mad we didn't live back in Chatham, while he was . . . what was he doing? Why was he so mean to my mother and me? Why did he turn on my mother after he married her? And why did he not embrace the little boy who had embraced him with open arms when we first met?

He would probably say it was because I turned into a brat, and I would say it was because he turned into a mean drunk. He is dead now, so I can't ask him why. But I still wonder. My being a brat and his being a drunk don't fully explain why he and I missed out on something that actually could have been wonderful for us both. I could have found a second father, and he could have found the son he never had. Instead, we became each other's nemesis. Finally, when I was ten, my mother decided to send me away from Charleston, out of the world of Uncle Noble and back to Massachusetts, to a boarding school near Boston called The Fessenden School.

The battles then ended. I was gone. The chance for anything good happening between Uncle Noble and me was over, as well as any more that was bad. My mother divorced him a few years later, but she never recovered from that marriage. She ended her days living alone in Chatham, trying to keep her spirits up, a broken, sweet, alcoholic woman.

This is the mystery of families: Why does so much that could be so good so often go so wrong?

Even more mysterious, why, when so much goes so wrong,

can life still work out okay, as it has done for me so far?

Uncle Noble failed to finish me off. I survived, even succeeded, with the help of many good people. I never saw Uncle Noble again after the divorce, nor did I talk to him again except for one time. I called him in 1987. I was thirty-eight, and he was about ninety. I had just sold my first book. I wanted this man who had so hurt my mother to know that his evil hadn't ruined me.

So I phoned information in South Carolina, tracked down his number and called the old goat. Sure enough, he answered the telephone. When I told him who was calling he must have felt ill but, to his credit, he didn't hang up. "What do you want from me, boy?" he asked.

You can imagine what I wanted to say. Instead, I simply told him that in the time since he last saw me I had graduated from Harvard (a school he had left early without earning a degree), I had graduated from medical school, I had finished my residency and fellowship, and I had just sold a book.

I can't print his reply. He cussed me out and told me I was lying. I could hear the old rasp in his voice; I could see him sitting in his favorite chair, drink in hand. I then told him that, although he had hurt my mother and hurt me, he had not destroyed us. I told him that my mother's best lived on in me. I told him that I had done more good for other people in my thirty-eight years than he had in his ninety. With each measured statement, I felt I was balancing a special scales of justice that I had not been able to balance as a child. It might even have helped Uncle Noble to hear my words. It might have been good for this old man to know, before he died, that his evil side had not prevailed. Who knows, maybe that knowledge would help get his cynical old soul into good-enough shape that St. Peter would give him a second look.

But Uncle Noble was not about to give me any satisfaction on the phone that day. He simply cussed me out again and repeated that I was a liar. I could tell he was drunk, but I like to think he was sober enough to understand.

I remember what I said in parting, the last words I ever spoke to him. "I know you know I am telling the truth. Now, we both can shove off for good." On the other end, there was a long pause. The snake had no more spit. I could hear his rattling, emphysematous breathing as he still clutched the phone. I could hear him trying to form a word, but his tongue for once was stuck, his mouth as dry as his heart. It was time to stop the fight. I hung up.

At that moment, I felt the great feeling of, "YES!" I knew that life's good guys had prevailed against the odds. All the people who had saved me from the influence of that man had prevailed.

And yet, I have to say I wish I could go back and make things right with that man. I wish I could go back and turn Uncle Noble into the kind stepfather and good husband he might have been, had it not been for alcohol and who-knows-what-else. I also wish I could undo the part I know I played in provoking him. I wish we could have found, somehow, the love we should have had for one another. It was in there, somewhere. We just never made it grow.

Despite all Uncle Noble's evil doings, I have never hated him totally. Maybe that's the gift he gave me. He taught me that something like love—call it hope—can grow even in the midst of something like hatred. He is the person I have hated most in all my life—and with good reason—but, in spite of it all, I know he wasn't entirely to blame.

He gave my life an ominous start. So what saved me from what could have been disaster?

The answer is this: good people.

What saved me is what saves millions of people every day. Human moments are what saved me—moments of connection blossoming forth to give me a feeling of strength, safety, power and hope.

What saved me is probably what saves us all.

Back then, there was my friend Bobby Hitt, who went to school with me down in Charleston. He saw Uncle Noble up close when I'd invite him over for dinner. Bobby hated him, too. That was helpful for me, that Bobby could see what a jerk Uncle Noble was, why I hated the guy. Bobby would also invite me over to his house, and I would have dinner with a normal family. His dad wrote for the newspaper in Charleston. Bobby had a noisy family with siblings and pets and a mom who looked worn-out, but everyone was pretty nice most of the time, and no one was drunk, at least as far as I ever saw.

Bobby and I rode our bikes all over Charleston, and we'd talk as we rode. He told me what a whorehouse was before I knew even the basics of sexual relations, so a whorehouse was a complete puzzlement to me. I didn't dare tell Bobby I didn't know what he meant when he told me what happened in a whorehouse; in fact, I almost thought he was making the whole thing up, but he usually was trustworthy, so I believed him. Now, about forty years later, I know he was telling the truth, but I do wonder what his sources were.

We played guns together a lot, which was the term for any

game involving toy weapons of any sort. We didn't have real guns, although a lot of the kids our age did. One fall, we went out to the mud flat and built a fort in an old fishing ship that had turned over on its side. We rigged it up with "lamps" that were just flashlights hung with string around nails in the walls, and "bunks" we made out of boxes and rags we brought from home, and "chairs" we made out of bits of wood from around the ship. We'd drink Pepsi and read comics down there in our fort and forget to go home until it was dark.

Bobby made me forget what a mess I lived in at home. Bobby showed me the power of having a friend.

But how about money? Isn't that the most reliable "friend" to have by your side as you face the worst in life? Isn't money—and its attendant advantages—a more useful and trustworthy ally than any "connection" or "human moment"? Connections and human moments may make for fine sentiment, the cynic carps, but give me money when times are tough and I'll find friends aplenty.

Early on, I learned otherwise. Money didn't help me in Charleston. Uncle Noble had plenty of money, and he was willing to spend it, even on me. But it wasn't money that I needed. I needed Bobby Hitt, and his family, and other healthy connections.

Most of us forget our childhood lessons, or we chalk them up to being mere fairy tales. After all, life is hard, and the mortgage must be paid. But I remember how much it meant to me then to have a friend, and how much it means to me now. When I find myself wishing for more—money, power, influence, whatever—I try to remind myself that I already have what I need, if I will but notice and value it, just as I had Bobby Hitt back then.

Friends can last a lifetime, but it takes effort to stay in touch. I have lost touch with Bobby Hitt. Bobby, if you read this book, would you please give me a call? And I will try to track you down, as well. Do you still live in South Carolina?

It seems to be harder to stay in touch for grown-ups than for kids. Some of my friends now have become too busy to make our friendship a priority anymore. I have reached out to them, only to receive polite acknowledgments of my messages, but no resumption of the deeper friendship. People tell me this happens inevitably in life as we grow older. People drift apart and become involved with families and careers, but I still try to hold onto my friends as vigorously as I can.

The alternative, as I see it, is emptiness.

Of course, I would feel this way. I have lived a life in which other people saved me from disaster.

Have you ever wondered who—or what—saved you? The question may take you aback, especially if you didn't have to overcome any great obstacles. "I'm not like you," you might say to me. "I didn't need to be saved."

But I bet someone, or many someones, or something, or some place, or maybe even some pet or team did help bring you to where you are.

Maybe it was a schoolteacher, or several schoolteachers, as it was in my case. Or maybe it was your mother. Maybe it was a business partner who rescued you, or maybe it was a doctor who made the right diagnosis at the right time.

We don't always like to think in these terms. We like to

think that we save ourselves. We like to think that we can do it all, that we are independent. But no one is.

Certain moments hang in my memory like treasured paintings, moments to which I return in my thoughts time and again. Snuggling in bed with my grandmother. Having a beer with my friend Peter Metz after our biweekly squash games. Watching my youngest son, Tucker, lie sound asleep on his bed, as the moonlight spills over his little face and turns it silver. Listening to my cousin-in-law, Tom, encourage me to go to medical school, when I was thinking I lacked the stamina and smarts. Asking Sue, now my wife, to marry me, as we sat in a restaurant in Paris, while the impatient French waiter, caring more for food than romance, urged Sue to stop crying and eat her meal before it got cold. Holding our first child and only daughter, Lucy, in my arms after she was born. Three years later, holding Jack, and three years after that, holding Tucker. These—and many others—are my masterworks of life, my human moments, masterworks all of us get, in one way or another, even though we aren't dealers in fine art.

Among the masterworks are painful scenes. Sooner or later we all face pain. When that happens, we need more than money. We may look to captains of industry as our everyday heroes—our Bill Gateses and Michael Dells today, our J. P. Morgans and Andrew Carnegies generations ago—but they are like schoolboys at play when it comes to addressing the ultimate questions.

We look elsewhere for help with life's pain. We look to each other. And we look to eternal wisdom, if we can find it.

I find it in these words of St. Paul [1 Cor. 13:8–13]:

Love never ends. But as for prophecies, they will come to an end; as for tongues, they will cease; as for knowledge, it will come to an end. For we know only in part, and we prophesy only in part; but when the complete comes, the partial will come to an end. . . . For now we see in a mirror, dimly, but then we will see face to face. Now I know only in part; then I will know fully, even as I have been known. And now faith, hope, and love abide, these three; and the greatest of these is love.

These words of St. Paul are familiar to Christians, but they speak to all people, whatever their beliefs. What saves us all, but faith, hope and love? Even if our faith is not in God, it is faith that someone will be there when we get home, or faith that a loved one will be true to us, or faith that the roof won't cave in as we sit under it!

The roof didn't cave in on me, even though it was a shaky roof to start off with! So far, it still hasn't caved in. What saved me was other people—their love—and the faith and hope that kindled in me.

Can you think of what is saving you?

CRAZY TALK

As a doctor now and, more specifically, as a psychiatrist, it is my job to try to save people. Or help them save themselves. Having started this chapter by telling what saved me, let me now give an example of how I participated in someone else's being saved, at least for a moment.

One Sunday afternoon when I was the psychiatrist-on-call at a mental hospital, a young woman walked in off the street and announced she wanted to kill herself. This event, in and of itself, was not unusual. People who walk into mental hospitals often are thinking of suicide. What made this woman unusual — and what has kept her in my mind to this day, some twenty years later — was what happened in the hour *after* she walked in.

Her name was Ruby, or so she told me. When I asked her her age she told me to square two and multiply that by the cube of two. I paused and asked her if she was thirty-two, and she nodded yes, while asking me for a cigarette. We did have a stash of cigarettes for people who came in off the street, so I gave her one. She sat in a chair opposite my desk, puffed on her cigarette, crossed one leg over the other, and started to swing the top leg up and down very fast.

I was in training, a rookie, new to the game of suicide assessment—new to the game of any kind of assessment, for that matter. Ruby was soon to become one of my most memorable teachers.

"Well, can you tell me why you want to commit suicide?" I asked as offhandedly as that question can be asked.

"Wow," she said, "what kind of a dumb-ass question is that? What do you know, you preppy-looking shrinklet, about life?"

They don't give you training for this sort of dialog. For this, your training is on the job. No one was watching me, except Ruby. No one was there to help me, and no one was there to reprimand me or redirect me if I messed up. I blinked a few times, and I bit my tongue. Then, I went on, "Well, I am pretty new at this, but I really do want to help you, if I can."

Ruby whistled in mock amazement. Then she leveled her eyes at me. "Do you really think that will cut it? Do you think you can save my life today by mouthing lame-brained goo-goo sounds about wanting to help me?" She grunted and repeated, now in a mocking tone, "You really do want to help me. Well, isn't that sweet?" Then, she announced, as if to an imaginary audience, "He really does want to help me. Bless my soul. I am saved." She took a deep drag on her cigarette, then dropped it on the floor and crushed it beneath her shoe. "Got another?" she asked.

"Yes," I replied and handed her one, hoping to win her over with cigarettes.

"What would you know about my life or how to help me?" she demanded.

My job was to see anyone who walked in, or was brought in by the police or an ambulance, evaluate the person, then decide whether to send the person back to wherever he came from or admit him to the hospital. This was a teaching hospital where I was a resident in psychiatry, but it was also a state hospital, so it was a run-down place. The people who came here were usually poor and homeless. They were pretty different from the trainees (like me) who were supposed to "evaluate" them. It made a lot of sense for Ruby to ask me what I knew about life, especially *her* life.

Ruby held the next cigarette unlit between her fingers as she began her next foray. "I know you *want* to help me. That is a given. But *can* you help me? That is another question."

"Will you let me try?" I asked.

"Do I have a choice?" Ruby zapped back. "I believe you are the only game in town, *n'est-ce pas?*"

"Ruby," I said, "look, you are smarter than I am. We can both see that pretty easily. So, the only way I can possibly help you is if you decide to *let* me help you. If you want to play games with me, you can run circles around me, just like you're doing."

"*Tut, tut, tut!*" Ruby exclaimed. "Never debase yourself like that. I am a mere lunatic, the scum of society, and you are an exalted doctor, in training at this famous hospital that is part of Harvard Medical School. It is I who should bow down to you, not vice versa." Clearly, Ruby knew about this hospital. She was probably a veteran of many admissions. I wanted to call security to see if they could track down an old chart on her while we talked.

"Have you been admitted here before?" I asked.

"Of course," she replied. "They know me upstairs. It's all in my chart. But that is not the point we have to resolve right now. Right now, we have to decide if I am going to kill myself with this little weapon I have." At that point, she pulled a handgun from her bra.

This was a career first for me. I had never had a patient pull a gun on me before. "Is that a gun?" I asked.

"Duh, Doc. It's not a Tootsie Roll."

There was an emergency button under the desk that I could push to bring security barging into the room, if I wanted to do that. But that seemed like a very bad idea. "Is that really a gun?" I asked. I simply did not believe my eyes.

"Well, punk, do you feel lucky?" she snarled in as much of a Clint Eastwood imitation as she could muster. Then she smiled and clicked the gun, which led not to a shot but a little flame. "It's my cigarette lighter. Did I frighten you, Doc? I'm frightfully sorry if I did."

"Okay, Ruby," I said, "I think you have told me enough so that I can let you leave."

"Now, now, now. You are going to discharge me to the street and let me kill myself as punishment for frightening you with my little cigarette lighter? Don't you think that is rather unprofessional?"

"Ruby, I think you are playing games with me. I think you came in here today because you were bored, not because you were in pain. I also think you have taken drugs."

Abruptly, she threw the cigarette lighter at me. It missed my head by a hair and smashed against the wall, breaking apart. "What do you know about life?" she barked at me. "What do you know about *anything*? See these scars?" she screeched, pulling her sleeves up to reveal a faded network of purple marks on both forearms. "I cut myself for fun. It's better than the pain I feel otherwise. I can't stop cutting. Do you understand that? Of course you don't. Don't you tell me why I came in here or what you think I've been doing today. I have been out there trying to be good, and I finally came in to get some relief, and you, you smug little self-satisfied preppy who hasn't suffered a day in your whole privileged life, you better not tell me I'm just bored and that's why I'm here. You don't know crap."

I sat in silence. I realized I had spoken in anger to her, and that that was a mistake. I also realized she was one smart woman, who surely did know more than I did. I felt a little defensive about the privileged preppy part, but I concluded it would not be appropriate to tell her about the troubles that I had seen. I was beginning to understand why some people call psychiatry the impossible profession. "You're right," I said. "I don't know much."

"Well, damn it, you better learn, 'cause I can't do this whole gig by myself," Ruby pleaded, then started to cry.

At that moment, the telephone on my desk rang. It was the switchboard operator, Barney, informing me that he was suffering from a severe headache. I told him I was engaged in evaluating a patient. He told me he didn't think he could manage the switchboard any longer, his pain was so intense. It was the worst headache he ever had in his life. He had called his supervisor who had told him she would come down to relieve him, but until then he should call me for help. I told him I would call him right back.

When I hung up the phone, Ruby looked at me

inquisitively. "The switchboard operator has a headache," I told her.

"Well, so do I," Ruby replied.

"But the operator says it is the worst headache of his life. That is a classic sign he might be bleeding into his brain, you know, having a stroke. I better go check him out. His life might depend on it. You'll need to come with me. I don't want to leave you alone just with security."

"Why? You afraid I'll hurt myself?" Ruby asked coyly.

"C'mon, let's go," I said, grabbing a stethoscope and blood-pressure cuff from the metal cabinet in the examining room.

The switchboard at that hospital was antiquated. The operator had to wear a headset and monitor a board that had hundreds of plugs, all with those long cords, like Lily Tomlin's character, Ernestine, used to operate on *Laugh-In*. When I got to Barney, he was sweating profusely and was obviously in great pain. Still, he had his headset on and was answering calls. "I can't take this headset off until someone else puts it on," he told me. "That's the rule. The board must always be manned."

Whenever people sneer at state employees, saying what goldbrickers they all are, I think of Barney refusing to leave his post, even as his life was in danger. "Barney, take off your headset. I'll take responsibility."

"Doc, you gotta put it on," he insisted. "I can't take it off unless somebody else puts it on."

"But I have no idea how to use it," I protested.

"That don't matter," Barney replied. "I'll show you."

"Okay, Barney," I said, "but first let's take care of you." I took a short history, then checked his blood pressure. It was sky high, way into the danger zone. This was a medical emergency. "Barney," I said, "call an ambulance. Tell them it is an emergency."

"Is this a Code Blue?" Barney asked.

"Yes, Barney," I replied. "It is a Code Blue. Follow the standard procedure."

In a flash, Barney was on the phone getting the ambulance, then he stat paged the doctor on call: me. Having followed standard protocol, he looked up at me as if to say, *What now, Doc?*

"Take off the headset," I told him. "Give it to me." Barney reluctantly obliged. The emergency room was just down the street, and the ambulance arrived less than a minute after Barney's call. As orderlies hurried up the stairs into the little alcove where the switchboard was located, I listened to Barney's instructions to me on running the switchboard. I seriously doubt he would have allowed himself to be carried out had I not listened to his instructions. I listened, but it was clear I was not a good student.

Suddenly, a hand appeared on Barney's arm. It was Ruby. "You gotta go, man. I'll take care of this. I've done this before. I know how. It's cool."

Barney smiled, as if a pediatrician had just arrived to take care of his baby. Now he was willing to leave. He lay down on the stretcher and was carried off to the ambulance.

As I watched him leave, I sat there, headset in place, while the switchboard flashed lights and made honking sounds that demanded a response. But who knew what response? If I was new to suicide assessment, I was definitely new to switchboard operation.

Ruby howled. Not in anger but in uproarious laughter. She

slapped her knee, she held her tummy, she bent over and moaned, she was laughing so hard. Standing next to me, she was having the time of her life watching me fumble around.

"I am glad you find this amusing," I said, as I tried, unsuccessfully, to put the right plug into the right hole.

Her only response was another shriek of laughter. She was truly beside herself. I played along, in part because I had no choice, but also because this was clearly having a more therapeutic effect on Ruby than any words we had been able to exchange up to that point.

"Do you want my help?" she asked, snorting as she tried to stifle her hoots of laughter. Her attempts to stifle herself just made her sputter and cough, as I replied, "Yes. I do want your help."

"How does it feel, Doc, to want my help? I can't resist asking you." I tried pushing a button that looked like it might open a line, so I could answer one of the many incoming calls. "You just disconnected that one," Ruby said, guffawing again.

"Ruby, please help me," I said, looking up at her. "These could be serious calls."

She took the headset off my head and nudged me to move out of the chair. As I got up, she slid in and started answering calls, while making the proper connections to the extensions that were lit up. In a few minutes, she had the whole board under control. A few minutes after that, Barney's supervisor breathlessly arrived and thanked me for helping out. When she asked who was that running the board so well for me, I told her it was a friend of mine who had come over to visit me while I was on call, and who luckily had some switchboard experience.

I also told the supervisor what a heroic job Barney had done, refusing to leave his post until he was confident the switchboard would be manned properly. Despite the humor of the scene, Barney, in fact, had risked his life. We then called the hospital and found out that Barney had arrived in time, that his hypertensive crisis was being treated and was under control. He would be okay.

Leaving the switchboard to Barney's supervisor, Ruby and I walked back into the examining room, where we had been what seemed like hours before but, in fact, was only a matter of about fifteen or twenty minutes.

Ruby sat down, and so did I. "You cured me, Doc. That routine was better than cutting."

"How do you feel now?" I asked.

"A whole lot better. That whole scene really scratched my itch."

We chatted some more, so I could be sure that Ruby was stable, and then she and I both decided it was safe for her to leave.

What I learned from Ruby that day, and from the switchboard situation, was the power of feeling useful. When people feel bad, it helps if they can feel they have some worth. A good way to feel that you have worth is to have someone else need your help. Ruby had come in that day feeling low on worth, and my initial interview with her only reinforced her feelings of being less worthy than others. I had control of the cigarettes, I had the power to let her into the hospital (or not), I was the one "evaluating" her, I was the doctor, she was the patient. All she could do was protest—which she did cleverly, as well as boisterously—or when at wit's end, cut herself, which she had done many times before, in order to feel something other than worthless.

But when, out of the blue, I became the one who was helpless, when I became the one out of my element, desperately needing help from the very person who had come to me for help, then—presto!—we had a cure, at least for the time being.

In that one, powerful human moment Ruby taught me a principle I have applied thousands of times since then. It is this: When someone—anyone, not just a patient of mine, but a friend, a child, even a stranger—feels down and sour on life, it often helps to put that person in the helping role, not only to give them a feeling of power and control, but also a feeling of dignity and worth.

LEAFLETS

As Ruby reminded me in the previous story, it is difficult to ask other people for help. It can also be difficult to help when asked. As much as people might say they like to help other people, when they actually get down to doing it, they can feel enormously awkward. I learned about this phenomenon one wintry day with my daughter, Lucy.

Early in December of Lucy's twelfth year, she and I did something together neither of us had ever done before: We handed out leaflets in Harvard Square.

I had always hated leaflets because, until that day, I had only been on the receiving end of them. They had been handed to me by aggressive leafleteers in Harvard Square, and just about every other square I'd ever been in. They also had often been pinioned to my windshield while I unsuspectingly took in a movie; they had cluttered up my mailbox and my front porch many times; and some even had flown into my backyard. I detested leaflets, as well as the people who produced them, mailed them and, most of all, handed them out. It was such an intrusion, to thrust a leaflet at me, a leaflet that deplored some form of injustice I already knew about, or offered some service I didn't want, or told me about a new business I had no interest in. I ranked leaflets and leafleteers right up there — or I should say down there — with subscription cards that drop out of magazines and mealtime telemarketers, as among the most annoying minor disruptions of my daily life.

Until that day with Lucy.

It was the day our church held its crafts fair. Artisans sold their wares, parishioners sold baked goods and sandwiches and large bowls of hot chili, and the choir sang Christmas carols, all to raise money for the outreach programs the church supported. It was a good cause, but when I was asked to support the cause by leafleting, I cringed. However, I felt trapped, having written a book about the importance of connecting with others. Now, I was being asked to practice what I preached, in a way I imagined would be most distasteful.

But the task got worse. Not only did the people at the church ask me to leaflet, they asked me to wear a sandwich board while I did it! I had never worn a sandwich board, and I certainly thought I never would. But now, I was being asked to walk around Harvard Square, advertising the crafts fair at Christ Church, thrusting leaflets into the hands of innocent bystanders, all the while wearing an absurd-looking sandwich board that was covered with exclamation points, spangles and other attention-grabbing graphics. Not only was I supposed to do this, I was supposed to do it with enthusiasm and with spirit, in an effort to infect others with a fleeting feeling of generosity and goodwill. And I was supposed to do it with my daughter.

When I proposed the idea to Lucy, she gave me the same look I had given the woman at the church who had proposed the idea to me. "You're joking, Dad," she dourly replied. Lucy had left the age where she would gladly look ridiculous in public and had started, like an adult, to assess each situation according to a very particular social meter.

"It could be fun," I pleaded, inwardly more aghast than she at the prospect of actually doing it.

Then, as usual, Lucy surprised me. After a long pause, she said, "You're right, Dad. Let's do it." Thus, the one person I had counted on to ally with me in resisting this embarrassing undertaking ended up cooking my goose.

The day of the fair was sunny and cold. As our sandwich boards were hung upon our shoulders and tied in place with ribbon, Lucy started to giggle. But, as I watched her, a new feeling rose up in me. I began to feel brave, even eager. I became a man on a mission with my daughter. We were on a Crusade. *Tally-ho!* I proclaimed to myself, as Lucy and I took our leaflets and headed out to the sidewalks of Harvard Square.

Lucy was wearing her powder-blue parka, with the sandwich board covering its front and back, and a pink feathery hair-holding device in her blonde hair. (What are such devices called? Not knowing is what makes us dads so dumb!) With the cold air crisping her cheeks, she looked, if I may say so, very cute. On the other hand, how I looked, wearing my New England Patriots jacket plus sandwich board, was a determination I desperately tried not to make.

As we reached the Square, we started to offer our leaflets to the people who filled the sidewalks. Some accepted our handouts gladly, while others rejected them as if they were radioactive. What happened in the next half hour taught me a major lesson in life.

I tried to give a leaflet to a man who was selling the homeless newspaper, *Spare Change*. I thought maybe he would understand charity and would like to drop in on the crafts fair when he was done with his own work. He looked at my leaflet, then looked at me briefly and said, "Are you kidding, man?" I guess I represented the competition.

But, then, I offered leaflets to two elderly women who were walking along, talking like old friends. "Oh, thank you," one said, as if I had offered her a finger sandwich at tea. "We'll be sure to drop by." The ladies kept on walking and talking, now with one of my red leaflets peeking from their black gloves.

Next, I offered my leaflet to a young man of Asian extraction who looked like he might be a grad student at Harvard. He was trim, in jeans and leather jacket, and he rejected my leaflet as if it were an extraneous piece of data in an experiment he was hurrying to complete. He was gone from my sight before I even could react to his rejection.

Lucy then ran up to me, informing me with great excitement, "I've sold three! Have you sold any?"

It did feel as if we were selling the leaflets, even though we were, of course, giving them away. This is because many of our "customers" were efficient people like me: people in too much of a hurry, and too preoccupied with themselves to be bothered by a little girl with a pink whatchamacallit or a fellow wearing a sandwich board, both handing out leaflets for a church fair. Lucy and I were just obstacles for these people to get around as they bustled on to Somewhere That Mattered. For these people-on-the-go, Lucy and I were simply in the way.

I would hand out a leaflet, and some distinguished-looking man—perhaps a Harvard Professor, or maybe a Proud Citizen, or a Man on the Way Up—would look not at me, but skillfully *past* me. Even when I tried aggressively to get in the line of sight of one of these People in a Hurry, they somehow were able not merely to avoid confronting me, but to walk past me as if they had not seen me at all. I felt they did not know that I existed, or if they did know, which they must have in order so dexterously to avoid me, they wanted me to know precisely what I had wanted all the leafleteers I had previously avoided to know: that they so wished I did not exist, that they would do their best to make me feel as if, in fact, I didn't. Ooooh, how I hated them! Which means, I guess, that I saw and hated for the first time that part of me.

Meanwhile, Lucy was having a ball. She was "selling" her leaflets to just about everyone now. She would cheerfully stick out her hand. If a Person in a Hurry ignored her, she would pay him no mind and eagerly offer a leaflet to the next passerby. She was able to renew her hope in a flash.

But I had trouble, at first. The process was humiliating. At one point, our foray to the Square took us past a trash can. Aha! I suddenly entertained the idea of ditching all my leaflets, telling Lucy I had "sold" them all, and inviting her to go back to the church for hot chocolate. Then, I could return to my role as an efficient Person in a Hurry and take off my cursed sandwich board.

But no. I stayed. And it was not just guilt that kept me leafleting. To my amazement, I was slowly starting to have fun. I had experienced the other side of leafleting and found it strangely pleasing. It gave me a kind of glimpse into people's privacy, a brief sampling of what people were like when they didn't know they were being watched. I was learning something about them, and about me.

Once I discharged my venom at the Great People who had no time for Lucy and me or our leaflets—by imagining them to be empty and worthless, though rich and powerful—I had to admit to myself that they were no different from me (except probably richer and more powerful). I had to admit that I had rushed through many a crowd just as they were doing, that I had rejected the leaflets of cute little girls just as they were doing, and that I had always felt my agenda certainly took precedence over leafleteers in Harvard Square or anywhere else.

I began to look at each person more closely. Lucy said she wanted to go sell some leaflets in the Kids Wordsworth Bookstore because she was cold, so I stood outside on the curb alone while she went in. Each Person in a Hurry started to look a little less evil as I saw some signs of suffering in him or her. (There were some hers in the category of People in a Hurry, though mostly they were hims.)

And I began to enjoy even more the people who accepted my leaflets. They wove in and out of the crowd like secret agents of connectedness. As I looked for them and focused on them, instead of on the People in a Hurry, I began to find more and more of them. I noticed the little smile in their eyes. I appreciated the millisecond they might take to look at me as they accepted my leaflet. In that millisecond, we exchanged a quick burst of energy, a moment of affirmation. It was as though we were part of a secret society that was determined not to let the Hurried Life consume our souls.

I started to notice details, like the spangled brooch on a woman's oversized coat, or the way a man had stuffed his scarf skillfully into his jacket, so it both looked stylish and held in warmth. I started to look forward to each encounter, each chance to find out what kind of person this next person would be. I started to see how much joy the People Who Paused seemed to take even in this mundane millisecond of their lives, during which they accepted a leaflet from a man or little girl in sandwich boards.

The leaflet seemed to give them an excuse to stop, rather than present them with an obstacle. Some even engaged me in conversation. "Oh, where is the church?" Or "Is that your little girl?" Or "Isn't it nice that Harvard Square is looking so Christmassy today?"

Others went deeper. One was a man who looked like an aging William Holden. He was dressed in worn, tattered but natty clothes. He was in need of a shave and his hair was matted down from need of a shampoo. He casually strolled up to me and took my leaflet, while shaking my hand—in and of itself an unusual thing for the recipient of a leaflet to do. "Well, well," he said, greeting me as if he were the Mayor of the People Who Pause, "you look a little lost out here. I've been watching you. But you are catching on. The key is to go with the flow. Don't let the bastards get you down. There's mostly nice people out here, you just have to catch them right. It's rather like fishing."

We chatted a little while. This man was an experienced beggar. But he was also a philosopher, a psychologist and a connoisseur of fine food he couldn't afford. For his fund of knowledge and quality of language, he might as well have been a graduate of Harvard University as a panhandler in Harvard Square. "I like the streets," he told me. "I like what I do and I like it out here. Each day brings surprises. I am never bored and I never suffer from stress."

"But how do you survive?" I asked this man, whom, in my mind, I had named Happy.

"Odd jobs. People know me at the stores. There is a lot of work that no one wants to do. Errands, weeding, window-washing, sidewalk sweeping. I keep busy. I earn more than I spend. You'd be surprised how much I have actually put away in the bank. For my retirement, you know," he added with a twinkle in his eye.

Then, he disappeared in a flash, almost as if he were a ghost. He didn't even give me the chance to give him some money. His last words to me were, "Keep up the good work. We're here when you need us. Cheerio!" Cheerio? This is the vocabulary of a beggar? I felt as if a mentor had just graced me with a message. I vowed to myself I would learn from Happy. And from the women with the black gloves. And from the other People Who Pause. I vowed I would learn to pause. And try to keep up what Happy had called my "good work." I felt chagrined that I had so resisted leafleting in the first place.

As I continued to hand out my leaflets, I wondered what Happy meant when he said, "We're here when you need us." Wasn't it supposed to be the other way around? What did I need from him?

As I stood there, lost in thought and a little dazed, I realized that I needed from him his example. I needed to believe him, first of all, and not dismiss him as some crackpot neo-hippie. Then, I needed to take him seriously, as seriously as

I need to take Thoreau or John the Baptist, fringe people who speak to the heart of life.

The irony is that those of us—like me—who live in the mainstream of life, can learn a lot from those—like Happy or Thoreau or John the Baptist—who live on life's outskirts. We are busy earning money, raising children, staying fit and "being responsible," while they are busy on another plane. Thank God they are there, as Happy reminded me, when we need them.

Soon, Lucy pranced up to me from out of the bookstore, proud that she had "sold" all her leaflets before I had. I split the leaflets I had left with her, and we dispensed the last few together.

As we meandered back toward the church and the hot chocolate that awaited us, I felt that I had changed. Oh, of course, at my age no one changes all that much. But, by golly—if I may borrow a phrase my grandfather used all the time—I had just seen something special. I would remember this day in Harvard Square and try to keep it in mind, as if I had been Scrooge just visited by the spirits of Christmas.

I had seen life from a new point of view. I had seen life from the point of view of Happy, a man the world sees as a bum but I now saw as a messenger, a prophet. I had also seen in others myself, at my worst: a Man in a Hurry. But I had also seen people who'd learned to pause long enough to open themselves to the unexpected in life.

In short, I had seen the human moment in a public square. It is now. It is there, and here. It is everywhere. Meaning and love reside in every moment everywhere like sap within a tree, waiting to be tapped. Messengers, like our children and like Happy, try to tell us how to tap into these moments all the time. If we can listen, we can learn. We can learn how to tap into every human moment. Then, we can live life as we're meant to live it.

ECHOES . . .

Sometimes, Often, Always

Messengers, like Happy and Ruby, appear in our lives regularly. We just have to see through their disguises. They usually do not show up with a sign around their necks that says, Prophet, *or* Person Who Can Add Meaning to Your Life.

The author of the following piece is one of the world's authorities on learning differences, and she gives memorably vivid and informative lectures on that topic around the world. In this piece, she tells of an episode that transpired before one of her lectures. In this case, the messenger was the person in need. In offering help, the author received a gift.

As you read this account, you should know that the author, whom I'll call Anne, is in her early seventies, has had breast cancer and is now more than ten years post-mastectomy. She has also seen her husband of fifty years have a stroke that robbed him of his mental faculties to such an extent that he has to live in an assisted-living home. Anne can visit her husband and be recognized by him, but he neither can look forward to nor remember the

*details of her visits. Still, Anne is as honestly upbeat about
life as any person I know or have ever known. She radiates
positive energy because she always seems to find the
warmth embedded even in the direst of circumstances.*

—E. H.

I thought I could predict every moment of that tightly
planned day. My note cards were in order. The outlines
were at the auditorium, ready for distribution. I looked forward to having a generous six hours for exploring reading
comprehension; helping readers connect with writers, with
ideas and with themselves, and how to join printed words
with the knowledge, emotions and the questions we carry
inside. While some kinds of comprehension develop sponta-
neously, most students need instruction from teachers who
understand the processes themselves.

I was wearing my Worry Doll necklace. Classically, these
individual, colorful, tiny Guatemalan figures are kept in a jar
or on a plate. When their owner puts a few under the bed pil-
low at night, their job is to worry on the sleeper's behalf, thus
providing tranquil slumber. But, lore says, when Worry Dolls
are joined in pairs on little bits of wood (as in my necklace)
they become Amigos, friends to the world and to each other.

With thirty minutes to spare before being picked up, I
planned to sit in the hotel lobby and polish the new introduction to my talk. As I relished this bubble of private time,
a man came down the hall, telling the woman behind the
registration desk, or perhaps the world at large, "I can't work
my phone. How do I get long distance?"

She replied, rather curtly, "It works just like any other phone. Just get into AT&T or whoever your carrier is. You'll have to use your PIN."

His face told me her words didn't make sense to him. "I have a family emergency. I need to make a call."

The woman shrugged and turned away. "Just use it like any other public phone."

He was pale, and he seemed perplexed and overwhelmed. I got up and crossed over to him, explaining that I couldn't help overhearing, that I had often been confused by telephone terminology myself. I held out my cell phone and offered to place the call for him. He stepped back, hesitant, but clearly wanting to say yes. I said that my prepaid phone plan let me call anywhere, any time, with no long-distance charges.

"It's free," I said. "Please just tell me the number so I can call it for you." When the number started to ring, I handed him the phone and turned away to give him the illusion of privacy. I heard him tell the person on the other end that his daughter had spent twelve hours in surgery, the doctors were doing their best but she was very weak and in grave danger of infection, so the children must not come to visit for the next several days. He said he didn't know when he would be able to call again, or how he would get the news to the rest of the family. Then, his voice cracked. He said he had to go and handed the phone back to me because he didn't know how to hang up.

He started to tell me about his daughter who had gotten her right sleeve caught in the machinery of a leaf blower; the machine had devoured not only the cloth of her jacket but had torn off her right forearm. With that, his whole body trembled, and sobs choked him. I put my arms around him and, with one hand, cradled his head against my shoulder. I didn't know what to say. How stupid it would be to tell him that everything would be all right. All I could think of to say was that I could tell he loved his daughter very much. That reached him. "Yes, I do. I love her very much."

He raised his head from my shoulder and stopped short. "I shouldn't be doing this. I shouldn't be crying like this. I should be strong. I'm a cop."

"Yes, you should be crying like this. You love her, she's hurt, you're worried and you're probably exhausted. How did you get here? Are you alone?"

He explained that his daughter had been brought to the hospital by a medevac helicopter, that he and his wife had come by car. His wife had seen the helicopter pass over their house but had no idea who the passenger/patient was. He told me that his wife was waiting in their room to hear whether he had been able to make a call. I asked him to bring her, and their list of family telephone numbers, to the lobby. I would place the calls for them, as many as they wanted, for the next thirty minutes. I emphasized it would be free. He looked at me, dazed, reluctant, embarrassed, ambivalent, frightened and aching for someone to make the decision for him. "Let's do this for your wife. We can help her."

Several minutes later, he reappeared, hand-in-hand with his wife. Her hair was rumpled, her eyes red from sleeplessness and tears. They looked like Hansel and Gretel, lost in the woods. I didn't press her with the manners of introductions; I just asked her to tell me the number of someone she thought they should call. When the connection was made, I gave her the phone. Her husband slipped his hand into mine, rather the way you fit a plug into an outlet to get power. I held his hand while his wife talked. For the next call, he talked. She held my hand. And thus it went, with them alternating who spoke on the phone, telling the news.

When bad things happen, we need to tell the story out loud. It's how we come to realize that it's true. Finally, they had called all the people on the list, and it was time for me to go. I kissed each of them and wished their family the best of luck.

At the podium, I put aside my carefully crafted introduction. First, touching my necklace, I told the conference-goers how the dolls had once represented worry but, coming together in pairs instead of alone, they were now Amigos, symbols of friendship.

Next, I told the story of the two frightened, grief-stricken people, and how, through them, I had just been given a great gift: A piece of black plastic, a cell phone, had been my passport into the inner reaches of two other human souls. I had been privileged to stand in the presence of so much love, from parents to child, and back and forth between husband and wife. These people gave me the gift of allowing me to help them when they were in trouble. Proud, habitually competent people often don't know how to do this. These two almost didn't dare but, in desperation, they took a chance.

Finally, I relayed the physician's credo that is carved on the base of a statue of Dr. Livingstone Trudeau in Saranac, New York: "To cure sometimes, to relieve often, to comfort always."

This same credo can belong to us all. With educators, parents and students, we can sometimes cure ignorance by offering knowledge. In classrooms, we can often relieve anxiety by demonstrating successful strategies. And, in our dealings with other human beings, we can comfort always by being intellectually and emotionally available.

There is no more solemn trust.

There is no greater privilege.

An Angel of Mercy

While Anne intentionally helped the people in the last story, the author of the following piece gave help without knowing she was doing so when she did it. Often, this is the case. We just do not know when the smallest gesture—like a thank-you or a pat on the back—can change a life.

For example, a friend of mine told me about a priest who was about to quit his job and leave the priesthood altogether because he despaired of the corruption he saw within the church, despaired of how little good he thought he was doing. Until, one day, he went to get a haircut. His elderly barber, who was a member of his parish, told the priest while cutting his hair that he had been thinking of suicide, but had stopped short of committing the act when he thought of the priest, and what a warm and genuine man he was. "I was fed up with it all," the barber said, "all the phonies that come and go around here, and since my kids are grown and my wife is gone, I thought I would go join her wherever we go after we die. But then, I thought of you." At that point, the barber stopped and put his hand on the priest's shoulder, just for a moment.

"That touch was electric," the priest told my friend. "Sitting there in that old-fashioned chair, seeing the reflection in the big mirror of Joe, my barber, with his hand on my shoulder, as he told me that he believed in me enough to turn away from suicide, well, what could I do? You'd have to be an awful cynic not to see a greater force at work in there, don't you think?"

Joe, the barber, had no idea how much he was helping the priest right then. This is often the way with human moments. Just as it was in the following account.

—E. H.

I have no training in retail sales, but every Christmas I help my brother out by working in his shop. One Christmas Eve day, I was behind the counter, gift wrapping, when my brother set a pair of magnificent, three-foot-high bronze candlesticks on the counter and asked me to write up the receipt for the woman purchasing them. Setting aside the wrapping accoutrements, I moved toward the lovely blonde woman standing at the opposite side of the counter, her slender hand resting on the base of one of the candlesticks. I smiled at the woman, wondering why she looked so familiar.

"Do you take American Express?" she asked, when I had tallied her bill and told her how much she owed. I nodded, marveling that I also found her voice familiar, with its musical sweetness and unmistakable European inflection. *How do I know this woman?*

Smiling, she handed me her credit card. I glanced at the name. The last name made no impression, but the first name, Leatrice, I recognized, indeed. I looked again into her still-smiling sapphire eyes. "Excuse me, but are you a hospital nurse?" I asked.

"Why, yes, I am," she replied, a bit surprised.

"Forgive me, please, if I get a little emotional," I said, already feeling tears welling up in my eyes. "Almost exactly two years ago today, I was in the hospital with an abscessed kidney, and you were the nurse on duty the night they admitted me." I remembered reading the name Leatrice on her nametag that dismal night, as she lay a cool, smooth hand on my feverish brow.

"Yes, I did work the night shift then," she answered slowly, her eyes widening as she scrutinized me more closely. "I remember you now. Renal abscesses are so rare, you know. We were all very worried about you," she added softly, reaching across the counter to take my hand.

"You were so very kind to me. I was so sick and in such pain, and you were like an angel of mercy. I blessed you for your kindness," I told her, tears flowing now at the memory. I had nearly died of that abscess.

"You're all well now, I hope," she said tentatively, still pressing my hand in hers.

"Oh, yes," I assured her, wiping away my tears with my other hand.

"You were very lucky," she almost whispered.

"I know. I was blessed with good care," I said. My gratitude for that care had not diminished over time. Especially at Christmastime, the anniversary of the event, I was particularly mindful of how blessed I had been—and was, still. "But, you're a wonderful nurse. I'm sure all your patients have blessed you."

"Perhaps," she smiled thoughtfully. I turned and processed her credit-card sale, handing her the receipt and helping her to the door with the candlesticks.

"Merry Christmas, and thank you," she said, reaching out to hug me.

"Merry Christmas, to you," I set down the candlesticks to return her hug. "Thank you for being such an angel of mercy," I added warmly.

"You were the angel of mercy, dear," she said softly, and I could see tears standing in her blue, blue eyes. "I'm crying because, as I was driving to work that night, I was questioning continuing as a nurse. I was feeling quite desperate, really," she admitted. "Then, I went in to check on you. You could barely move, you were in so much pain, but you blessed me. I'll never forget that. I've had so many patients over the years. You were the only one who blessed me. You changed my life that night." She kissed my cheek, picked up the candlesticks and turned toward the door.

I bid her good-bye, and she smiled at me over her shoulder in parting. Then, she was gone. We had, by chance, encountered each other on two occasions in as many years, but I knew neither of us could ever forget the other. We had saved one another, each in our own way.

Ice

While in the last piece, a key human moment came when one person said thank you, in this piece, written by a man who is now a teacher, a key moment comes when one person gets angry. Sometimes, the most powerful and useful human moments bristle with conflict, even rage. (And be forewarned, the rage here is expressed with some off-color words.) This is because intimacy always includes conflict. Conflict is not the opposite of connectedness. The opposite of connectedness is indifference. When you care enough to get angry, you are still connected.

—E. H.

My relationship with my father was always strange in some way I can't put a name to. Not early on, of course. We were very close when I was little. But, as time went on and I moved clumsily into adolescence, I grew apart from him in ways that I know (particularly now that I'm a parent) hurt him. I grew to not respect him in ways that I chide myself for now, especially since his death two years ago.

I am the middle child of five, but the first boy, and there were a great many expectations associated with that. My father was a frustrated athlete, especially in the realm of hockey, where he always claimed that he hit his peak after thirty. He always blamed his mediocrity (one year of third-line varsity at Taft, one year of freshman hockey at Yale, and out) on the fact that no one ever spent any time working with him. His father, a highly successful surgeon and professor emeritus at Harvard (also a recruited star baseball player at Yale) never once saw him play anything, never once worked on my father's skills in the yard. I know, because he told me so many times.

I was having a bad game. My coordination was off, for no reason I could figure out, and I couldn't do anything right. My father had suffered another bad day at his failing business, and he started yelling from the stands as he always did. My father was such a yeller in hockey rinks that none of the other parents would stand with him. I went down at center ice and dropped my stick. "Get up!" he yelled. (When he yelled I couldn't hear anybody else.) I fumbled for my stick and dropped it. "GET UP!" I dropped it again. He yelled some more. I couldn't get to my feet, I was trying so hard.

And then I snapped. I actually calmed down as the game went on around me. I picked up the stick, ignoring everything else, and skated slowly past the stands. At the top of my lungs, I screamed, "F--k off, a--hole!" as I skated by, pumping my arm in a victory gesture. Everyone turned silent. I went to the bench and put my head in my hands. The coach came over as everyone on the bench stared at me, dumbstruck. "You okay?" Coach asked.

"What did I just do?" was all I could say.

It was a long, silent ride home, one I'll never forget. We didn't speak for a day-and-a-half. I remember how sad I was during that time. I was in ninth grade, a good hockey player, but bad at everything else. I was mired in a battle for my identity, having recently come into a high school of four thousand kids, and I was losing. I was smoking pot, drinking, intentionally failing algebra, getting Cs everywhere else, even though I was capable of much better. I was failing my father in every way. And now, I'd publicly humiliated him, and we were not speaking.

Finally, my father and I talked. He initiated the conversation, and he set the tone. He was calm. I could tell he was sad, too. He didn't need to say that. His opener—"We need to straighten some things out"—was calm and loving, not what I thought I'd deserved. But it was an open door, and I needed that open door. I stayed calm, and I told him that I needed space as an athlete, that I needed to play for me, not for him. I had to tell him that he needed to respect the fact that I was an athlete who had worked hard at his game, and that I knew when I was having a bad day. I didn't need him to tell me, especially not in that way. I told him also that I had grown into a good hockey player because he had worked with me, and that I still wanted to talk about the game with him—it was our only connection—but that the relationship had to change.

My life did change after that, although it was another year before I quit drugs and started achieving in school. I later realized that it was my father's doing. He backed off. He never yelled at me during a game again. After games, he would ask me what I thought, not tell me where I had erred.

We could talk again. There was still much we didn't talk about, but he gave me the power I'd needed, and I think it was hard for him to do that.

I have always respected that moment of connection between us when he stepped back and gave me the reins of my life. The moment comes back to me often.

I think about this in working with adolescents. They can be so difficult, but so often what they're after is what they're being denied: power. If I can create classroom strategies and one-on-one interactions that give them that power in a way that teaches them how to use it, then I'm on my way to getting to them.

I thanked my father for that in my eulogy to him.

1-800 . . .

While in the previous story we were able to see what happened over the long-term, life doesn't give us that opportunity if the people involved are strangers. Some of the most memorable human moments—like mine with Ruby or Happy—take place with people we never see again. Then, we are left guessing as to what will happen next, as was the author of this piece.

There is no logical reassurance I can give this author, or anyone else. After all, bad things do happen. And yet it is my deepest belief, borne out by my experience, that if you add positive energy to whatever is going on, even just a little bit, as can be done with a smile or a short conversation, that somehow helps. Sometimes, it helps a lot.

—E. H.

It was below freezing one day in early February, when I noticed that my vacuum cleaner was malfunctioning. Or, as I preferred to think of it, dysfunctioning. *Dysfunction* is a word I learned from reading self-help books. At the time, I owned at least 150 of these, but none of them could help my vacuum cleaner remove crumbled rice cakes from the crevices of my sofa. My entire environment was blanketed with a beige layer of rice-cake crumbs. I ate rice cakes everywhere. I was a fanatic about health foods, hoping that the right food could keep me safe from unpredictable illnesses. It is a comforting illusion that I nurture. We all need some sort of illusion to get through the day.

I called the 800-number on the warranty card, which I had never mailed to the manufacturer. I was not a fanatic about mailing in warranty cards. When my call went through, an interminable voice-mail menu led me into a series of instructions that finally resulted in the arrival on the line of an actual human voice.

People excite me. I love strangers. When I talk on the phone to people I don't know, it is fascinating to me to imagine the details of their lives. The theater of my imagination improvises instantly. Where *is* this person? In a cubicle? In a gigantic roomful of desks? Working at home? Are colorful plastic toys strewn about while a stew slowly simmers in the crockpot? What kind of stew? Beef? Chicken? Tofu? All these questions make me long to connect with these people, to know them a little and to sense that I have touched and been touched. To me, there is a feel of the exotic about this, like the thrill of traveling to a distant land.

The human voice on the other end of this line was female, nasal and hoarse.

"This is Charlene, how can I help you?" it said.

Charlene was clearly from Country-Western land. Her twang suggested that at any moment she might sing to me, a rendition of "Stand by Your Man" perhaps. I love English spoken in some way I don't often hear.

Outside my window, the sky was that unreal blue it often becomes in February in my northeastern beachside community.

"Where are you, Charlene?" I asked.

"Ah'm in South Cah'lina," she replied.

"Is it warm there?"

"It's a gorgeous day heah," said Charlene.

"Do you have a bad cold, Charlene?" I asked. She sounded as though she belonged in bed with a stack of *People* magazines and boxes of honey-lemon lozenges. I was hoping there was someone in her life who would bring her cups of tea and plates of buttered toast on a tray.

"Ah have the WORST cold of mah life," she said. "But how can I help YOU, ma'am?"

"My vacuum cleaner is not vacuuming," I said, "but that does not compare to how miserable you must be feeling. You sound awful."

"My daughter's wedding is tomorrow night, and Ah just feel terrible."

"Did you ever hear of echinacea or golden seal?" I asked. Since early childhood, I had been a major hypochondriac. Accordingly, I had spent countless evenings reading books about vitamins, herbal medicine and homeopathic remedies while my peers were polishing their toenails and watching TV. "Do you have any Vitamin C where you are right now?" I asked. *Even FedEx could not get her the vitamin fast enough,* I thought. *She has to take a huge dose NOW, and then repeat that dose hourly for the whole day!*

"Ah do have some Vitamin C," she said.

"Can you take some now?" I asked anxiously. "Can you take two thousand milligrams? Right now?"

"Ah could do that when Ah get off the phone with you."

"Good," I said. "What about the echinacea? What about the golden seal? Echinacea can jump-start your immune system. Golden seal can kill bacteria. You need them. Get them after work. Take them." I felt embarrassed about how controlling I was being, how what I was doing, I knew, would be interpreted by someone from Al-Anon as a "boundary violation." I was attending Al-Anon for my "boundary and control issues." But I couldn't let Charlene suffer so much!

"Thank you for helping me," she said. "Ah really feel miserable."

"Will you get the herbs?"

"Ah wee-ill," she replied. The way she said "will," it had two syllables. I loved it. I wished she could teach me to talk like that.

"I'm glad I could help," I said. "How do you think you got so sick?"

"Ah have no ah-DEE-yah," replied Charlene with the wonderful Southern flavor in her voice.

"How do you feel about the man your daughter is marrying?" I asked. I am really shameless about just jumping in and asking questions like this of total strangers. I can't help myself. As soon as I get a theory, I just have to see if it works. I was trained as a scientist, but I believe in astrology and tarot cards.

My theory (I usually have a theory) was that she was not happy about some aspect of her daughter's impending marriage, and that this distress had compromised her immune function.

"Ah don't trust him," said Charlene. With the stuffiness in her head, it sounded like, "Ah dote trust him."

"Does your feeling that your daughter will somehow not be safe with him make you lose sleep?"

"Yeah, it does. Ah'm jus tossin' and turnin' all naght long." It sounded like, "tossid and turdid all daght logg."

"Why don't you trust him?"

"He cheated on his last wife." It sounded like "waahf" the way she said this. "He didn't make his child-support payments. He was drinkin' then, though. He's sober now."

"Recovered alcoholics are good people, Charlene."

"Not all of 'em. What if he starts up the drinkin' again?"

"I know how you must feel," I said.

"Mah supervisor—she is goin' to write me up if Ah talk to you too long. Ow cahlls have to be a certain length."

"Oh, Charlene—I'm so sorry!"

"It's all right. You helped me. Now how can I help you with that vacuum cleaner of yours?"

CREATING
CONNECTIONS . . .

Invitation to reflect: Through the power of love and imagination, we turn ordinary moments into human moments. I have defined human moments as those moments when we feel closely connected to someone or something outside of ourselves, and in the presence of something that matters, which we call *meaning*.

Where or with whom do you reliably find your human moments? Maybe with your children or grandchildren? Or with your spouse? Or a certain friend? Or maybe in your garden, or in church or temple? Maybe in a special chair in a certain corner of the reading room of your local library? Maybe alone in the woods where you take long walks? Maybe with your dog? Or with certain memories? Or maybe all of these?

Common obstacles to connection: Anything that blocks love or imagination blocks human moments. The block can be simple, like being in too much of a hurry. It is difficult to have a human moment if you are rushing to go somewhere else. The block can be complex, like having been badly hurt by a certain group of people. Resentment can then rein us in and prevent us from reaching out. Habit can also block human moments. You get used to seeing the world in a certain way, and so you do not open yourself up to a new view. Your imagination falls asleep.

One obstacle to love is that we place in our own way, on purpose. Oddly enough, as much as we crave close connections and the human moments they create, we also fear them. We fear anything new, we fear getting close to others and we fear opening ourselves up. As much as we want to, we also do not want to. So, we choose to hold back. The obstacle to love, in this case, is our own choice. How much easier it is to play the seasoned cynic, dryly commenting on the sentimentality of others, than to let down your guard and open your heart for others to see!

This is perhaps the greatest obstacle of all: a person's own choice to hold back.

Possible steps you might take: If you find that you are holding back more than you wish you would, if you find that fear takes over when you try to connect, then what you might do is pick a safe situation—like a conversation with a friend—and talk about your fears. One of the amazing facts of human nature is that we solve problems—even without seeming to solve the problems—just by talking about them to interested others. Once you address your hesitation as a problem, and once you start to talk about it in confidence with trusted others, then the problem will start to shrink away. You will start to come up with strategies and solutions. Furthermore, just the fact that you are having a close conversation with another person will begin to give you more confidence—confidence you can use to widen your circle of connectedness. I know this works, because I have used it in my own life.

Chapter Two

CHILDHOOD

WHERE'S MY DAD?

I n the middle of the night, I heard a noise.

I woke up and listened, and heard another noise, like a clank. It was dark out, but I had no idea what time it was. I was three years old, almost four.

As I lay in bed, I continued to hear clanking sounds. I called out for my mother. In a moment, she appeared by my bedside.

"What's going on?" I asked.

"Dad is leaving," she replied, stroking my forehead with her hand.

I don't know how I understood that she meant he was leaving for good, but I must have on some level, because I then remember asking her, "Is he taking all the tools in the shop with him?" Dad had set up a wonderful little wood shop in our basement on Seaview Street in Chatham. He and I would play down there for hours on end.

"Yes," Mom said. "He is packing up the shop right now." It was the clank of the tools being put into boxes that had awakened me. I started to cry.

"But he is just moving up to Gammy Hallowell's, and he is taking the tools with him so you can play with them whenever you visit him—and you will visit him often."

I sat up and looked out my bedroom window. By the light of the moon and streetlights, I could see my dad carrying a cardboard box, with hammers and planes and a hand drill sticking up out of it. I saw him put the box into his car, an old Willys.

Like a film clip, that's all I remember of that night. Dad moved out. He took his tools with him. I cried. Mom comforted me.

Until that night, I lived within what my nearly-four-year-old mind imagined was a happy family. My two older brothers, John, who was twelve, and Ben, who was sixteen, may have known better, but I had no idea (at least not consciously) Dad would be leaving home for good. On the other hand, I must have had some idea, because I instantly got the picture that night, with almost no explanation.

Why was he leaving? Because he was sick. Gammy—our grandmother—could take care of him. He still loved us, but he was sick and needed to move away. That was what I was told, and that was enough. I didn't fight it. It was not until years later that I learned that "sick" meant insane; years later still I learned that, in Dad's case, insane meant manic-depressive, or what is now called bipolar disorder.

Looking back, this was the first real crisis of my life. I lost my dad, at least my live-in dad.

What saved me back then was the family I found outside my own house, the family I found with my cousins, Jamie and Lyn, and my aunt, my mother's sister, whom I called

Duckie, and her husband, my uncle, my father's brother, whom I called Uncle Jimmy. That's right: A pair of sisters had married a pair of brothers, so these cousins Jamie and Lyn were double first cousins, the genetic equivalent of siblings. Since my actual brothers were so much older than I was, Jamie, who was only two years older, became my brother in practice; and Lyn, who was four years older, became my sister. This was the first of many small miracles of connection that saved my life.

How is it a miracle, you ask? Because, when your father goes insane and leaves the house in the middle of the night never to return, the usual next step is not that an aunt and uncle and pair of cousins lovingly adopt you, while your mother tries to sort out her life and regain her bearings. Had I not found Jamie and Lyn and Duckie and Uncle Jimmy, I can guarantee you that I would either be dead today, or on Skid Row, or in jail, or barely bumping along.

But I did find them. I would go across the field and down the hill from my house to their house every day. Chatham was a little town, and it was safe to walk everywhere. As I got a bit older, Jamie taught me how to ride a bike. I can remember how patient he was with me. He was, and still is, as kind a person as you'll ever find. Although he was only five when my dad moved out, he knew that something bad was going on, and he paid extra attention to me. So did Lyn. So much so that I never really felt the pain. I only cried the night Dad moved out—and it still makes me sad to think of it, as it would have been great to keep Mom and Dad together forever—but Jamie and Lyn made me a member of their family so quickly that I never felt really sad.

At my fourth birthday party, the first birthday after Dad moved out, I am told I was a terror, bossy and rude and just a brat. But Jamie and Lyn didn't give up on me, why I don't know. They kept asking me to play with them, and play we did, every day. I watched TV with them in their basement, I fed their dogs with them, and I slept over more often than I slept in my own bed. I went to kindergarten in Chatham, and on to first and second grade. Jamie and Lyn and I were a family now. (We still are.)

My childhood may have been stormy, as were so many in my generation, but it was also filled with the excitement that fills every childhood, and the jagged edges of adventure. I remember one time being desperately afraid as I hid under a bed in a strange house while the police searched for Jamie and me. Room to room the troopers marched, I imagined with guns drawn, their muffled voices drawing nearer and nearer to my hiding spot beneath that bed on the second floor. I thought I was going to be arrested and taken to jail if I was caught. I was about five. I held my breath as I lay under the bed. I remember the policeman's flashlight scanning the floor and stopping when it hit my ankles. For sure, I was done for. But the policeman must not have made out my feet in the light. He left. I let out a long sigh, but only once I determined the policeman was far enough away not to hear me.

Years later, I discovered that that event, which ranks as the most intense moment of fear in my life, was staged. The older sister of one of Jamie's friends was friends with one of the Chatham cops. She had arranged for them to come "search" the house while Jamie and I were playing in it, having first told us that the police were going to arrest anyone they found. Why did we believe her, and believe her so deeply that to this day I have never been so scared? This is childhood. No perspective, no skepticism, no disbelief. Just wide-eyed wonder.

Jamie and Lyn and Duckie and Uncle Jim gave love to me, and even the town itself gave, as towns do to children everywhere. I remember standing on the white lines in the parking lot at Harding's Beach on hot days, so as not to burn my feet on the blacktop as I waited in line for a hot dog. I remember radios, suntan oil and bikinis. I remember the smell of grass as it was being mowed. I remember so many smells from Chatham: honeysuckle, salt air and seaweed chief among them.

Childhood transcends happy or sad, good or bad. By objective standards, my childhood was not a stable one, but I loved it nonetheless. I also sometimes hated it. Like most people, I have many wonderful memories and some pretty rotten ones. But what counts is having had that time of life, not whether it scores high or low on a scale of happiness and stability. Whether we were traumatized in childhood or treated quite marvelously, it still is the time that underpins all other times; it is still the time from which we came, the time that calls us back, now and again.

Let yourself be called back. What do you hear? What do you see? Your dad moving out? A policeman's flashlight scanning a room as you hide under the bed?

Oh, how I wish I could go back. Not to do it all again, but just to see the town as it was: see Benny Nick, the patrol cop, standing at the intersection outside the Mayflower, waving to each of us kids as we walked by; see Mr. Parmenter look down at me from behind the counter at the drug store when I asked him where I could find something called Tampax for Lyn; order a pistachio cone at Howard Johnson's (without knowing what pistachio was, but ordering it on a dare); watch the town team play baseball from Uncle Jim's Jeep parked out atop the hill in center field, while he sipped Pabst from cans he'd opened with what he called a church key.

They had beer in cans with no pop tops then. Chatham had a telephone operator who came on the line and asked, "Number please?" No one locked houses or even cars.

It was safe. But it was dangerous, too; dads moved out, after all.

I would like to go back now and see that town as it was, but I can't. None of us can. But we can do something that is maybe even better. We can live those moments again in memory. We can see the town now as it was, in memory. We can hold what has long since died and disappeared and make it live again. Some of the most beautiful human moments look best in reruns, in memory.

We may not literally be able to go back in time, but we can go back and pluck our childhood moments like fruits from off the memory tree, and eat them to their fullest in our maturity.

ECHOES . . .

To Kiss a Boy

In the last story, I wrote about my memories of my father moving out. How I remember it now is different from how I lived it then. I am unable to know, now, what I felt then. I can only guess, and my guess is probably off the mark, at least a bit. In this way, time changes all human moments.

In the story that follows, we hear from another man who is looking back on his boyhood. The way we raise boys today is changing, and in a good way. But until recently, most boys could recall a moment from their childhoods like the one this author describes. It is so ironic that we raised boys to be tough, only to complain that as men they couldn't show emotion.

Every day, I hug and kiss my two sons, as well as my daughter. And, even though the boys (and Lucy) usually wipe off the kiss or turn their heads so I end up kissing their hair instead of their cheeks, I am glad I am giving them the idea that it is okay, even manly, to kiss—not to mention hug!

—E. H.

Like most of their era, men in my family were loath to show their emotions. In fact, there was a moment in the family's raising of a boy child when the big shift took place. I shall never forget mine.

Little boys were allowed to cry—show pain, disappointment or hurt when it occurred—just as girls were. But the day came when we boys had to stop all that if we were going to grow up to be like our fathers or grandfathers. If we were going to be real men—something we, of course, wanted to be—we could not continue to express our emotions like our sisters could.

My day took place at Washington's National Airport. Washington was my home, and my grandfather traveled there on business from his home in New York quite frequently. We always went to the airport to meet him and to see him off. The terminal wasn't particularly crowded then, and we could walk out on an observation deck to see the "Connies," as my dad called the Constellation planes, come and go. I adored my grandfather. When he came down the steps of the plane and onto the runway, I waved from the observation deck and couldn't wait to run to him for a hug and a kiss on the forehead.

One day, as he was leaving to go back to New York, I stepped forward for my usual hug and kiss. I was about nine or ten years old. He gently pushed me back, smiled and extended his hand to me. "You're a man now, Ralph," he said.

As I think back to that event some forty-five years ago, I can still feel the sense of bewilderment and hurt. I didn't feel like a man, and I felt a huge sense of loss.

But my grandfather and father were men of their time. Trying to navigate through my teens and young adulthood, I never remember either of them telling me that he loved me. I knew they both did, but it went unsaid.

There was one occasion, however, when I witnessed an outpouring of emotion from my father that astounded me. I had not seen such a thing before from him and am so grateful that I was present to be a part of that moment.

Dad and I had quit smoking together. I had smoked for ten years when we made the joint decision, and he had smoked for forty.

Two decades later, I was at a professional meeting in Ohio and called him to see what the doctor's diagnosis was of a long-standing breathing problem he had. He could not even say the word to me, nor could he tell me how he felt about it. He merely spelled it out over the telephone: "C-a-n-c-e-r." The doctor told me when I called that 5 percent of the patients who had his form of lung cancer survived the five-year anniversary of diagnosis. Dad was not one of them.

Our immediate family had gathered around his bed for a couple of days and knew that the end was near. He had been in a sort of coma since I arrived home to join the family and be with him. He hadn't spoken to me. I have been a singer all my life, and Dad was a very accomplished musician. I had brought an audiotape of a Bach mass I had recorded a year or so earlier with a wonderful choral group to play for him. I wasn't sure what—if any—of it he actually could hear, but it made me feel better to think that I was playing something he would have loved to hear.

When the "Qui Tolis" movement began, with me singing

the baritone solos, we all were astounded to see him actually sit straight up in the bed, his eyes opening for the first time in days and seeming to stare at something the rest of us didn't see in the room. I was moved beyond words and felt incredibly loved.

Shortly thereafter, Dad seemed to get better. He was awake and talked with all of us—his children, their spouses and his wife, my mother. He asked us if he was going to die. He still hadn't come to terms with that reality. When we told him he was, he began to tell us all how much he loved us. He repeated it over and over again, as if trying to make up for all the years when his commitment to manhood prevented him from doing it. He then turned to my mother and reached his arm out to her with what seemed to be every ounce of his strength. "You are my love," he said. I couldn't believe that he was saying that with all of us present. I had never heard him talk to her like that, and imagined that he must have been unable to see that we were there. "I have loved you for most of my life, and always shall. You are the love of my life. I love you so much."

There was this man whom I had never heard utter such things pouring out a lifetime of passion to my mother. A few hours later, he took his last labored breath. We all were present. We had a hard time leaving his side, and told him over and over again how much we loved him, just as we had told him when he could hear us.

What lessons I have learned from the men in my life! I thought when I was ten years old that a true man couldn't show the people he loved how much he loved them. As a child of the 1960s, I rebelled against that idea and openly lavished love on my own children. I had made the vow that my relationship with my own son, in particular, would be different. I would hug him and give him a kiss on his forehead until he asked me not to, and would tell him I loved him every day. He now is twenty-eight years old, and I guess it hasn't occurred to him to ask me to stop. It makes me smile just to think of that.

Finally, as an older adult, I saw my male role model express a passion I never thought was there. Since then, I have spent much of my professional life as an educator trying to help other dads find that passion in themselves and share it with their own children.

Rescued

This story, told by a woman who is both a poet and a daughter, captures one of the universal moments of childhood: when you are scared and you need help from your mother or father. As you read this, I'll bet you think of such a moment of your own with your mother or father when you were young. I hope so.

—E. H.

I remember myself, age eight, asking to be excused after an interminable Sunday lunch, and taking myself outdoors for a walk. Sundays in Illinois in the 1950s were dangerous to young children: You could die of the boredom if you weren't careful. I remember walking along, desperate for adventure, and coming upon a stand of tall pine trees. I climbed to the top of the tallest one, whose branches were so beautifully spaced that they formed a ladder that even a child could climb. I scrambled up, with the joy of competence and strength, and admired the view from the top. My Sunday boredom vanished, and I could see for miles. I was simultaneously a watcher and a hider, an eagle and an angel. I could feel the thin top of that tree begin to sway with the breeze, and I wrapped my fingers more closely around its branches. The world began to sway, and the tree felt suddenly fragile and my hold on it precarious. I couldn't loosen my grip enough to begin my descent. My hands became slippery with holding on, my breathing came faster and my stomach began to churn. So, I waited—for what I have no idea, any miracle would do. And then, far below me, I saw my father walking along in his three-piece suit and his long overcoat and fedora. How had he known I needed him? How had he known which way I'd gone? I didn't dare call very loud to him for fear the inhalation of deep breath would dislodge me, but I breathed, "Daddy," and he heard me. He called out to ask where I was, and I guided him with small noises until he located me at the top of the highest tree, backlit against the sun.

He scaled the tree, hand over hand, up the ladder of the branches until he reached me and put his hands outside my hands on the same branches and his feet outside my feet, my body cupped inside of his. And he walked me down.

In my memory, my father is always dressed in a three-piece suit, with a gold watch in his pocket and a watch chain across his stomach. He must have had other clothes. He did, after all, sleep in pajamas and paint the picket fence each summer in khakis and an old shirt, but those were exceptions that simply proved the rule of the three-piece suit.

He was an ideal father: loving, reliable, kind. He taught me my prayers and listened to me say them every night as he put me to bed. He taught me how to shine shoes properly and paid me a dime for every pair of his I shined, no matter how they turned out. Every winter, he took me to the nearest man-made hill in all of that vast Midwestern prairie so that I could practice skiing. It was bitterly cold, and as that was the only hill for a thousand miles, the wind came across the great plains with nothing to stop it. It whipped the snow off the hill, so that even a land that was knee-deep in snow every winter had to make artificial stuff to keep it on that hill, and my father would stand at the bottom in his three-piece suit with the long overcoat and the fedora and the gold watch chain winking in the sun, and wait for me to come down the hill, over and over again. And I thought nothing of making him wait.

My father was an observer: careful, predictable, already old by the time I noticed him. He wasn't like the other fathers. He watched me skate and sail and play softball, but he didn't do any of those things with me. Except for that one afternoon when he climbed a tree, and then I knew he loved me.

Drums

In the previous story, the father was not like other fathers, but he was a wonderful father nonetheless. In this story, the child is not like other children, but he is a wonderful child nonetheless. I think I find this story particularly moving because, as a child psychiatrist, I have met many children who have to struggle to find their way. Almost always, those who make it have at least one adult in their lives who sees their strengths before their limitations, and makes them feel loved and special for who they are. Such adults are not always easy to find.

John Q. Thompson Jr., the father of this boy, is such an adult. He makes his son feel loved in a world where such a feeling is hard to come by. I don't think a person can do anything more important.

—E. H.

I have an adopted son, Will, who is eighteen years old. He has been diagnosed with various conditions. He is so much more than these diagnoses, of course, but for the sake of brevity, I will mention that he has acquired over the years the diagnoses of Tourette's syndrome, obsessive-compulsive disorder, and attention deficit hyperactivity disorder, but the overriding diagnosis for him is that of high-functioning pervasive developmental disorder and Asperger's syndrome.

He functions well in a number of areas, but the most notable is that of playing percussion. Since he was three years old, he was always banging on multiple pots, pans and cookie tins. At the age of thirteen, he announced that he wanted a drum set. I countered, "I know you like to beat on things and 'drum,' but let's start out with some lessons, you know, like with one drum, the snare drum."

He said, "No! I want a drum set." Finally, I relented and bought an old 1962 beat-up Ludwig drum set. To my astonishment, he sat down and played it. I play guitar, and when I played with him I found that he could intuitively play whatever appropriate rhythm was needed, be it rock, blues, march or big-band music. How this boy, who has multiple learning disabilities and the other diagnoses I mentioned and who can't tell you what day of the week it is and still believed in Santa Claus until he was seventeen years old, could immediately coordinate his four appendages and play like a pro can only be explained by inborn talent. For all his problems, he was born with a brain that could play drums with the best of them.

With this background, I'll now tell you about a special moment of connection. (Connecting is, of course, a problem for him, connecting with us and others. He doesn't like to brag [won't], delivers only fleeting eye contact, has no real friends, just friendly circumstances, and abhors tender words of affection like *love* and *sad*, though he can tolerate the "coarser" *mad*.)

When I was growing up, I always dreamed of having a family band. Well, my wife played the French horn in high school but hasn't stayed with it, and my daughter plays flute but isn't really into it. But I have played in various types of bands and, with my son on drums, I now play electric guitar.

One day, my son and I were playing a set upstairs at our house. Mark Gorena, a youth minister and a friend of ours, was at the dining-room table speaking with my wife. At one point, there was a pause in their conversation. Our music was bearing down from above. Mark looked and pointed upward and said to my wife, "That's how your son hugs his daddy, isn't it?"

My wife, agreeing, with tears in her eyes, nodded back.

CREATING
CONNECTIONS . . .

Invitation to reflect: Who from your childhood stands out in your memory as particularly positive and kind? Can you bring them into your mind right now?

Common obstacles to connection: Often, old pain separates people from the happy parts of their childhood. As one who knows about this firsthand, I can tell you my painful memories from the past are more gripping, often—and more dramatic—than the harmonious ones. Therefore, many people never hold onto the happy, affirming, strength-giving memories of their childhoods because the painful memories basically scare them away, and they end up with little or no memory of childhood at all.

Possible steps to take: Not long ago, my five-year-old son, Tucker, discovered, to his total amazement, that he could pass his finger through the flame of a candle and not get burned. He was terrified to do it at first. Even after he watched me pass my finger through the flame several times, he still felt afraid. But, after I coaxed him and reassured him and showed him how safe it was, he gave it a try. "WOW!" he shouted. "That was easy!" And he passed his finger back and forth through the flame a dozen times.

A painful childhood can serve as a wall of fire, separating you from the good parts, as well as the painful. If you have a friendly guide—like a spouse, a friend, a sibling, a relative or a therapist—you can reduce the power of that wall of fire. You may not turn it into the flame of a candle, but you can keep its blaze from cutting you off from your childhood altogether. It doesn't have to burn you up as you pass through it anymore.

Go back, reconnect with what was good, find the faces that cared and the people who helped. Swim in the old lake again, play on the old ball field, march in the old Fourth of July parade. Just imagining these happy aspects of your childhood can turn on their positive power, power that you may not have tapped into for years.

Even if your childhood was wonderful, you may have turned away from it and forgotten what positive energy it can feed you. Let yourself reconnect to that time of life; let yourself feel the hope and energy that is the natural gift of childhood. Simply go back in your mind, sit under a tree or by the fire, and take in what was good. It need not be lost. You *can* go back again and find a dose of renewal.

Chapter Three

FAMILIES

Hockey Night

For a few years back in the 1950s, the Boston Bruins hockey team played on Christmas night at the Boston Garden. For the four or five years that they did this, my grandmother got tickets for the whole family to drive from her house in Wiano on Cape Cod all the way to Boston on Christmas night, watch the game, then drive home. We did this every year, even after my dad moved out. This practice lasted from when I was about three to when I was about eight, just before my move to Charleston. Thanks to my grandmother, a family tradition survived a divorce.

This tradition made for deep magic in my life. You have to understand, Christmas at Gammy Hallowell's was special to begin with, but to top it off with a long trip into the night to watch a professional hockey game, and end up with a long drive back home so that I didn't go to bed until well past midnight, this was life better than best. This was magic.

The day would start with my brothers, my mother and I joining up with my cousins, Lyn and Jamie, and Duckie and Uncle Jim to drive from Chatham to Wiano, about a forty-five-minute drive. Dad had already left home and was living at Gammy's, so we would meet him there. We would open our presents from each other at home, but Gammy's presents would await us in Wiano. Gammy, being the only wealthy member of the family (and being a grandmother), always gave the most special presents.

But it wasn't the presents alone that made for the magic. It was the whole atmosphere of her grand house, with the snow-drifted grounds, the long curving driveway, the blue-gray bay out back, and the huge, crackling fire inside. Gammy had the biggest fireplace I had ever seen. Three or four people could easily have sat in it, not that they would have wanted to! She had a huge mantel above the fireplace, as well, marked by massive port and starboard lamps on each side of the mantel. Stockings, of course, adorned the mantel when we arrived, a huge tree stood in the gathering room between the dining room and the living room, and the aromas of the Swedish cook Gerda's great cooking permeated the air.

After we had the treat of opening presents, and after we watched Uncle Jim, as the oldest man present, carve the turkey, and after we ate the turkey and whatever special dessert Gerda had concocted, and after we had taken a little nap or pretended to do so, then Dad and Gammy would herd all of us who wanted to go into cars for the trip to The Game.

Uncle Jim, Duckie and Mom usually drove back to Chatham at this point. I never could understand how they could pass up the hockey game. In retrospect, I am sure it was awkward for Mom to be at Gammy's house at all, since she and Dad had divorced. Looking back I give her a lot of credit for how she handled it, so gracefully that I was never aware of any tensions in the air at all—even though there must have been quite a few.

Dad, Gammy, Jamie, Lyn, my brothers John and Ben, and I, and sometimes our cousins, the Heckshires from Philadelphia, would pile into as many cars as we needed and start the drive.

I remember those drives as if they were transcontinental expeditions. To my young mind, Boston was far, far away, and the arena called the Boston Garden was an enchanted kingdom. We would play twenty questions or a geography game for some of the trip. How many countries, states, cities and regions do I know that begin with the letter *a*? Many, thanks to that game. Dad, not long out of the War, always used Alsace–Lorraine for his first *a*. I always thought it sounded like a girl's name, not part of a country. To this day, when I hear "Alsace–Lorraine," I think of my dad and those trips to the Boston Garden.

Dad would also teach me about hockey as we drove. I learned about the red line and the blue lines and offsides and everything else I know about hockey from Dad, who was an All-America right wing at Harvard. I was very proud of him for that, and when I visited her house, I often looked through the scrapbooks Gammy had made from those days.

When we got to Boston, Act Two of the magic show began. The city. Parking. The dark streets with bright lights. Dad telling me to hold on tight to my ticket so no one would snatch it out of my hand (what a thought!). My brothers and cousins and Gammy and I walking up the many flights of stairs to our seats in the balcony. I am amazed that Gammy could handle all those stairs at her age, but she was a trouper.

She always managed to get us balcony seats near the front row, so we could look down on the whole ice. When the

Bruins came charging out of the dressing room and onto the ice, I would let out a whoop with all the other fans and feel transported to another state of mind: Pure Pleasure. Act Three of the show. I was enthralled, from the first second of action until the end. After each period, I would wish that I could turn back the clock and see it played all over again. I wanted the game to last forever.

It seemed the Bruins always played either the Montreal Canadiens or the New York Rangers on Christmas night. The red-white-and-blue uniforms of the Canadiens looked crisp and royal, while the black-and-gold of the Bruins looked tough and streetwise. And the Rangers' dark-blue uniforms, with "R-A-N-G-E-R-S" written diagonally down the front in white letters, highlighted in red, looked imposing, just as a team from New York should.

I can remember Jean Beliveau, number 4 for Montreal, as vividly as I remember John F. Kennedy. Beliveau had charisma. He was a gentleman, or so it seemed to me, in a rough-and-tumble game. He played hockey the way I imagined my grandfather, Skipper, would play—like a gentleman.

But I loved the fights, too. The Bruins had a bunch of tough guys. Leo Boivin, one of their defensemen, looked like a six-foot fire hydrant on skates. It was said he was the best hip-checker ever to play the game. Teddy Green, another defenseman, was the best fighter on the team. Although the Bruins usually lost, Teddy Green won his fights. I remember Vic Hadfield of the Rangers leaving the ice with blood streaming down his face after a battle with Teddy Green. The blood scared me, but Dad told me it looked much worse than it was. This was back when the league only had six teams, no one wore helmets, and Jacques Plante, goalie for the Canadiens, was stirring up a controversy by being the first goalie to wear a mask.

After each twenty-minute period, a truck called a Zamboni would roll out onto the ice. The Zamboni picked up all the ice chips and sprayed down a thin film of water, giving the rink a shining, new surface. I loved to watch the Zamboni as it swept away the junked-up ice and replaced it with what looked like pure glass. On Christmas night, the Zamboni driver wore a Santa Claus hat, and we all gave him resounding applause as he drove off the ice, waving his hat to the crowd. I remember thinking he was a very nice man. I once asked my dad if I could drive the Zamboni someday. I don't remember what he said; I don't know that I cared; I was just so glad to be at the game.

After it was over, Act Four of the magic began. The Bruins, usually beaten, would skate off the ice, but we all would applaud, win or lose. Sportsmanship was a big deal when I was growing up. Then Dad and Gammy would usher us back down the many, many stairs out onto Causeway Street next to the North Station. Most of the crowd would head off into trains for their trip home, but we headed for the parking lot and our cars. Now, I had no ticket to hold tightly onto, just my dad's hand, as he guided us through the crowd. Usually, there was old snow or slush to step around or jump over, and, of course, there were Boston drivers to dodge.

Once tucked into the back seat of the car, I found my cocoon, safe from the cold and the snow and the dangerous drivers, safe in the back seat of the big Chrysler Dad would now safely negotiate back to Wiano, all those many miles away. Off into the night we set, as I curled up, with Lyn or Jamie or one of my brothers, and listened to conversation for the few minutes it would take before I fell asleep. I can still see the red taillights of the cars ahead of us, an undulating column of red specks heading south.

In later years, I went with Dad and Jamie and Lyn and her husband, Tom, to see the Bruins many more times. I had the pleasure of watching another number 4, a young player named Bobby Orr, come into the league and dominate more than anyone ever had before. As classy as Jean Beliveau, as innovative as Jacques Plante, Bobby Orr was the most exciting player I've ever seen in any sport.

But, as much as I loved watching Bobby Orr play hockey in the Boston Garden, and after him Larry Bird play basketball, it is the magical glow of those Christmas nights before Orr and Bird that burns brightest in my imagination. For a few years, we had a family tradition. For a few years, I had my dad on Christmas night. For a few years, I had all that I ever wanted.

I have learned since then that a few years is all it takes. A few years can last forever. A few years can even reappear.

Would you be surprised to know that I have started taking Lucy, Jack, Tucker and Sue to a Bruins game once a year? The Bruins don't play on Christmas anymore, which allows the players to be with their families for the holiday. But whenever I take my kids to see the Bruins, even though they don't play in the Garden but in a new arena, it feels like an old Christmas to me. I can see the old guy riding his Zamboni, I can see the shadow of Jean Beliveau, I can see Gammy's spindly legs taking the stairs without faltering, and

I can see Boivin, Green and the rest of the old team that ate nails for breakfast. I'm thinking about seeing if I can find a 1950s Chrysler for next year's trip.

MY BROTHER,
JOHN HALLOWELL

I want to focus on a moment in the year 2000 when I cleaned out a half-inch of encrusted dust, grime and dead insects that had collected inside a glass fixture covering the ceiling light in my brother's bedroom.

My brother, John, whom I call Johnny, is eight years older than I am. He lives with a woman named Anne in a small apartment in Cambridge. For reasons that I will explain, the two of them are not able to keep house very well. The family helps Johnny in various ways. One day, Jamie told us how much of a mess Johnny's apartment was becoming, so Lyn, Tom, Jamie, Sue and I descended en masse for Operation Clean-Up. Since Sue and I were the last to arrive, the light fixture was my reward.

In order to explain why Johnny couldn't clean up his own place and why the lamp fixture was such a mess, I need to provide some background.

When I was a little boy, Johnny was so much older than I that I barely knew him. He was kind to me, but we were so

far apart in age that we didn't play together. I do remember
his transcribing letters that I dictated to Santa Claus, and I
remember his telling me bedtime stories, not only because
he told them well but also because he often burped during
the telling, causing the aroma of whatever we'd had for dinner to fill the air for a few rancid seconds. I thought that was
a reasonable price to pay for a story from Johnny.

Johnny went before me and paved a stellar academic career,
culminating at Harvard. When he was there, he became a
celebrity within the family, receiving the accolades of our
grande dame, Gammy Hallowell, for the credit he brought to
the family name. He achieved Phi Beta Kappa in his junior
year, an honor only sixteen juniors receive each year at
Harvard. Then, in his senior year, he wrote an honors thesis on
Charles Dickens that earned him a degree summa cum laude,
the highest grade possible. He graduated among the top few in
his class and earned a fellowship to go study in England. He
spent a year there under the tutelage of C. P. Snow and his
wife, the novelist Pamela Hansford Johnson. Lord and Lady
Snow—they were Peers of the Realm—doted on my brother
and gave him every reason to believe, as Harvard also had
done, that the rest of the world would soon dote on him, too.

When Johnny returned to the United States, he eschewed
an academic career and went to work for *Life* magazine
instead. Loving the theater and the heady world of "stars," he
went to work in Hollywood, and he did well there, writing
many cover stories for *Life* as well as a book, *The Truth Game*,
about Hollywood and its stars.

He was a gifted writer. As a writing student eight years his
junior, I admired his talent. Johnny had a reporter's eye, but

a poet's touch. The combination of the two is rare in writing about Hollywood, and I think that is what made Johnny's writing so good.

But, after a few years in Hollywood, his brain circuits got crossed. He inherited our father's manic-depressive illness and, when it struck him, it struck hard. Johnny went crazy fast. He was put in Camarillo State Hospital in California and given electric-shock treatments, back in the days when these were often done without anesthesia. The procedure amounted to torture. To this day, Johnny feels outrage about his treatment at Camarillo State.

The family soon got him out of that hospital and brought him back to Cambridge. I was a sophomore at Harvard then. I went with Jamie and Duckie to the airport to meet Johnny. I had never seen him like this; in fact, I had never seen anyone like this. It scared me how crazed he looked. Glaring right and left, chain-smoking, he paced around, drawing all kinds of false conclusions, blaming us—his family—for his predicament, and muttering half-sentences about complicated plots against him, some set up by Howard Hughes, others by Hollywood moguls, agents, stars and writers, one he even imagined concocted by me. This delusion was prompted when he saw a pack of matches on the floor that read "King Edward Cigars" on the cover. (My true name is Edward; Ned is only my nickname.)

"You think you're a king, Edward, don't you?" he snarled at me. "Well, we'll just see about *that*."

Johnny was crazy. This is part of my family's genetic heritage. After he went crazy, Johnny's life changed, forever. Never again would he ride so high. But maybe that wasn't so bad, considering where his riding was taking him.

He was diagnosed with manic-depressive illness and put on medication, to which he responded well, thank goodness. Gradually, his crazy thinking subsided, and he was discharged from the hospital. Soon after that, he also came to terms with the fact that he was alcoholic. He joined A.A. This was where he met the woman who turned out to be the love of his life.

The relationship in itself was odd because Johnny was, and is, gay. But when he met Anne, an older woman who had her own grown children and was divorced, something extraordinary happened: They fell in love. Anne is a very bright and witty woman who loves literature and movies, as Johnny does. But their attraction went much deeper than that. Obviously, it wasn't sex that drew them to one another. Rather, I think it was that they knew they could help each other, in their own peculiar ways. You might say they were brought together by the grace of God.

I don't know what the bond was based on for sure, but Anne is sort of a caricature of my mother. In any case, Johnny and Anne have been living together now for more than twenty years. Anne needs a lot of physical care, and Johnny provides that for her. Johnny takes her to the hairdresser and, when Anne can't walk, Johnny wheels her down the sidewalk in a wheelchair. Anne has cardiac and circulatory troubles, so Johnny massages her feet and brings her to the doctor on a regular basis. In her own right, Anne dotes on Johnny, giving him her considerable love and affection.

Jamie, who is closest to Johnny among our family members, has been checking in on Johnny and Anne every week for years, usually having lunch with Johnny on Sunday, making sure he is okay, and intervening when something needs to be done, from arranging a psychiatrist's appointment, to helping them buy clothes, to giving emotional support. Jamie has been like their guardian angel, while the rest of the family has also helped when Jamie let us know we needed to.

Anne and Johnny have physically weakened with age, but their love has strengthened. They are quite a sight to see—Anne heavy on the lipstick, John usually a few days late for a shave—but they are not out to win a beauty contest. "We are just a pair of old crazies," they proudly state, not the least ashamed of what they've struggled through. Quite to the contrary, they are proud of what they've conquered, as well they should be. Anne has been sober for thirty years, and Johnny for twenty-five.

Recently, when I was driving down Huron Avenue in Cambridge, I passed a pedestrian who caught my eye. He was wearing baggy navy-blue Bermuda shorts, a red plaid shirt, sneakers and white socks. He walked haltingly, as if he were lame or short of breath. He was my brother, John.

I drove up next to him, honked and waved. For a half-second, we went back in time. I was ten years old again, and Johnny was eighteen, as he looked up, gave an affectionate smile that said, "Hi, Neddy," and waved. Life was still ahead of us.

But then I turned back to fifty years old, and he to fifty-eight. He kept walking, and I drove on. I didn't stop, as I knew he was just on his way to the corner store and he liked to have this walk. I shook my head in wonder. There was Johnny, frail and lame, out on one of his provisions runs, getting something or other for Anne, and oh-so-pleased to be doing it. He had found the love of his life, and he was happy making her happy. Love was what Johnny's life was all about now.

For years, even after he went crazy, there had been more. Johnny taught creative writing at the Harvard Extension School, where he was a very popular teacher. He also worked secretarial jobs, one at the Massachusetts Mental Health Center, where I also worked as a psychiatrist for some years. Following that, he did a stint as an attendant at the Pine Street Inn, one of Boston's shelters for the homeless. He was never too proud to take a job, any job. While some people would say that being an attendant at the Pine Street Inn or a secretary at a mental hospital is beneath a summa-cum-laude graduate of Harvard, Johnny took the jobs and performed them with pride. He needed to support himself, and his love, Anne.

But, when he was fifty-seven, he suffered a stroke. The residual damage left him unable to work. At last, this brave, brilliant, unusual man had to quit his jobs. He applied for public assistance, which he deserved and was granted. Now, he and Anne live off of that, with some additional help from Lyn, Jamie, Sue and me, and Anne's children. Johnny is still able to get around on his own. He still goes out to the store. He still rubs Anne's feet. He still reads books and writes. But he has had to slow down. He can't do what he used to do. He speaks more slowly now, he misses some words, but even now he can tell you more about the works of Charles Dickens than most anybody can. Whatever is asked of him, he tries to do. He just can't do it all.

Which is why the family came to help clean up his house that day. Once Jamie put the word out that help was needed, the effort was spearheaded by Lyn, who has in many ways taken the place of Gammy Hallowell as our matriarch.

It was not the most pleasant job. As I held the light fixture under running water, I couldn't believe how much crud had collected on it, so deep and viscous it was like the chunky curd of cottage cheese, only black. Insects must have been rotting up there for years. I showed it to Lyn and Tom, and they told me the nooks and crannies behind chairs and tables and bureaus had been even worse. They had been there much longer than I.

Lyn had known Johnny longer, too. She was his special friend growing up. Johnny had taken the worst of our early family turmoil, and he had found in Lyn one of his best allies. Uncle Noble, in his twisted way, had accused the two of them of having an incestuous relationship. That accusation was totally false, but it drove Johnny completely away from Uncle Noble, Mom and me, while Uncle Noble and Mom were still married.

Later on, Jamie also became Johnny's close ally. Being the youngest, I was a newcomer, one who Johnny never really got to know well. But we loved each other, from a slight distance.

As I scrubbed crud, I, the newcomer, took my place among the family helping Johnny. It was an especially difficult day because Lyn had just received news that she might have multiple myeloma. She and Tom showed up to help out anyway. As it turned out, Lyn did not have multiple myeloma, but, on that day, she didn't know the results of the tests. Still, she was there, cleaning up for Johnny and Anne.

I cast a glance over my shoulder at Lyn and Tom and Jamie and Sue, and I sneaked a peck at Johnny and Anne, sitting on their bed like frightened cats as we all worked, and I thought of how much I loved my family. Here were Lyn and Tom, facing the possibility of a fatal illness, helping out

Johnny and Anne who had been dealing with possibly fatal illnesses for years. There was Jamie, Johnny's old faithful buddy, doing his part. And here was Sue, new to the clan, but jumping right in.

This old WASP family, coping with our genetic inheritance of alcoholism, mental illness and politeness, had hit enough hard times through the years to have lost our spirit and spunk, but that never happened. Scrubbing the light fixture, I felt proud. Proud of us all. None of us was famous, but we all had done our share of scrubbing at one time or another. We all had hung in there for each other, as we were doing now.

A sociologist might look at our family and say over the past two generations we fell—from a position of health, wealth and influence to a place of mental illness, little money and no influence. But, in the ways that count—in stoutness of heart and depth of effort—we still fly high.

Johnny and Anne have hung in there for each other for over twenty years now. They have overcome greater odds than most people ever face. I look at them in awe, Johnny and Anne. Not married, but as faithful and devoted to each other as any two people could be. Here is this man, John Hallowell, who had been a star at Harvard and a star in Hollywood, ending up his life living on a shoestring, out of the public eye but in the eye of the one he loves. Here is this brother of mine, whom I call Johnny, fulfilling his role as a good brother not by bringing riches and fame back home to the family, but by showing us all an example of a life lived, at least in its second half, for love; a life lived against huge odds, a life in which he faced two potentially killing conditions— manic-depressive illness and alcoholism—and prevailed.

Here Johnny is, winning, living a life in which he did not fulfill the promise he showed as an undergraduate at Harvard, but instead did much better. He fulfilled his promise of love.

Johnny, hooray for you. Hooray, hooray, hooray.

Johnny, I am proud to be your brother. Very, very proud.

And family, crazy family, I am proud to be one of you.

MY OWN MOM

I can see my mother now as clearly as if she was still forty and I was still six. There she is, standing in the doorway of our house on Bridge Street in Chatham, waving good-bye to me as I get on the school bus. She is wearing a pink blouse, a white pleated skirt, a navy-blue belt and a string of pearls. I feel, in that moment, without knowing I am feeling it, the absolute truth of what my mother always said to me: "I'll love you always, no matter where you go or what you do."

Now, as I look back and see through the eyes of my little face looking out the school-bus window at my mother, I can feel again what I felt then: the warm touch of her unconditional love. When you are six, if you know your mother loves you totally and unconditionally, that is one of the most valuable assets you'll ever have in life. It might be all the protection you'll ever need.

What makes it so good is that it is indestructible. You can find out later, as I did and most of us do, all kinds of facts that reduce your mother in your eyes, that prove her to be human, or even evil. But, if you have felt that unqualified love early on, it is an inoculation against despair, a permanent shot of faith-in-life. I can see in my mother's eyes now, as I saw then, a look that says, *No matter where you are, no matter what you do, I will always love you.* It is my belief that God sends His message of love through such eyes. It is really all any of us ever needs.

That look from Mom, as if inspired by God, did more than gaze. It wired my mind forever. It set off a lengthy chain reaction of neurotransmitters, hormones, endorphins, growth factors, immune globulins and other nourishing substances that combined to fill me with a feeling that life was good, no matter what the next hop, skip or jump might bring. While, in the years to come, I would contend with many doubts, and slog through periods of insecurity and personal upheaval, I've never completely lost the feeling that look from my mother instilled.

In isolated moments, mothers, fathers, grandparents, teachers, coaches, even pets, can give these looks to children. All it takes is a few looks to do the job for a long, long time.

I don't know why I remember Mom and even her outfit that day, but I do. Memory of childhood is funny; we often do not remember what we intended to remember, while we do remember what we thought would make no lasting impression. That day, when I was six, was just another day in my life as a first-grader. But I can see Mom, the white clapboard house, the lilac hedges, even the lilies of the valley nestled beneath the lilacs, as vividly if they were going to be there when I get home today.

But they are gone. Mom is gone. The house is still there but under new ownership many times over. The lilacs are still there, and even the lilies of the valley. But I am not there.

Neither is my childhood. However, the look Mom gave me is still there, and is here with me today.

The woman herself, my mother—Dorothy McKey Hallowell, called Doffie by her friends—was the happiest, but also the saddest, woman I ever knew.

The basic facts—her first husband, my father, went crazy, while her second husband turned out to be an abusive alcoholic—don't jibe with what should have been. This is what was said about her in her high-school yearbook in 1934:

Dorothy McKey

June 26, 1915   "Doffie"   7 years

45 Ledges Road, Newton Centre

"Did You Ever See a Dream Walking?"

All police forces out—riot in Ledges Road by Harvard! The cause? Why Doffie McKey, of course—look at that hair, that face, those eyes, and that—figure. But in spite of all Harvard and a thousand other engagements, Doffie appears at all school functions. The gym owes much to her energy and pep, and where is Class Eight without her cheery greetings Monday morning? We are more than sorry for you all next year, for in the weeks Doffie has not been with us this year, we have learned how hard it is to struggle without her gay, vibrant and energetic nature to help us out of the most doleful situations.

Unfortunately, my mom's own life became a rather doleful situation. My mother was born to be a happy bride and lead a happy life. She was born to raise kids and make a husband happy. The woman's movement never reached her, nor did she want it to. She just wanted to fluff up pillows, smile coyly and give warm words of encouragement. But the dream never became reality, at least not for very long.

She described herself as a "cock-eyed optimist," and as her life careened from trouble to trouble, she never lost that sense of a-better-day-is-coming.

She believed in what she called the bluebird of happiness. She believed in God and taught me early that God is everywhere and God loves us all, no matter what. But she rarely went to church. After her second divorce, she rarely went out at all. She drank, became alcoholic, and ended up her life living on public assistance.

But she never lost her sense of style (she had once, indeed, been a beautiful debutante on the society pages of the Boston papers, much as her high-school yearbook describes), nor did she ever lose her insistence that the high road was the only road, that goodness resides in everyone and that the Boston Red Sox were the world's best team.

Mom took me to a Red Sox game one cold, drizzly April day when I was about twelve. By the bottom of the ninth inning, the Red Sox were losing, five to nothing. I said, "Let's leave." But Mom said, "Oh, no, you never leave a game until the final out." I made fun of her and told her that if she knew anything about the Red Sox she'd know they couldn't catch up. She replied, "Just you watch and see."

The next thing I knew, they scored three runs and had the bases loaded. But, there were two outs and Roman Mejias was coming up. The Red Sox had traded one of my favorite players, Pete Runnels, to get Roman Mejias, and I thought Roman Mejias stunk. "C'mon, Roman!" my mother shouted, shocking me by knowing his name. "He's no good," I mumbled.

Strike one. Roman just watched as a curveball froze him solid.

Strike two. Roman swung like a drunk in a bar brawl and hit nothing but air.

Then, just as I was getting up to leave disappointed and disgusted, Roman Mejias smashed a screaming line drive, long and deep into right center field, over the helpless center fielder's leap, and off the wall in the farthest recess of Fenway Park. Roman jubilantly sprinted around the bases for a triple, as the winning runs scored. The Red Sox won, six to five.

Mom looked over at me and said, "I am never a person who says, 'I told you so,' but . . ." Her look of victorious determination will stay with me forever.

She never gave up hope, this cock-eyed optimist. She gave a lift to all who knew her, even at the end of her life, when she had so little strength.

Her loneliness and sadness later in her life left me feeling guilty. Why couldn't I have made her happy, somehow? And what right did I have to a happy life if she was back in Chatham drinking, wishing a man would come into her life who she knew would never come?

Mom did meet Sue, and loved her, but she never met our kids. She died too soon. That is really too bad. She would have been a wonderful grandma.

My mother died at the age of seventy-two. In the years since, I have often thought of that image of her standing at the door, waving good-bye, when I was six and she was forty. As hard as her life was, and despite the many disappointments she endured, she always let me know that she was on my side, no matter what. I knew my mother loved me just as surely as I knew the sun was hot. There was no qualification, no question, not even one half-second when I doubted her love for me. She couldn't give me money, she couldn't give me a stable home, but what she could give me she did give me, the greatest gift a parent can give a child: unwavering, unconditional love.

THE END OF AN ERA

Gammy Hallowell, the grande dame of my family, held court from her home in Wiano. While I could visit Skipper and Gammy McKey easily, visits to Gammy Hallowell were orchestrated affairs. We had to drive from Chatham to Wiano, about thirty miles, a long trip for a little kid. It was like visiting a special kingdom.

Gammy had many of the trappings of the rich. She raised roses. Her estate was right on the water. She had a croquet court out beyond her lawn and gardens. Her house was vast, staffed with servants. I could "order" my breakfast in the morning, and I still remember the scrumptious scrambled eggs Gerda would make. (Her secret was using cream, not milk, in the eggs, which made them come out smooth and rich as pudding.)

Dinners were complicated productions. I will always remember my first encounter with finger bowls. Jamie and I were visiting for the weekend, having come up from Chatham. Dad had already moved out of my house and was now living with Gammy. She had some other people over for dinner, so there must have been eighteen of us around her long, shimmering dining-room table. Candles flickered, and servants served, as I was taught how to transfer food from a plate held by a servant standing to my left onto my own plate. I was four. This was all quite strange.

Jamie, my experienced guide, was six. He did fine through the soup course and the main course. But a problem arose when, after the main course was cleared, a bowl of water was put down in front of me with what looked like a dandelion floating in it. I noticed everyone else was getting a bowl of water with a dandelion, too. I looked at Jamie, who was talking to the woman sitting on his other side. Not knowing what to do—as Jamie, my guide, was otherwise engaged—I picked up my spoon and began to ingest the water, as if it were soup. I figured this water with a dandelion in it was what we were having for dessert.

Well, didn't the whole table get a chuckle out of that. It was one of those moments when all the grown-ups just can't get over how cute and adorable the innocent child can be. I was duly embarrassed, but quickly appeased and very, very pleased by the actual dessert, baked Alaska, that soon replaced my little bowl of water. To this day, I cannot see a finger bowl without thinking of Gammy Hallowell.

Looking back, I realize how much I owe Gammy Hallowell. It was her money that sprung me from the clutches of Uncle Noble and put me in a boarding school, where I then grew up. So, her money mattered, of course. But it was her love and grand style that have lasted in my imagination, long after the money has gone. If I ever become rich, I want to build a cavernous fireplace as deep and wide as Gammy Hallowell's was, put huge port and starboard lanterns on the mantelpiece, and invite all the children I can find to sit around that fire and open presents at Christmas. Maybe I'll have them stay for dinner and give them all finger bowls, as well.

I remember when Gammy died. I was sixteen, watching a football game on TV, home on vacation from school. My mother called up the stairs, "Gammy Hallowell just died." We had been expecting it; it was just a matter of when the actual moment of death would come. "Oh. Thanks for telling me," I called back down the stairs. Then, I went in and lay down on my bed and thought for a while.

I wondered what would happen. I wondered who would hold the big Thanksgiving and Christmas celebrations, who would preside over the extended family, doling out opinions and judgments for us all to chew on and be united by—sometimes, if only by opposing them. Gammy was like the central government. Now that she was gone, there would be no unifying force, or so I feared.

My fears proved true. After Gammy died, the family split apart. I didn't see nearly as much of my older brother, Ben, after that. Family members squabbled over the dividing up of Gammy's estate, and that created further rifts.

It also turned out there wasn't much money left when she died. She had spent it on all of us, on her many charities, on maintaining her grand lifestyle. But there was enough to put me through medical school, and for that I will be forever grateful to her and to Uncle Jim, who advised her to provide for my education, even as far as medical school.

With the money gone and the estate divided up between feuding siblings, an era came to a close in the life of my family when Gammy died. A certain grandeur disappeared. It would be replaced later by a new and better magic, the magic of the children we, Gammy's grandchildren, would bring into the world.

But, on the day of her death, I knew a big change had come. Something special would be missing now. No more finger bowls. No more late-night drives in plush automobiles to Bruins' games. No more croquet games with Gammy, nor roses cut while her charm bracelet tinkled.

It wasn't just her money that was gone, and the trappings that went with it; also gone was the sense of importance her presence cast over the whole family—at least from my vantage point—and the feeling of togetherness. On the day of her death, the world felt less special to me. How I missed her imperious judgments based on nothing but her undeserved yet unshakable confidence. How I missed that confidence, even though it was best that I lose it, lest I become the snob as an adult that I have to admit Gammy Hallowell frightfully was.

Families change. We went from being Old World, Boston Brahmin, WASP aristocrats to being this-world, gotta-find-a-job proletariat on the day my grandmother died. It was the best thing that could have happened to me but, at the time, it felt frightening. I had to grow up. I had to get a job.

ECHOES . . .

Coming Together

As you have seen, my family has its share of craziness. Most families do, if truth be told. At our most unguarded and honest, we are often most idiosyncratic, if not crazy. This essay, written by a woman who is a writer and lives in the Boston area, shows some of the warmth and wonderful craziness of her family, especially in her father who wore red high-top sneakers in his old age.

When I read this the first time, I marveled at the power of the process of growing old and finally of dying, not only to bring families together, but to deepen our own sense of what it means to be alive.

—E. H.

My father was a doctor who wasn't sick a day in his life. He was from the old school: Gargling with salt water was his cure for a sore throat, and soaking in a hot tub full of Epsom salts would relieve any pain. He spent all of his career working at a state hospital, choosing to get by on a state salary and live in state housing rather than make a mint in the outside world. He had grown up in an abusive, neglectful home, and I think the cocoon of the state hospital—where all your needs were provided right there on the grounds, from housing to groceries to laundry to cut flowers—offered the security he'd never known.

Dad was fifty when I was born, and I have a twin brother and two older sisters. Whereas "older fathers" are a dime a dozen today, in the 1950s, they were fairly rare. My father was an aloof Englishman. He was a good twenty years older than many of my friends' fathers.

Dad was a strict disciplinarian, known to reach for the hairbrush if we got out of line. My mother was a warm Southerner, gregarious and chatty. The two of them went together about as well as kidney pie and grits. It was a tumultuous marriage, ending for all intents and purposes when my mother took the four of us children and moved back to her native North Carolina when I was twelve years old. Dad would come visit during vacations, and we would spend summers in New York with him. Except for a couple of brief trial periods, my parents never lived together again.

In 1973, my father retired and headed to south Florida, where he thought he'd live just a few years of the good life before passing away. He was seventy-two at retirement: Because of his skill as a pathologist, he'd been given an extension on the mandatory retirement age of sixty-five. I think he would have preferred to work until he dropped, but he was not given that choice.

In Hollywood, Florida, he found a garage apartment, where he did what he vowed he'd do in retirement: He never drove a car nor owned a phone again. Every day, he'd walk a mile and a half to the beach, where he swam for an hour and visited with other retired beach bums before walking back home. With his full white beard and his red high-top sneakers, Dad became a singular sight around Hollywood Beach. The word *character* was often applied to him.

After attending our out-of-state weddings, Dad announced that he had traveled enough. He would never leave Florida again; in fact, he did not stray much outside a two-mile radius of his home. My sisters, brother and I would visit him two or three times a year, taking our children along. In his old age, "Grandpa" had mellowed, and I have several sweet photographs of him leading my toddler daughter by the hand, her dimpled one tucked into his gnarled one, his other hand clutching a plastic sand bucket.

The years passed, and Dad did not die, as he had predicted he would, sooner rather than later. Until his late eighties, he continued his daily swim at the beach. But the truth was, he could no longer care for himself. His garage apartment had become a pig sty; the local board of health condemned it. Against his will, we found him a retirement home, a lovely converted patio apartment building that was clean and breezy and run by a caring couple. Dad had his own room, but he no longer went to the beach, except during our visits. His eyes and knees were giving out; his memory was going. He was, simply, tired.

"I'm ready to go," he would announce, all fact, no self-pity. As his child, I did not want to hear this, and I would offer up such platitudes as, "Dad, you're not going anywhere anytime soon. You have a lot of life in you yet." With each succeeding visit, as he grew more silent, I stopped spewing niceties and spoke more frankly with him. "It must be very difficult," I would say, as he would grope for a word or memory. "It is," he would agree.

It's rare for our entire family—all four siblings and our children—to get together at Christmas. But there we were, in Hollywood, Florida, in 1997, with Dad in our midst. It was not a particularly happy time. People were edgy. My brother and one of my sisters got into a huge argument on the beach. My brother-in-law snapped at me in a restaurant. The two little boy cousins were not getting along, and, worst of all, Dad was in poor shape. Limping and wheezing, he managed to get out to the beach with a walker, and the help of several pairs of hands. When we all left, my sister cried. I wrote in my journal: "I can't wait to go home." I'm sure everyone else felt the same way.

A month later, I got a call from Stella, the kind woman who, with her husband, ran the home where Dad lived. My father was in the hospital. When I called the doctor, he asked me if Dad had a living will. All three of us sisters headed for Hollywood. For a week, we sat at his side for twelve or fourteen hours a day, holding his hand, talking to him, rubbing lotion on his feet, whatever little or large gesture we could offer. It had never been easy for my father to give or receive affection, but now he had no choice but to give in to us. It made us feel better, and I feel sure it made him feel better, too. He was in bad shape, and it was difficult to watch. He was hooked up to all sorts of tubes. His chest rose and fell with effort. His breathing was aided by an oxygen mask, his waste delivered through a catheter. The doctor asked us what our "wishes" were. No heroic efforts, we said. Dad had been clear on that.

Each day, we sisters would get up early and head to the

hospital by seven to catch the doctor on his rounds. We shared a motel room, taking turns on the cot. We'd take shifts at meals. We sat and talked to Dad or to each other, catching up on the big and little things in our lives in a way you can't do over the phone or in letters and e-mails. At one point, my oldest sister and I got hold of a tape recorder and taped a reminiscence about our childhood, happy days that we thought Dad would enjoy recalling. Who knows how much he heard or understood, but whenever I play that tape, I swear I can hear him responding.

It was the first time the three of us girls had been alone — without husbands and/or children — in years. I am grateful for that time with my father, and with my sisters. There were no meals to fix, no kids to entertain. There was just time . . . and a dying father. It made for some heartfelt remembrances, shared tears and gratitude that we could share this privileged task of delivering our father to whatever comes next. He was there when we were born, and it seemed only natural that we should be there when he died.

When the doctor told us that "there would be no miracles," and that we should "let nature take its course," we cried. I whispered in my father's ear that I loved him. "Can you hear me?" I asked. Dad, his eyes closed, nodded his head. They say hearing goes last.

But then my father "rallied," to use a favorite hospital term. The doctors were even talking about releasing him to a nursing home. My sisters and I went and looked at a few. We also cleared out his room at the retirement home: We knew he would never return. Dad had come into the world with nothing, and he left pretty much the same way: just a few boxes of papers, a drawer full of old clothes. He had always traveled light. I saved a few pictures and his medical-school diploma. Then, with two young children at home, I returned to Boston for a few days.

Five days later, Dad took a turn for the worse. I flew down, arriving at the hospital at midnight, praying the entire way that I would make it in time. When I got to his room, my sisters were already there. We cried as we held Dad's cold hands. His eyes were open but vacant. He could not see us, but I feel sure he could hear us. We sang all his favorite songs. We did a guided imagery of his beloved beach. When we paused for breath, his roommate, an emaciated young man dying of cancer, begged us to continue. Dad died three hours after I arrived. I really believe he was waiting for me, the youngest, to arrive.

Dad's only family, ever, were his children. He was a loner, with no real friends except for his beach acquaintances, most of whom had already died. My brother arrived the next day, and the four of us children arranged a simple "memorial service" in the small dining room at his retirement home. We set out some wine and cheese and crackers, and with our children, sat around a table sharing memories. His former landlady and her husband came, as did an aide at the home. My six-year-old son said, "Please give Grandpa a nice rest." We sang, "Amazing Grace," and "Kumbaya." When it was over, we drove to Dad's favorite spot on the beach, and got his favorite ice cream. Any hurt feelings from Christmas were gone with Dad's ashes, which my brother scattered—illegally—into the wind at his favorite beach spot.

We didn't mention the unhappy Christmas, but I think we

all realized that any trivial differences we'd had just six weeks earlier were erased by the power of love, family ties and history that the death of a parent brings. I feel blessed—and I know my siblings do, too—that we had a second chance at a family reunion, to do it right this time, at my father's passing. I think Dad knew all about it; in fact, I sometimes wonder if he planned it that way.

Unconditional Love

One of the universals of childhood is Grandma. Of all the treasured connections and human moments that people have told me about over my many years of asking about them, moments with grandmothers are the most frequently cited. I can see why, as grandmothers seem to specialize in love of the most generous kind. I could fill an entire volume with stories just about grandmothers.

One reason is that grandmothers seem to love us, no matter what. One memory that most adults who describe themselves as happy have in common is that there was someone — anyone — in their growing-up years who made them feel special, someone who loved them so much that the child knew — absolutely and positively — that, no matter what he did, no matter how much trouble he might get into, that person would still love him. No matter what.

If someone feels that way about you, that feeling is transmitted into you and gives you a special strength. In a sense, you become invincible. Nothing can totally bring you down, because you have that person's love to sustain you. Truly religious people will tell you that the love of God

To Sow with expect
of return ? ~~return~~
Special Harvest

Mike_smith2074@
Yahoo-com.

gives them such invincibility. But, even from a mortal human being, unconditional love can confer special strength and security.

A famous man was once asked to tell how he had achieved so much in his life. His reply was simply this: "In my mother's eyes, I only saw smiles."

In the following story from childhood and adulthood, a woman tells of how her grandmother gave her this invaluable gift.

—E. H.

My grandmother and I had a special relationship. I was her oldest grandchild and the light of her life. She was the anchor for me and a source of unqualified approval. Periodically, my brother and I would go to spend a week with our grandparents. They played with us, told us stories of our mother's childhood, and spoiled us with their love and undivided attention.

Each evening, after an early supper, my grandmother took me on her lap, while my grandfather took my brother on his lap as they sat and rocked and listened to the evening news. It was a time of feeling safe and protected and invincible. Nothing could happen to us when we were cuddled and rocked.

We played under the dining room table and made elaborate set-ups of towns, which we demanded were to be left alone. So, we ate at the kitchen table during our visits.

Grandma's huge feather beds were hot in the summer, so she made us pallets on the cool floor. We would lie just inside the screen door, where we would catch any stray breeze, and go to sleep lulled by the noise of the cicadas and watched over by the star-sprinkled heavens.

My grandmother did not complete her schooling, because she was the eldest girl and was needed at home to care for younger siblings. She saw no need for girls to go to college, but there was no one more supportive and proud when I went to school.

We named our first daughter after our two grandmothers. I think my grandma conveniently forgot our daughter was also named for my husband's grandmother: Jo Beth was named for *her!* However, she didn't call her by her name either when referring to her or to her face. She was always, "Grandma's little angel."

My grandmother died of cancer when I was forty years old, having never said a harsh word to me in my entire life. My husband and I were taking our three children—ages nine, seven, and three—and going on sabbatical to New Zealand for a year. During our last visit with her a few weeks before we left, she was so loving and caring, and, as always, support-ive of whatever I wanted to do.

She stood on her front porch waving to us as long as the car was in sight. Then, she went inside, went to bed and never got up again.

Marge and Tom

There is a death in this story, as there was in the previous two stories. But this death, as you will see, is of a very different kind.

When you read the following piece and you find out who Marge and Tom actually are, you will understand why this is one of the most unusual stories in this book, and one of my favorites. After reading this, I'll bet you'll have a new appreciation for . . . well, you'll see.

—E. H.

As my five children finished high school and headed off to colleges, I spent more and more time gardening. Instead of watching soccer and field-hockey games, I planted perennial beds and moved rocks around and generally redesigned our entire landscape. Although I missed the kids and the company of other parents a lot, I did find consolation in the company of a pair of unusual pets: two wild turkeys. We have a collection of ducks, geese and chickens, as we live in a little country town with quite a lot of farmland. I've always been drawn to farm animals, but not to barn work. Poultry takes a minimum of effort, and the birds make me laugh.

I felt our turkeys were extraordinarily good-looking. Tom, the male, was a classic Thanksgiving picture. Big and fat, with glossy purply-brown feathers and weird crimson wattles, he strutted around behind Marge, the love of his life. Marge was sleek and glossy brown, but without Tom's ostentatious tail feathers. She had a bald, vulturish-looking head covered with hot-pink protruding bumps. I felt she looked as though she had been drawn by Disney, although a few relatives did tell me she was not exactly beautiful.

Perhaps what I saw as beautiful was her personality. Marge liked me a lot, so how could I resist her? She followed me around, gobbling away. When I was kneeling headfirst under a bush, in no time Marge would have her little pinhead stuck in there with me pecking at bugs or slugs or whatever it is turkeys like in the dirt. I began having conversations with her, and she would reply. Basically, she told me not to worry so much. She was a bit of a pain in the neck because she liked to eat delphiniums, and I'd have to shoo her out of the beds from time to time. This would annoy Tom, who made thumping sounds and kind of rushed at me advising me to back off, but that was mostly all bluff.

Never one to hold a grudge, Marge would come running whenever I appeared. She would lope across the lawn like a dinosaur from *Jurassic Park*. During the winter, Marge and Tom huddled together on a tree limb in their pen. They didn't seem to mind the cold and waited patiently with me for spring and our gardening routine to begin again.

The year our youngest child went off to college, I was pretty depressed. My oldest son had gotten married, however, and had moved near us with his new wife. I liked my new daughter-in-law very much, but she was hard to get to know. She was naturally quiet and somewhat shy, and she tended to stay at her own house involved with gardening herself. I was a bit afraid that she looked at me like the eccentric I was becoming, the crazy old mother-in-law who talked to her turkeys.

Gradually, we became friends, and I learned a lot about her sorrows. Her parents had divorced angrily when she was quite young, and then her mother, whom she adored, had died of breast cancer only the year before she met my son. Her deep sadness touched me. I wanted to help, but I didn't know how. I hoped that, in time, I could become her good friend and that she would learn to trust me.

This past spring, my husband and I were returning from a long weekend visiting our youngest son in college. As we were driving home from the airport, the car phone suddenly rang, which nearly caused us to veer off the road. I'll never get used to phones ringing in cars. I answered and was surprised to hear my daughter-in-law's quiet voice asking how our trip had been. Since she rarely talked on the phone and hardly ever initiated a phone call, I was certain something was wrong. Sure enough, she gently said that she had bad news.

"Daisy?" I asked, thinking that our old German shepherd had finally come to the end of her days.

"No, it's Marge," she replied. My heart sank. "And Tom, too."

"What? Not dead?"

"Yes. I didn't want you to come home and see an empty

pen. Something happened to them this morning. Each was in a separate corner, sort of huddled up. Each is dead. They have no marks on them. I don't know what could have happened."

Well, we'll never know what killed both of my beautiful turkeys. My suspicion is that, somehow, they were poisoned. The house sitter may have inadvertently given them something that had turned moldy. We don't know. I was terribly sad. What would gardening be without Marge to cheer me on and Tom to protect her?

But at the same time that I felt this loss—and it was a huge loss, even though they were turkeys—I realized that I had gained something wonderful. It must have taken a lot for my daughter-in-law to make that phone call. She had to have checked when our plane was landing and then planned to call us before we actually arrived home. To tell someone that their favorite pet has died is almost worse than actually hearing the news. She was determined to make it easier for me, and, in fact, she succeeded. I realized then that she and I had become real friends. It took tremendous courage, caring and trust to make that phone call.

And now, a year later, although I miss Marge and Tom as I crawl around in the dirt, I find myself chatting with Marge even though she is in turkey heaven. Eccentric is eccentric. When I'm feeling a little sad about the turkeys or the grown-up kids, I think of my daughter-in-law caring enough to try to cushion me from loss. It was the beginning of our becoming a true family.

Taking Care

If the death of turkeys can work to bring a family closer together, as in the last story, then I think my point is proven that almost any event can contain within it the seeds of human moments, moments that lead us toward meaning and love.

But it can be awfully hard to see anything but the sadness or the gloom. In the following vignette, a young woman faces the transition from being taken care of by her parents to taking care of them and the rest of the family. It all happens so fast, as she crosses over from being a child to being a grown-up herself.

—E. H.

Spring. Exams. Yale. Sophomore year. As I now realize is a habit, I spent many moments throughout the spring thinking about the summer. It would begin with a tour to England and France as part of the Glenn Miller Band to participate in the fiftieth commemoration of D-Day. Then, in mid-June, I would return to Connecticut, move the belongings that had filled my dorm-room home, and quickly join my sister in Boston. Her husband of four years would be on an internship through business school in Spain, and she would be living alone in their quiet apartment in Cambridge that I had come to know as my Boston home, as she'd been living there for five years.

But first, exams. Three history, two something else. Lots to do. Then, pack. Get that whole crazy room into boxes and bags. Be sure to have it ready when Dad arrived, impatient as he would be to get it into the truck to drive home. Worry about moving with Dad. Things had not been good.

Dad arrives. We load the truck. Dad is quiet. No "How can there be this much?" Or "Who needs this many clothes?" Or "Why do you need to keep, own, pack, move all these books?" Relief. Worry. Why is it so smooth, so quiet? In the car. On College Street. He shifts from first to second gear. "How did exams go?" he asks. I tell him. I'm tired. Ready for rest, then ready for summer. Excited about spending it with Ellen in Boston. He shifts to third. Not on the highway yet. "Glad the exams went well." Pause. "There's something we need to talk about. Didn't want to worry you during exams." Pause.

Cancer. WHAT?! I'm awake, alive, scared. He calms me with the breakdown of what it is, the diagnosis, the plan. Surgery. July. He draws analogies. An orange. The pulp needs to come out. The skin is still good. Caught it early. Prognosis excellent.

Suddenly, we are home. I am calm. He is calm. There will be surgery, but, as always, he is going to be okay. He's not leaving. He won't die. Like his friend, Sam. Like his friend,

Al. Like his friend, Ken . . . almost. These are all my "uncles." But he's not going anywhere. He will be okay. He's proven this to me by telling me all the medical details.

We are out of the car. No hugs. No tears. Why should there be? He's just going to the hospital to have it removed. We each carry an armload into the old house, up the creaking, winding stairs to the attic. On the way down. "Mom? Where's Mom?" Another load from the car. As I walk through the kitchen, arms full, she emerges. I say hello and climb the stairs again. As I come through the kitchen once more I say, "How about a hug?" I'm calm. No worries. She says nothing. We embrace. Her knees buckle. I hold her weight. She cries. Terrified, she and I. She of it, I of the realization that she and he will need me to care for them. She is not calm. She is a weight in my arms. I am her mother.

I don't go to Boston. I am the link between the two of them and between them and my siblings. I mow the two acres. I cook the meals. I do the laundry. I resent it? I know they need me. I love them for needing me. I see them as human. I see him suffer physically. Catheter. Dependence. Exhaustion. I see her suffer emotionally. Is she going to lose him? What will she do? I love them. We are a family.

We emerge from that summer stronger. Six years later, no cancer. Got the whole orange. Lost most of his sight a few years later. But we had all practiced. She is stronger. She can help him. He can ask for help. I can be their daughter without being their parent. Family.

Rhoda Lee

The following account was given to me by a lovely woman named Terri Alexander, who attended one of my lectures. She sat off to the left, and had a hat that came down around her eyes, so it was difficult to see the expression on her face. However, after she wrote this piece, she got up and talked to the audience about her subject, Rhoda Lee. She stood tall, smiled and spoke with pride. Then, I could see her face just fine.

She told us all that her great-grandmother Rhoda Lee told her always to keep love in her heart. She told us she had tried to do this, and, while maybe she didn't know every bit of knowledge that social workers were supposed to know, she had kept alive that love, as Rhoda Lee had urged her to do. She also told us that by keeping that love alive and telling us about it, she was keeping Rhoda Lee alive, and she was doing her part in keeping the spirit of love alive in the world.

When she sat down, there was a hush in the room. Then, we all broke out in spontaneous applause.

It seems to me what this young social worker—and her

great-grandmother, Rhoda Lee—said is the most impor-
tant lesson of life: Love conquers all.

—E. H.

The most profound connection I have ever had in my entire life, before the birth of my daughter, was with my paternal great-grandmother, Rhoda Lee Jones.

My great-grandmother had about a third-grade education and was born to parents who were born into slavery and later became sharecroppers. Rhoda Lee (that's what I always called her) was a very dark-skinned and stocky woman whose heart was of pure gold. She never said to me the words, "I love you," but I felt her love throughout my being every day.

Both of my parents were abusive, but Rhoda Lee never bad-mouthed them or made excuses for them. She just loved me as much as she could. What I remember most about her was her sweet, tender way of handling some of the most horrible situations.

Rhoda Lee instilled in me a love for reading very early in my life by reading (every night!) the Holy Bible to me before bed, or during the day if I would listen. Oftentimes, this woman with a third-grade education would use the stories in the Bible to help me understand and solve problems in my own life.

In my twelve years of knowing my great-grandmother, I never heard her speak an unkind word about anyone, even those who were terrible to her. Rhoda Lee raised other people's children, down on the Eastern Shore of Maryland, and was known to be a lifesaver when it came to abandoned or abused children. To this day, if you ask my people down on the Eastern Shore about Rhoda Lee, they will speak with deep love and great pride. It has been an honor for me to be a blood relative of this extraordinary woman.

Rhoda Lee's dream was for me to attend Washington College. She used to tell me to be proud of myself and use my sometimes-harsh life to help other people, especially children. I wasn't able to attend Washington College, but I did graduate from another school with a master's in social work at the age of twenty-three.

I wish everyone had a Rhoda Lee Jones in their lives. Once, she told me that if I told people about her, her memory would live on, and I would give someone else the gift of love.

The Single Most Important Person in My Life

When I was handed this vignette the title immediately caught my eye. Who would it be? Mother, husband, wife, friend . . . who? I should have been able to guess. Can you?

—*E. H.*

Without exception, the single most important person in my life was my grandmother. I visited her in Ohio every summer of my life until she died.

The last summer of her life she visited me, instead of my visiting her. I remember so vividly sitting with her on the swing in my front yard. She held my hand and told me that she was tired of living. She wanted God to take her home. I immediately protested, and she just squeezed my hand and told me that she had a few things for me. She gave me a pair of her earrings and her engagement ring. She never had much materially, but she wanted me to have the few pieces that she did have. I remember talking more, but I cannot remember what we talked about.

My grandmother died in Ohio two weeks later. I did not cry at her funeral. I knew she was happy. I put a picture of her holding me as a baby into her hand in the coffin. I wanted always to be a part of her, and I am to this very day. She loved me so much. She never "told" me much, but she "showed" me everything. She will forever be a part of me. I want to be a grandmother just like her.

Moët & Chandon

In the previous two stories, two women—a great-grandmother named Rhoda Lee and a grandmother whose name we are not given—stand strong as major influences for good. If you are lucky, somewhere in your family you had someone who meant as much to you as those women did to the authors of those pieces.

In this story, the focus is on the author's father. I met the author of this piece when I was giving a seminar to a group of trustees of various independent schools. She was—and I trust still is—a warm, strong woman with a vibrant presence. When she handed me this short vignette, I read it right away and resolved at that moment to follow through and write this book. I had been thinking of this book for quite a while, but when I read this brief story something in it spoke to me so powerfully, so vividly, that I felt a tremendous desire to celebrate human moments in a book.

I wanted to entitle this book Moët & Chandon, *in honor of this story, but no one would have known what the title meant before they read the book, so I didn't.*

> *This is a very simple story, about one of the moments we all hearken back to—if we have lived long enough—the moment of the death of a person we love. The author of this piece and I corresponded with each other after I first read this, and I include a later note she sent me as a postscript.*
>
> *—E. H.*

It was a dark December evening. I felt a foreboding as I stood on the stoop of my parents' home, waiting for the phalanx of cars escorting my father home from the Eastern Shore. I was numbed, not by the coldness of the evening, but at the prospect of our final farewell.

My father, my hero, had been given a death sentence four weeks before. A sinister tumor had attacked his brain and was now robbing him of his life. He faced this with utter dignity and chose to die at his newly purchased retirement home on the waters of Maryland's Eastern Shore. As it became increasingly difficult to care for him, the family voted (without me) to bring him home to Baltimore.

As the cars slowly pulled in, I caught eyes with one of the most magnificent people I have ever, and will ever, meet. No words spoken, just an amazing, knowing understanding ran between us. We always had a special connection and, oftentimes, exchanged few words. I had not seen him in several days, so once he was settled, I was given the privilege of private visitation. Those rosy cheeks and deep-blue eyes calmed me as I approached the bed. His speech was severely impaired by now: One-word sentences were all that would come out, but I understood everything.

He said, "Moët," and I said to him, "You want some champagne?"

He said, "Us."

Something moved me to his liquor closet and there, on the shelf, was a bottle of Moët & Chandon with a bow on it. I knew instantly what he meant. He had saved the bottle from my wedding and was giving it to me.

He died the next day at 11:45 P.M., fifteen minutes before my fifth wedding anniversary and his thirty-fifth wedding anniversary. I thank God every day he was in my life.

Later, the author sent me this addition to her original piece:

Dear Ned,

I wanted to give you a follow-up on the lovely bottle of Moët & Chandon. Trust me, it did not go to waste.

Several days after my father's death, my family took his ashes back down to the Eastern Shore. We hired one of the few remaining ferry boats on the East Coast, The Oxford/Bellevue Ferry, and traveled to the front of his waterfront property. It was there that we spread his ashes. Afterward, I pulled out the bottle of Moët & Chandon from my carry-on bag, my husband passed around glasses and we gave a fitting tribute . . . a toast and fond farewell to an amazing man.

Thanks again for reconnecting with me.

Sincerely,
Tina

Santa

In the previous story, a bottle of champagne took on much greater meaning than it had when it was purchased. This is what memory does to many objects and events. What seemed trivial at the time may bring us to tears years later. And what seemed important at the time can become important in an entirely different way later on, as did the bottle of Moët & Chandon in the previous story, and as does Santa Claus in this vignette.

As kids, we naturally never imagine how deeply our childhood memories will stir us when we grow up. Back then, we had no idea. Back then, we didn't know the magic each event would later hold. This vignette, by a woman from Maine, provides a good example.

—E. H.

When I was very small, his was the voice I thought was Santa's. Every Christmas season, about two weeks before Christmas morning, the phone would ring, and my mother would call to my sister and me, "Girls! It's for you!"

Who could it possibly be? we wondered. Barbara would get on the phone (she was four years older) and tip the earpiece so we both could fit our ears there, and we'd listen. Bells ringing. Sleigh bells, a lot of them, enough for eight reindeer, we were sure. Then, "Ho! Ho! Ho!" Santa would ask us what we'd done that was good, and what wishes we had for presents under the tree. In the background, we'd hear Mrs. Claus prompting Santa to write down our wishes so he wouldn't forget.

It was years before we knew it was our godparents at the other end of the phone. I so loved that moment. Every Christmas season I would wonder, *Will he call this year? Will he remember? Suppose we're out when he calls?* But, no need to worry. Every year, like the sunrise, he never failed me.

Later, when he was diagnosed with cancer and confined to bed, I flew to Florida with my thirteen-month-old son to see him. My son had not yet met the man I called Uncle John. When we arrived, my godmother came out and said we should wait; apparently, my godfather did not want us to see him in bed. With enormous effort he'd gotten up, my godmother helped him dress, and he came out and sat at the kitchen table.

It was a brief visit. I put my hand over his hand on the table and told him I loved him. Then, it was time to go. He insisted on getting up and standing in the doorway to wave good-bye, just as he had always done every other time I visited. We blew each other a kiss.

The next morning, my godmother called to say Uncle John had died in his sleep. We were the last people to see him alive. I was so grateful we'd been able to say good-bye.

I can see him now, standing at the door, blowing us that kiss, looking for all the world like Santa Claus, my very own Santa Claus.

CREATING
CONNECTIONS . . .

Invitation to reflect: In what ways do you take strength from your family?

Obstacles to connection: If there is conflict in your family, take heart: This is a good sign! The opposite of connection is not conflict; the opposite of connection is indifference. Connected families naturally squabble and disagree. Perhaps the greatest obstacles to connection in families these days are practical ones: time and distance. People don't seem to have time to sit down for dinner together, or they live too far apart to get together very often.

Possible steps to take: In my life, I try very hard not to rush past human moments. In other words, I try to be present when I say good-bye in the morning, and not have my mind already out the door. Often, this is hard to do. Like everybody else, I have many problems and obligations pushing down upon me each and every day. But, I find over the long haul, the quality of life in my family is the most important part of who I am. I have to make time for my family. I have to tend to it and fuss over it, like a precious garden, if it is to grow well. And not just my immediate family, but my extended family, as well.

Take the time. That is my most cogent suggestion.

In terms of family conflicts, a good therapist can work wonders. Family therapy has come a long way. Skilled practitioners of that art save families every day. Your primary-care doctor should be able to refer you to a good family therapist. Often, the best family therapists are social workers; that specialty gives the most training in family therapy.

Short of seeing a family therapist, a good motto is simply this: *Try to grow.* Families often get stuck, repeating the same patterns, year after year, decade after decade, so that seventy-year-old cousins are fighting the exact same battle their fathers fought with each other. I have seen this in my family. But, if you try to seek growth—in other words, if you try to do things differently—even if you don't succeed, at least you will have the sense that you are making a worthwhile effort. And you might just succeed! Families can, and do, change for the better!

Chapter Four

TEACHERS
AND
SCHOOL

I AM HERE BECAUSE THEY WERE THERE

This is a love story, but it is not about the usual kind of love. It is the story of me and my teachers. My teachers have shaped my life more than any other group of people outside my family. I think that is the case for many people, actually.

The first teacher I can remember is Mrs. Eldredge, whom I met when I was six and in the first grade in Chatham. I was unable to learn to read. As my classmates started to catch on to phonics and the sounds that letters stand for, I didn't catch on. I was unable to look at letters and make words. I was unable to keep up with the other children in the class.

In another classroom, I might have been labeled stupid or slow or even retarded. After all, during the years of my growing up—the 1950s and 1960s—there really were only two descriptors of a child's mental ability: "smart" and "stupid." Because I was very slow to read, I qualified as stupid. As a result, I might have been ridiculed, put in the corner, told to try harder or simply forgotten about. In a public school in a small town on Cape Cod in those days, people didn't know much about diagnosing children beyond identifying them as smart or stupid, good or bad. Along with stupid and bad, came the standard treatments of shame, pain and humiliation. Rare is the child who grew up in my generation who didn't have at least one teacher along the way who specialized in memorable methods of shame, pain and humiliation.

But Mrs. Eldredge was not a shamer. She was a kindly soul. I remember her as being an old lady, and very round. Everything about her was round: her face, her cheeks, her body. She even wore dresses that had round, red apples on them. She had no formal training in helping children who couldn't read, except that she had been teaching first grade for about a hundred years.

What she did to help me was simply this: During reading period, she would sit down next to me and put one of her big, soft arms around me and give me a little hug as I tried to decipher the words. I would stammer and stutter, because I just couldn't do it. But none of the other kids would laugh at me. This was because I had the Mafia sitting next to me.

That was my "treatment": Mrs. Eldredge's arm. That was all she did for me, but that was all she needed to do. She made it safe for me to fail. She made it safe for me to have the brain I had. She couldn't give me a brain transplant and take away my dyslexia, but she did do what she could do: make it so I didn't feel ashamed. Her method worked so well that I actually looked forward to reading period. I'll never forget Mrs. Eldredge. I think her arm has stayed around me ever since—through high school, college, medical school, residency, and into my life as a writer, public speaker and therapist. I feel it around me, even now.

After first grade, I found a teacher every year who made a difference to me. One of them, Mr. Slocum, a teacher I had at Fessenden (the boarding school I was sent to starting in fifth grade), took me to my first live Red Sox game, at which I caught the only foul ball I have ever caught, off the bat of Earl Battey, catcher for the Minnesota Twins. I have been to hundreds of ball games since then, but that was my first, and Old Man Slocum had me and a bunch of other kids in tow. Mr. Slocum didn't have to do this; it was a day off for him. But he liked bringing up kids.

Then, there was Mr. Magruder, another teacher at Fessenden, who gave me a JFK button. I was eleven and knew nothing about politics, but because of that gift I became a Democrat on the spot. It was 1960, the year Kennedy was elected.

Only a few years later, I would be playing soccer one bright fall afternoon, and Mr. Magruder would come up to me and give me the news that JFK had been shot. The world as I knew it has not been the same since that day. I guess that means JFK was one of my teachers, too, in a way. He certainly instilled in me an affirmative sense of the wider world out there, a kind of positivity-without-cynicism that national politics has lacked, at least for me, since he died.

My high school was Exeter, a prep school in New Hampshire. There, I encountered the life of the mind in full force. All the classes were held at round tables. Kids learned by discussion. Every teacher probed and questioned; Socrates in every classroom.

The winters were cold, my family at home was as crazy as ever, and I found myself becoming what I guess you could call depressed. But my teachers never let me fall. Each year, one of them took an interest in me. Nothing excessive, just enough interest to make me feel I wanted to do well.

When I was in the eleventh grade, I fell in love with the novel *Crime and Punishment*. My English teacher responded by giving me Dostoyevsky's notebooks for *Crime and Punishment*. I felt honored beyond belief. A teacher give a student a present? Wow!

The next year, the single most influential teacher I ever had entered my life. His name was Fred Tremallo. Of course, I called him Mr. Tremallo then. He and his wife, Ellie, became my parents away from home my senior year at Exeter. Mr. Tremallo was my English teacher. He told me I could write. He was round, too—not like Mrs. Eldredge, but like a linebacker. He had a mustache and had served in the Secret Service. He was of Italian descent and from New Jersey, and I don't think he knew much about the WASP triad, but he seemed to take a shine to me. Why? I don't know.

The process by which he changed me more than any teacher had before or has since was simply this: He told me I could do more than I thought I could, and then he drew that more out of me. The first week of school, I wrote a three-page story, our first writing assignment of the year. The story came back with a comment. I can still see Mr. Tremallo's red-pen–written lines slanting slightly upward in the space at the bottom of the last page: "This has promise," he wrote. "Why don't you turn it into a novel?"

A novel? I thought to myself. *A three-page story isn't enough?* Not for Mr. Tremallo. I asked him after class if he really meant I should turn this story into a novel and he replied, "Yes," his mustache opening and shutting around the word matter-of-factly. I waited for him to say more, but he didn't. The next class filed in and took their seats around the round table, as I left excited and aghast. Was I really going to write a novel? The idea seemed as out of reach as flying to the moon. Come to think of it, it's probably how skeptics felt when JFK first told the country we were indeed going to put a man on the moon.

But, by the end of the year, I had written a novel of some four hundred pages. It won the Senior English Prize, still the honor I value most of any I have ever received, because writing that novel had seemed so impossible at the start of the year. It had seemed not just out of reach, but truly undoable, like defying gravity or becoming invisible. Yet, it got done.

The novel itself was not very good—it was never published, thank goodness—but it did meet the basic criteria of being a novel: It did cohere, it did carry a narrative thread from a beginning to an end, and it did contain characters who took on lives of their own. I suppose you could say about a twelfth-grader's novel what Samuel Johnson said about a dog's dancing on its hind legs: "It is not often done well, but one is surprised to see it done at all." That I did it at all changed my life.

How? It gave me an identity. I became a *writer* that year, not only in my own mind but in a public sense: in the minds of my peers, and a highly critical bunch of peers at that. They accepted and acknowledged me as a writer. If they accepted me, I figured I must be legit. It was all because in the school year 1967–68, Mr. Tremallo brought out of me more than I thought I had.

I went to medical school and became a doctor and then a psychiatrist and then a child psychiatrist, but all that was built on the confidence I developed in my ability to do difficult tasks. That confidence was always somewhere deep inside me, but Mr. Tremallo reached into the cloudy waters of my adolescence and pulled it out for me, and others, to see. By getting me to do what I did not think I could do, he enabled me to prove to myself that I could do hard jobs. That belief has proved invaluable to me.

Wherever did he get the idea that writing would be my passion? Wherever did he get the idea that this twelfth-grader could write a novel? I don't know. But week by week, as I wrote the book chunk by chunk, he red-penned his comments like a coach building the skills of an athlete. Most of the comments were quite specific, like, "Why do you make this passage limp along pluperfectly?" How memorable, turning "pluperfect" into an adverb. Because I remember that comment, I never use the pluperfect tense without first thinking of the poor sentence limping. Some of the comments were more general, like "Rework this," or "Vague," or "Try again with this." He was demanding, but I always felt his arm around me, like Mrs. Eldredge's. I never doubted that he knew best, that he believed in me, and that I should run through walls to do what he asked. The human connection made all the difference.

So, senior year, when other kids were outside catching rays, listening to Bob Dylan, the Beatles, or Simon and

Garfunkel, I was inside in my "loft," a spacious study above the school church, writing away. The novel grew. I remember when I hit page 100, I thought maybe I'd actually do it, maybe this cockamamie idea of *me* writing a *novel* would actually come true.

Mr. Tremallo also stressed technique and discipline, giving me Wayne Booth's *The Rhetoric of Fiction* to read, a book I studiously underlined, comprehending almost none of it, but feeling very writerlike for being asked to try. I didn't realize it at the time, but I think Fred was trying to give me the tools of the trade as part of the experience of achieving a writer's goal. He was giving me the writer's equivalent of the black bag and the stethoscope, even before I really knew how to use them, just as years later in medical school I would be given an actual black bag and an actual stethoscope before I really knew how to use them.

When my twelfth-grade year was over, and the job had been done, I said good-bye to Fred and Ellie. Now I was a writer, for better or worse. But deeper than that, I had the knowledge that I could do more than I had ever believed I could.

Although I saw Fred and Ellie Tremallo a couple of times after I graduated, it wasn't the same. He was a very private man, shy and perhaps even suspicious. He didn't go in for sentimental reunions with alums. He had new writers to train. We had our time together as teacher and student, and that was that.

Until the time of his death.

In the winter of 1999, I received word from Charlie Terry, a teacher at Exeter with whom I had stayed friends after my graduation, that Fred had lung cancer and only had a few months to live. I called the hospital in Exeter, spoke to Ellie, got in my car and went to visit.

When I walked into the hospital room, there sat Fred, in bed, bare-chested, typing away at his laptop on the hospital table. "College recommendations," he stated, rightly assuming I wondered what he was working on. "Got to finish them up before I die!" Then he chuckled, and I winced. As ever, he broke the ice immediately.

We walk into these moments that we know are especially significant in our lives without a cinematographer and a symphony orchestra to underline for us the importance of what's happening. Somehow, second by second, we underline these moments for ourselves. Sometimes, we underline them with tears; sometimes, with ceremonies — but, usually, simply with slightly awkward conversation and no other special effects than the sound of the traffic outside or someone coughing in the next room.

Fred, Ellie and I sat and talked, me sitting on the edge of the bed and Ellie standing next to Fred's head, on the other side of the bed from me. I told Fred about Sue and my kids, and I told him about my practice as a psychiatrist, and I told him about the books I had written.

"When are you going to write the great novel?" he asked me.

"I don't know," I replied. "Maybe never."

"You could do it, if you tried," he replied. A challenge, once again, as in twelfth grade. Who knows, maybe someday I will.

"I don't have a novel," I said, "but I did bring a piece of my writing for you." Then I told him I wanted to read aloud to Ellie and him what I'd written. It was an earlier version of this very narrative. When I finished reading it, he cleared his throat and said, "Well, my emotions aside, that is an excellent piece of writing." There he was, teaching and encouraging, right up to our last moment together.

It was time for me to leave. A whole line of students had formed outside the door, and they were waiting to come in. "Others are waiting," I said, "I'd better go," and Ellie nodded.

"Let them wait," Fred said. I knew he meant the others outside no disrespect, he was just giving me one last gift: his time. I held his hand. It reminded me of when I held my grandfather's hand, just before he died. I shook Fred's hand just as I had shaken Skipper's. Fred gave me a look, a look I knew well, in which his eyes softened and brightened simultaneously, and you could feel him beaming toward you a message too positive to be put into mere words.

I then gave Fred's forehead a kiss, I gave Ellie a hug, and I left the room, never to see Fred or Ellie again. Except in my memory, all the time.

ECHOES . . .

Fitting In

The struggle to fit in: Is there any drama more central to childhood, at least after the age of eight or nine? As a parent, I worry about my kids' popularity, even though I try not to. I get upset when one of them is not invited to something they wanted to go to, or when I perceive some social slight on the horizon. And yet, working these issues out is a private matter, one that needs to happen within the child, and not be overly supervised by us parents. I love this woman's account of how she began to listen to her own internal drum.

—E. H.

As a girl of fourteen, I closely resembled a spineless jelly-fish, and not an attractive jellyfish; perhaps one of those limpid four-leaf-clover things that drift with every tide. I had been with the same classmates since junior kinder-garten, which means eleven years with the same kids, all of whom disliked me and, therefore, whom I disliked in return. It hadn't always been as bad as it became by ninth grade. When the boys were still a part of our class, we girls had gotten along better, but all the boys had left for their respective boarding schools at the end of eighth grade, leaving a class of nine girls to wait another year before we would leave, as well.

Just because I told my parents I didn't like my classmates did not mean that I wouldn't have happily given my eyeteeth to fit in. If I could have been popular, I would have even thrown in a few molars. But I was hopelessly nerdy: meaning "different without the courage to pull it off." It means ignoring the beat of your own drummer and trying to dance to a tune you cannot hear by watching where others put their feet. I spent half my time sullenly disdaining my classmates and the other half trying to get them to like me, which confused all of us and made me the poster child for the self-loathing adolescent. I hated myself for being left out, and I hated myself for trying to fit in.

Walking down a school corridor one afternoon with two other girls, we passed the teachers' lounge while my classmates were in full swing about how much they hated the Latin teacher: a pale, plump, insecure young man whose book bag had been stuffed with icicles periodically all winter. Without thinking, I said "Shhh," assuming he might be in the lounge and would hear them. Acting as one, they turned on me and said measuringly, "What did you say?"

Thinking quickly, I said, "I was going to say 'shit' if you hadn't interrupted." They seemed mollified and went back to ignoring me, as I returned to sullen self-loathing.

By the end of the year, I was given one more chance to fit in with my class, and I jumped at it. We were taught ancient history by a man named Mr. Ward, whose only real interests were coaching the boys' football team and reminiscing about his experiences during the Korean War. At this point in my life, I remember very little about Egypt and a lot about how to kill a man in a foxhole when you're in a tank. Apparently, you drive the tank over the enemy in the foxhole and spin your gun turret. This slowly sinks the tank into the foxhole and squashes the soldier. It seems unlikely to me now, of course. In retrospect, I also realize that he wasn't a very good teacher.

Mr. Ward taught history to both the seventh and the ninth grades and, with the logic of early adolescence, we all decided that, since we didn't like him, we should cheat on his exams. It was a simple method of cheating: We were just going to bring our study notes into the cafeteria, where we were to take the exam, and refer to them as needed throughout the test. This method presupposes that you have studied pretty hard anyway, because you have lots of notes to cheat from, but that's not the point. The point was that, whether we needed to cheat or not, we were going to. If you think that I was going to be the only girl in my class to say no to this idea, I haven't explained myself very clearly to you yet.

So I studied, prepared lots of notes which I put in the back of the pad of paper we each brought in to the exam room, duly referred to the notes appropriately throughout the exam, and got away with it. Then, two days later, the seventh grade snitched on us all. The news raced through the school, and we knew we were in trouble hours before it actually arrived. Mr. Mason, our headmaster, the man who had taught me sixth-grade arithmetic, who had given me a gift-wrapped box of tiddlywinks to remind me to pay attention to decimal points, who was a personal friend of my father, and whom I loved, arrived in our classroom. He solemnly asked our teacher to step outside, sat down in a chair in the front of the room and simply looked at us. I was sitting in the back row, but when you are in a class of only nine girls that's not nearly enough camouflage. He told us that when confronted with accusations of cheating, the seventh grade had admitted to it and had implicated the ninth grade, as well. He was here to ask us about it. No one said a word. As the silence stretched on, tears began to stream down my cheeks. Mr. Mason could see me, but at least my classmates were all facing forward. Before I would give myself away by sniffling, I stood up and, keeping my back to my classmates, I walked out of the room. Mr. Mason let me go without comment, and after looking desperately up and down the empty halls, I fled into the girls' bathroom, locking myself into a stall. Finally, I had enough time to stop and think. I realized what a good place I had chosen: I had water, a toilet and a small, high window to the outside world that I could climb through just as soon as it was dark. In the meantime, Mr. Mason couldn't come in here to get me because he was a male.

Every time a girl entered the bathroom, I stood on the toilet seat and kept absolutely silent. I was beginning to relax when a small girl entered and called my name. Naturally, I answered. It probably seemed strange to her to be answered by a voice when there were no feet showing under the stall, but I was in so much trouble by now I really didn't care what she thought. "Mr. Mason wants to talk to you," she said. There was no recourse; I was trapped. I climbed down from the toilet and followed her to a small office down the hall, where Mr. Mason was waiting for me.

It was just the two of us, and we began again the conversation that I had walked out on.

"Did you cheat?" he asked calmly.

"Yes, I cheated," I replied.

"Why?"

"Because everyone else did."

"Do you understand that I have to give you an F for the entire year of ancient history?"

"Yes, I suppose so."

Mr. Mason was calm and gentle, but as clear as day. I was in a lot of trouble, and the way out of it would not be easy, but it was possible. He told me that my first step was to go home and tell my mother what I had done, and he would call Concord Academy where I was already accepted for the next year, pending the successful completion of my ninth-grade work, and try to explain that the F that would appear on my transcript should not result in the withdrawal of my admission. I longed to throw myself on Mr. Mason's broad tweedy chest and cry my eyes out, but I was getting an inkling that he was teaching me something I desperately needed to know: how to deal with problems. We were taking care of business here, and I was expected to carry my own weight.

Eddie Dugan, the janitor and all-around children's friend, drove me home in uncharacteristic silence, and I found my mother sitting at her desk. I waited until she was finished with her phone call to tell her why I was home at one-thirty in the afternoon and what I'd been doing.

I don't know what Mr. Mason said to Concord, but they decided to let me enter the tenth grade there in the fall. I arrived at school, lost and homesick, and realized when I looked at my course schedule that I had been assigned to ancient history once again, and that they were even going to use the same textbook that I'd had all of last year. Now, I understood that, given the F I had received for that course last year, it would make sense to them to make me repeat it, but I did know the material and I really didn't want to take it again. I gathered up what Mr. Mason had taught me about accountability, straightened my embryonic spine, listened to the first faint beats of my own drummer, and requested an interview with Mrs. Hall, the headmistress.

It was a strange conversation that we had that September day forty years ago. I stood before her desk clutching my class schedule and explaining my dilemma about ancient history. I kindly absolved her of any responsibility in this mishap. I remember telling her that I quite understood her mistake, that anyone could be excused for thinking that a girl who got an F in ancient history in the ninth grade should take it again in the tenth, but what she might not have known is that I had failed it, not because I didn't know the material, but because I had cheated on the exam. And I respectfully requested to take any other history course being offered.

As Mrs. Hall was a teacher much like Mr. Mason, and understood that accountability is the redemption of many a floundering adolescent, she looked me over, nodded once and changed my class to American history.

My Miss Mackey

Lots of people never get the credit they deserve in life but, in my estimation, teachers top the list. Teachers are the great, unacknowledged benefactors of humankind. Sure, there are lousy teachers. But, my goodness, the good ones are so good—and they get so little recognition!

Here is a story about a couple of lousy teachers, and one angel. This story was written by Paul Hostetler, a retired minister in Pennsylvania.

—E. H.

The late widely known educator, Dr. Ernest Boyer, stressed the importance of early education. He stated that kind, skilled early-childhood teachers should be among the highest-paid educators in our classrooms because they make the biggest positive difference in their students' lives.

I agree. But I also feel deeply that unkind, intolerant teachers at that level can bring about much damage to young learners. Let me illustrate.

When I went to school as a very shy first-grader in Canal Fulton, Ohio, in 1931, my first language was Pennsylvania Dutch. As a result, my classmates made life miserable for me. And my teacher added to my woes by being obviously amused with my "Dutchisms" and mistakes in English grammar, calling attention to them in front of the whole class. Is there any wonder I can't remember her name?

She and the second-grade teacher were friends. One day I overheard them discussing my situation and laughing about it. I can still feel the pain.

Since the second-grade teacher was so friendly with the first-grade teacher, when I moved on to the second grade, I experienced many of the same indignities from first grade all over again. And—would you believe it?—I can't remember my second-grade teacher's name, either.

During that year, I vowed that I would overcome all my grammar problems, become a teacher and embarrass my pupils, too. How ironic. Well, I overcame the grammar deficiencies but I abandoned the second part of that vow—due, in large part, to what happened during the next school year.

Our family moved to an adjoining school district during the summer of 1933. That fall I started the third grade in a country school about a mile west of North Lawrence. It was a one-room building, and the teacher was named Miss Mackey. She obviously loved each boy and girl she taught. I came to love her with all my heart.

Miss Mackey taught me to enjoy school, especially reading. Each morning, she stood in front of the eight grades and read to us. We all joined her on her "magic carpet" and flew to faraway places to discover Alice in Wonderland, the

Arabian Nights, Abraham Lincoln, Ebenezer Scrooge, Oliver Twist, King David, Tom Sawyer and many others.

When I eagerly responded during reading lessons, she would get me additional books to read on my own. I learned some years later from one of her neighbors that Miss Mackey "begged, borrowed or stole" books from all possible sources to keep her pupils reading. In this way, she gave each of us our very own magic carpet.

After my completion of grade three, our family moved again, to the North Lawrence school district. A few years later, when I was in the sixth grade, the country school was closed, and Miss Mackey came to the North Lawrence school as the teacher of the first three grades.

I wasn't aware of this until I saw her out in the school yard one day, soon after the opening of school that fall. She was surrounded by happy, playing children. When she saw me, she rushed over and gave me a big hug and kiss.

Coming from a very undemonstrative family (I never saw my father kiss my mother, although it was always clear to me that they loved each other very much), her gesture both greatly pleased and deeply alarmed this eleven-year-old. The boys in my class snickered and hooted.

Through the years I have kept my magic carpet, and it has brought me to numerous high adventures. I have believed and questioned. I have rejoiced and mourned. I've been stretched and I've been squashed. In time, I joined the ranks of those who help "manufacture" the carpets.

Several years ago, I went back to Ohio to visit this remarkable teacher. She was an older version of my beloved Miss Mackey, but her eyes glowed with the same love and earnestness I knew so well. She had been happily married for many years and was now Mrs. Amstutz. My boyish love for her caused me, even then, to feel jealous of her husband.

I told her I was at long last getting around to thanking her for the great positive influence she had on my life. I mentioned her care, her skills and the passion for reading she had instilled in me more than fifty years before. We reminisced together as time stood still.

When I was on my feet, ready to leave, I reminded her of the time she embarrassed me in the school yard. I told her I was going to "embarrass" her in front of her husband. I then hugged and kissed her. We were both in tears. Her husband smiled his approval.

More recently, I called Principal Robert Horner of the Tuslaw High School on Manchester Avenue, near Massillon. We laid plans, at my suggestion, for me to present a citation in honor of Miss Mackey, then eighty-one years old. The event was a dinner where various honors and scholarships would be presented to graduates. I eagerly looked forward to that evening.

About a week before the dinner, my Miss Mackey disappointed me for the first time ever. She decided not to be involved in the big occasion, after all. I urged her to reconsider, but teachers have the last word, it seems.

A few days later, I received a picture she had taken of me at the schoolhouse door six decades ago. Only a mother and a devoted teacher could have loved that ragtag lad.

Here's to my Miss Mackey! Three cheers for her and for all other good teachers. May God help them understand that there are many, many of us, riding about on enchanted magic carpets, forever grateful for their investment in our lives.

Regrettably, most of us haven't done very well at expressing our appreciation. Maybe this story of mine will spark others to thank their own Miss Mackeys in their own personal way. Even though teachers don't always make it easy to thank them and often feel embarrassed by a big fuss (after all, Miss Mackey wouldn't come to the occasion planned in her honor), I know deep down they must treasure the thanks. I'm just glad I said thanks before it was too late.

Sister Agnes Louise

A teacher who scared the daylights out of you: Who didn't have one of those somewhere along the line? But most of us didn't get the chance to see beyond the terror, as the author of this piece was lucky enough to do.

—E. H.

Sister Agnes Louise. Just the mention of her name sent the teenagers in my small Catholic high school running in terror. This tyrannical nun was our English literature teacher. She had the face of a bulldog and the temperament to match. She seemed to delight in humiliation, which was especially traumatic for a typical self-conscious teen. In the classroom, she would call on whomever she had chosen to "torture" that day. The poor soul would be commanded to stand up in front of the class and recite whatever passage she expected them to know. Pity the teen who didn't have the selection memorized exactly—*and* spoken in Old English! If the task wasn't done to the nun's satisfaction, she would berate and insult the child until he or she was almost in tears.

In fact, a few people *did* collapse in tears! Needless to say, I never made the mistake of being unprepared for her class. Fortunately, she knew me to be a good student and didn't feel the need to call on me very often.

That's why I was caught totally off-guard one afternoon as I stood at my locker. I was up to my usual task of trying to figure out what books I needed for my next class, when I suddenly heard a voice behind me say, "Susan, I would like to speak with you."

My heart started racing. I would know that voice anywhere! It was Sister Agnes Louise. What had I done? Why would she seek me out? I prayed she wasn't going to humiliate me in front of everyone in the hallway.

"M-m-me?" I stammered. "You want to talk to me?"

Was that a slight smile of satisfaction I saw on her face at the sight of fear in my eyes?

"Yes," she replied. "I wanted to talk to you. I heard that you traveled to Japan last summer, and I wanted to hear about your trip. I've also been to Japan, you know."

Japan? She wanted to talk about Japan? I breathed a visible sigh of relief.

But, after taking a few moments to recover, something hit me with surprise. I realized that Sister Agnes Louise's whole life didn't revolve around making us all miserable. She was a real person with outside interests, who maybe once in a while just wanted to have a nice conversation with someone. It was a moment of clarity for me as I saw my teacher in a whole new light.

Later, we had a pleasant discussion about Japan. I never learned why Sister Agnes Louise liked to terrorize her students.

Maybe she felt she was toughening us up for the real world. Or, possibly, that was the only way she thought she could gain respect. But, even if none of us ever learned to speak in Old English, she taught me that there's always more depth to people than they show to the outside world. And, if you take the time to get to know them, you might find that you like what you see—at least a little bit.

The Empty Stairwell

When I give workshops and lectures, I often tell audiences that teachers not only change lives, they save lives. Sometimes, I see people in the audience roll their eyes at that remark, as if I were exaggerating. But I know that I am not exaggerating when I say teachers save lives. Not only did teachers save my own life, I hear stories like the one that follows all the time. Teachers do indeed save lives.

—E. H.

Practically no one ever used that stairwell. So, that was the stairwell where I could have some privacy when I killed myself. I had taken to studying in that stairwell during my senior year in high school. I could sit on one step and use the just-higher step as my study table. The stairwell had a sturdy handrail at the top of its winding three-tiered spiral. Probably, I calculated, sturdy enough for me to hang from.

I studied here because it was quiet. My life was anything but: varsity swim team, lead actor in the plays, senior prefect, honor-society grades, captain of the speech-and-debate team, columnist for the newspaper, and happy, happy tour guide. But, as I said, no one ever used this stairwell . . . almost never during the day, and never, ever at night.

So, there I was, another overachieving, self-loathing, closeted gay boy, sitting and studying his stupid A.P. biology, and thinking about what rope would be best.

Hollywood would want this tale to end a bit more at-the-last-moment-ish, but what happened was that Mr. Crawford came walking up the stairs as I sat in the stairwell one night, and he asked me how I was doing. I said, "Great!" I was very convincing. He told me that he wanted—no, that he was ordering—me to come to see him in his office the next day, and that I had done enough studying and I had better get back to my dorm room (it was pretty late). He told me he'd see me tomorrow. He told me he was worried about me.

I went to see him the next day and knew that I could go to speak with him as many times as I wanted.

I'm a teacher now, but I haven't told him what he did for me. I must do that.

"Why'd You Tell?"

How do teachers know when to break a trust? I guess they get it wrong now and then—sometimes, with disastrous results, no doubt—but, most of the time, they seem to get it right. At least, that has been my experience. Teachers watch out for kids. Like the teacher in this story.

—*E. H.*

"Why'd you do it?" I asked Ellen in the parking lot. "Why did you have to tell them? I knew this would happen!" I was furious. Ellen was an English teacher at my private boarding school, and I had trusted her with some struggles that I was enduring that school year. I was seventeen, rarely trusted adults and brought up in a family that doesn't believe in therapy. Nonetheless, I had realized that what I was going through was a lot more than I could handle on my own. I chose Ellen, a teacher I knew only from being a student leader in the dorm, to confide in.

Ellen told the dean of students, who wanted to tell my parents. As a seventeen-year-old, I saw this as complete betrayal.

I saw this as vindictive and only caring about "school rules" and liability. I stormed out of the office that the dean of students and Ellen were cohabitating. Ellen followed. As we reached the parking lot, she touched my arm. I felt my face turn red. I turned around and began to yell at her. I told her she ruined everything and that I would never trust again. I asked her why she did it when she knew I had trouble trusting. She didn't speak. She let me scream. I began to cry. She let me cry. She respected the boundary that I was creating, and she never attempted to justify her actions. As I turned and walked away with a sarcastic, "Thanks, Ellen. Thanks a lot," I prayed she wouldn't follow me. As I got to my dorm room, I mourned the loss of the teacher and friend I had confided in.

That night at dinner, I was late. My friends were already at the table, and at the vacant spot, there was a blue envelope labeled, *Leslie*. I opened it, and inside Ellen had written a short inscription. "I'm sorry you are hurt. I care about you, and that is why I told. You will understand this someday. As I've said before, my apartment is open and my shoulder is here for you to cry on, my hand to hold to get through everything . . . even this."

That night, I cried in her apartment for hours.

Today, I understand.

The Rose Cane

Just as a teacher can intervene strategically and secretly, as in the previous vignette, a parent, of course, can do the same. Here we see a mother helping her daughter work through one of the most treacherous of childhood moments: the moment of being excluded and teased.

—E. H.

I looked forward to my elementary school's Halloween costume parade every year—except the year when I was eight years old. Still recovering from injuries I had sustained as a result of an accident two years before, I had to walk with a cane. A group of six girls in my class had plagued me with their teasing since I'd first returned to school after the accident, restricted to a wheelchair and with a cast on my right leg from instep to thigh. Most recently, The Mindy Gang, as the rest of the class called this group of girls in deference to their "leader," had devised a favorite, daily pastime of imitating my walking with the cane. Because of the cane, I had come to dread not only every regular school day, but one of my favorite school activities, as well.

My mother, who knew how much I adored wearing costumes and participating in the parade, grew concerned about my lack of enthusiasm for Halloween. I had been unusually reticent about the daily tormenting, but my mother still knew something was amiss. One afternoon in mid-October she casually asked, "Have you decided on a costume for Halloween? We'll have to start making it soon."

"Mom, you know I can't be in the parade. I have this *cane*," I answered, pronouncing "cane" as if it were "leprosy."

"Hmmm," replied my mother, "I don't recall the doctor telling you that the parade was out this year. Last year, when you still had to use the walker or wheelchair, of course, he did say the parade wasn't a good idea."

"I know the doctor didn't say I couldn't," I began evasively, ambivalent about disclosing the details of The Mindy Gang's activities. Every day, I silently endured their merciless teasing, praying that the next day they would leave me alone, but they never did. I knew that if I told my mother, she would fix everything, but it would be a hollow victory. "It's something else," I finished, hoping my voice had just the right measure of vagueness and apathy to stop my mother's inquiry cold.

"Mmm-hmmm," pronounced my mother after a beat. Suddenly, by the inflection of her voice, I realized that my mother knew all about The Mindy Gang's diversions. (Her omniscience is a given in family lore to this day.)

"The other kids make fun of me because of the cane when I'm just *walking*, Mom. What do you think they'll do if I'm in the parade with it?" I demanded.

"All the other kids?"

"No, just The Mindy Gang," I replied, a bit irritated, since I realized she already knew the answer.

"Well, if you're going to let them spoil it for you, I won't force you to go. I hope they deserve to be that important to you," my mother said pointedly. Then, she added casually, "The cane could be part of your costume, you know. If you're interested. It's just a thought."

"That's really dumb, Mom," I responded. "And I'm not going to be in the parade." But my mother knew better. I was hooked on the idea of the cane being part of my costume, even though I wouldn't admit it. She had seen the sparkle come back into my eyes.

Unbeknownst to me, my mother, undeterred, got busy. She created a flamenco-dancer costume, using one of her old horsehair crinolines and some of her colorful silk scarves. The morning of Halloween, she presented the costume to me, complete with a pair of castanets she had received as a souvenir and combs for my hair that she had fastened with handmade, red crepe-paper roses. I was so excited about the costume that I momentarily forgot my misery as I hobbled the few feet between us to hug her.

"Oh, I almost forgot the best part!" my mother exclaimed.

I gasped aloud when she handed me my utterly transformed cane. She had wrapped it completely in green crepe paper. At the top, where it hooked, she had attached a larger version of the red crepe-paper roses she had made for the combs.

My mother gingerly set down the cane and wrapped her arms around me. "I know how hard it's been for you since the accident—having to learn to walk all over again, and being teased all the time in school—but just remember that you have as much of a right to be in this parade as anyone else."

"Even The Mindy Gang?"

"Especially The Mindy Gang," my mother answered firmly. "People are just mean sometimes. But they can't make you feel bad about yourself. Only you can make you feel bad about yourself."

"That's easy for you to say," I shot back. "They're not making fun of you every day." Then, I looked in my mother's eyes and realized, for the first time, that if she could change places with me she would do it in a heartbeat.

"Well, you can't make them stop making fun of you. But you can choose whether or not you're going to let it bother you. It's up to you. And," she added matter-of-factly, "if you really don't want to be in the parade, that's up to you, too."

Honestly, I wasn't so sure my mother was right, but nothing—not even the dreaded Mindy Gang—was going to keep me from wearing that costume and walking with that transformed cane.

Once in my classroom, I discovered, to my sheer delight and amazement, that my costume was the most admired. Even the legendary Mindy herself had her turn with the castanets.

Of course, predictably, the teasing began as soon as we started marching.

"I don't want a cripple walking in my parade," taunted Mindy.

"Cripples can't walk," I informed her, "and it's my parade, too." I held her gaze for a few seconds, then proudly limped onward, gleefully incredulous that, for once, Mindy had nothing to say—or to imitate.

I returned home that afternoon, triumphant and ebullient, regaling my mother with every detail. Finally, I solemnly confessed, "You know, Mom, it was the rose cane that did it."

"No, sweetheart," she smiled, "it was you."

CREATING
CONNECTIONS . . .

Invitation to reflect: Which teachers helped you the most? Are there one or two you might like to get back in touch with now?

Here is an example from a man who is now a senior administrator in the Scarsdale, New York, public school system looking back on one of his own teachers:

> *Recently, at a lecture about education, I got to thinking of all the teachers that were so important to me as I was growing up in Boston—in a family wracked by alcoholism, moving from one part of the city to another because we did not pay the rent.*
>
> *I was particularly reminded of Mrs. Powers, the principal of the C. C. Perkins School in Boston (it's a condo now, near the Prudential Center). She was my sixth-grade teacher, as well as principal. Before you got into class, you saw her directing traffic in the building, an imposing, even slightly frightening person, with her hair in a bun and her face red. All I remember is the vague sense of a wonderful year—with one specific memory.*
>
> *In the spring, she called me out of class into the central corridor of the building and told me I had won the prize*

for politeness, and that the prize was five dollars, that I should tell nobody about it so as not to brag, and that I should run right home and give the money to my mother for safekeeping, then return to school. I was so proud and happy.

It probably took me twenty years or more to figure out that there was no prize for politeness, only a wonderful teacher who cared about me.

Obstacles to connection: For many people, school was a time not of warmth and growth but of humiliation and pain. Because of social difficulties (who wasn't dissed in school by at least some "in" group?), or undiagnosed learning problems (having ADD and dyslexia myself, and being an expert now on these conditions as an adult, I can tell you millions of people have suffered, and still suffer, from these conditions without ever knowing it), or severe problems at home (rare is the family that doesn't go through at least one or two hard years), the years we spend in school can be years we'd just as soon forget.

Possible steps to take: You might take this opportunity to change your perspective on those years. You might look back now with the eyes of an adult, and say to yourself, "I no longer need to feel that way." For example, a while ago, I spoke to my friend Jon Galassi about our years together in high school. I told him I still felt intimidated at the thought of going back to a reunion because of some of the kids who always seemed so much more confident and with-it than I was.

"Ned," Jon said to me, "that was then. This is now. I know how you felt. I felt that way, sometimes, too. But all that is changed. I can promise you, they would be delighted to see you, and I know you'd have fun with them." Here I was, at age fifty, being coached by my friend as if I were still sixteen. These vulnerabilities last.

"Even ———?" I asked, inserting the name of one of the class movers and shakers.

"Him?" Jon replied, laughing. "Especially him. I just saw him. He's turned into a really nice guy. And don't worry, he's got all kinds of problems. No one is perfect anymore, not like we thought they were back then."

I loved what Jon said, "No one is perfect anymore." It is good to remember that, as you look back.

Chapter Five

FRIENDSHIPS

FACT: I'D BE LOST WITHOUT MY FRIENDS

To this day, as my wife can tell you, I feel self-conscious when I dance. Everyone else looks so much more "ept" — if that is the opposite of inept — than I do, that dancing reminds me of what a staggering gap there is between, say, George Clooney and me.

But, even though I still feel less than cool, at my present age of fifty, it doesn't bother me much anymore. I guess that is one of the perks of getting older. I have to admit, though, that I do wish I had been a football hero. Oh, that would have been nice. I wish I could have made a broken field run during a key game at Exeter and talked about it in The Grill the following Monday, having kissed one of the unapproachable goddesses at the dance that Saturday night. But that only happened in my dreams.

I have led not a storybook life of dreams-come-true, but a down-to-earth life of finding good people when I needed them, every step of the way, a life of reliable friendships and warm connections. That has turned out to be more wonderful than the storybook, because it is true. Ironically, for a guy who often felt on the outs growing up, and still feels out of the in-crowd, it is my connections that have made my life rich beyond my dreams. Because of Sue and my kids; my friends like Peter, Jon, Michael and John; my relatives like Lyn and Jamie; the people I work with, like Christine, Ellen, Debbie, Judy and Theresa at my office, and Jill, my agent, and Paul, my partner; and because of my connections with my patients and my readers and with the Being I call God, my life has blossomed more beautifully than I ever thought it would or could.

As a child, I was not a natural friend-maker, being wrapped up in my crazy family and not schooled in the ways of "normal" life. I had to learn how to make friends, just as I had to learn what normal was. I hated being left out, but sometimes, I retreated to my room anyway to read a book or watch TV, rather than deal with the rancid feeling of not fitting in, a feeling that often plagued me when I was in groups of people. I would find some pleasures on my own — the life of the imagination can be rich — but I would often as not find sadness and gloom — my imagination could turn on me and use its power to tell me I was an incurable loser. But I knew I couldn't live very well just going off to my room all the time. I figured I *had to* join other people if I were ever to be happy in life. It didn't come naturally, but I decided I had to do it.

To tell the truth, I never have overcome those fears altogether. Maybe because of my genes, maybe because of my unstable childhood, or maybe because it's just the way it was meant to be, I never have dispelled my fear that wherever I go someone else is judging me and finding me lacking, or that the in-crowd doesn't want me, or that I can't measure up to the people I want to measure up to.

I acknowledge this because I do not want to give the impression that life is all hunky-dory for me now. Insecurity still stings me when I least expect it. But, at the same time, life is oh-so-much better than it was years ago. Those of us, like me, who live a lifelong struggle against our fear of judgment and disapproval need some tips on what to do to cope. Finding good friends is at the top of the list.

Friends make life better; you can take that to the bank.

One of my most important friends is a man I didn't like when I first met him. But he ended up showing me how to get out of my own way. He showed me how to take action, rather than fret. Fathers usually do this for their sons. My father, through no fault of his own, wasn't around enough to do this for me, and my stepfather only made matters worse. So, my friend Tom Bliss did this for me instead.

He was not my dad; he was just my friend. But there aren't many people who ever have helped me more.

He will wince when he reads this, because he is a man who hates to receive credit, and he gets very uncomfortable at direct emotional exchange. He feels things deeply, but he would rather not talk about himself.

When I needed a friend to show me if not *the* way in life, then *a* way, Tom did it.

He came into my life when I was a senior at Exeter. He married my cousin, Lyn. When I first met him I thought he was too quiet, too formal and had too big of a nose. But he nonetheless befriended me. I was an usher at the wedding. When, in my toast at the rehearsal dinner, I said I was glad to be gaining a new friend in Tom, I thought I was just being polite. Little did I know how pivotal a friend he would become.

As I went through college, I didn't know what I was going to do to make a living. There was no clear path for me, like going into a family business or fulfilling some lifelong dream. The thing I had done that had distinguished me most was write a novel at Exeter, so I thought I wanted to be a writer, but how could that translate into making a living?

The problem went deeper than economics and a profession, though. I didn't even know how to be in the world. Oh sure, I was a good student, I had friends in high school and college, I felt strongly about politics and religion, and my hormones raged for the opposite sex, but I didn't know what to do.

I didn't know how to *do life*.

I didn't know what trousers to wear, what words to say, how to introduce myself to girls, or how to drink without regretting later what I did or said. I didn't know how to talk or when to leave or who to call or what to think or where to go. You'd think a kid would know this by his college years, but I really didn't have a clue. Those clues are what I didn't get growing up.

Then Tom stepped in. Without knowing he was doing it, or doing it so subtly that I didn't know he was doing it, he began to show me what to do. Tom was a jock, a high-school star, and he was as good-looking as George Clooney. My judgment that his nose was too big was just my way of finding some-thing—anything, please!—about him that I could denigrate. I thought, of course, he would be too cool to actually like me. That's where I was wrong.

Whenever I would visit Lyn and Tom after they got married, Tom would talk to me as a peer. Even though he was a medical student and I was a mere freshman in college, he treated me like a friend. I began to watch how he dressed and how he talked, and, the next thing I knew, I was using some of his mannerisms, like saying, "you know," between phrases as I searched for the next word, or leaning forward to listen when someone else spoke, or rising up a bit on my tiptoes from time to time when having a conversation and holding a drink.

Tom was a rugby player. He wore a belt sometimes that had stitched into it the phrase, *Rugby Players Have Leather Balls*. I was not a jock, nor did I imagine there was anything even remotely leathery in any part of my anatomy. But, one day, when Tom and I were throwing a football around on the beach (I did this sort of thing with him, trying to learn) he told me I was a fast runner. He didn't know it, but that compliment promoted me to a new level. Here was a jock, one of the in-crowd, telling me I could run. It was as if I'd just made the team.

That was just one moment. Others have followed.

I was an English major. And proud of it. But Tom gently suggested I might want to try medical school, just in case my life as a writer didn't develop as quickly as I hoped.

Medical school? *Impossible*, I thought. *I can't do all the science. I can't get up early every morning and stay up all night the next day. I am not dedicated enough. Plus, I am an artiste, not a crass professional.*

"You can do the science," Tom said. Then he told me he got a D in organic chemistry and still got into Georgetown Medical School.

"You can get up early," he told me. Years later, he would confess to me that this was the one bit of reassurance he hadn't been so sure of.

"No one is as dedicated as medical schools make it sound like you are supposed to be," he told me. That was a relief.

I hadn't dared tell him the part about being an artiste, and not a crass professional. This is because I was starting to learn what he was inadvertently teaching me: how not to be defensively pompous and pretentious, how to do life right.

So, I began to take premed courses. Tom graduated from medical school in Washington and started his residency in orthopedics at Rhode Island Hospital, in Providence. Since I was living in Cambridge, now I could go to Providence to visit Lyn and Tom a lot. I often went more than once a week.

Sometimes, Tom would take me to the hospital with him. I would go in, feeling nervous and insecure, like an outsider visiting the cool dudes, but Tom showed me these were just people, too. Tom never treated me like I was anything but a good guy. Slowly, I began to feel like a good guy, and maybe even to become one.

Tom told me he had been insecure with girls, too. He told me that when he met Lyn, he couldn't believe how lucky he felt that she liked him back as much as he liked her. "It was the best day of my life, the day we met," he would say. "Don't worry about it. You're a good-looking guy. You'll meet someone, too." A good-looking guy? And I could run? Tom had no idea how much those chance remarks really meant to me.

We would go out and drink beers. Not too many, but enough to loosen up and talk even more. Lyn was very good at drawing Tom out, so we would have long conversations about everything under the sun.

What he really did for me was just show me how to *be*.

He showed me how to do life, in a normal way. No one else had the ability or took the time to do that for me before. Tom showed me that life did not have to be twisted and strange and uncertain and full of worry. He showed me life could be fun and productive and good.

There was no one moment in which Tom changed my life, just a long series of them. He was always there, handing out the presents every Christmas, cooking the chicken at every barbecue, offering support and reassurance at every turn along the way.

Tom is my relative by marriage, but my friend by choice. He has been my friend now for thirty-five years. I never would have become a doctor were it not for him; nor, I daresay, would I ever have learned how to do the many other things that go into living in a reasonably happy and responsible way. As a psychiatrist now, and as a parent, I wish I could prescribe a Tom Bliss for lots of people. But there aren't many like him to be found.

We were, and are, different from each other. He is an orthopedic surgeon. I am a psychiatrist. He is strong and silent. I am insecure and talkative. He is a jock. I am a jock wanna-be.

But we have a true and equal friendship now, not just a relationship based on me learning from him.

I think what I give him is exactly what he gives me: I like him. He likes me. We respect one another. When we met we were so different, but we gave each other a chance, and, the next thing you knew, we had become friends. Brought together by Lyn, we found, much to our mutual surprise, that we had good stuff to offer each other.

I needed him more than he needed me, but that doesn't matter now. Now, we will be friends forever. This is how friendship happens, sometimes.

My great hope for my children is not that they get good grades in school or become stars in other ways, but that they find friends like Tom, and become friends like Tom for others, too.

NAKED MEN

I want to tell you what happened when a naked man wearing a bathing cap came up to me and insulted me. But first, you need some background.

My friend, Peter Metz, is a child- and adult-psychiatrist, as I am. He is the godfather of my daughter, Lucy, and I am the godfather of his daughter, Sarah. We were college classmates and we did our residencies in psychiatry together.

Since 1981, we have played squash together on Tuesday afternoons. These regular games started in an unusual way. You might say it was a matter of life or death.

Peter and I hadn't known each other in college. Even though we were in the same class, there were twelve hundred members of that class, and no one knew everyone. But during residency, since there were only twelve residents in the class, we all got to know each other.

One day, I saw Peter present a patient on rounds. In psychiatry, where the whole point of the field is to understand a person, how you present a patient to other professionals during rounds is a good indicator of your skills in understanding other people. Peter did a brilliant job. Even better than brilliant.

He did such a good job, I wanted to kill him. He made me feel so competitive that I wanted to remove him from the program and from the planet. I knew I was good, but I could see that he was much better.

However, I didn't dare murder him. I didn't even dare to maim him or generally besmirch his reputation by whatever means I could think of. The problem was, as much as I hated him, I also liked him. His presentation of that one patient was so good, it wasn't merely brilliant, it was heartwarming. It was winsome. It made me like both the patient and the presenter. As much as it filled me with envy, it also filled me with a desire to become this man's friend.

So, after rounds, I told him, "Peter, you were awesome. I wanted to kill you, you were so good. But, since killing you would do neither of us much good, I wonder if we might try being friends, instead."

He must have been glad to have his life spared, because he agreed.

The next question was, how do we become friends? Life is extremely busy in medical training, even in psychiatry. How would we find time for a real friendship? I proposed we play squash. Peter enthusiastically agreed, as he loved exercise and he had played some squash in college. I hated exercise myself, but I knew I needed it, and I, too, had played some squash in college.

Also, a game had competition built into it. If I couldn't kill Peter, maybe I could beat him at squash. As it turned out, we were very evenly matched, so we could take turns winning. After the games, we developed the habit of going to a nearby tavern for a few beers and conversation. That was where we really connected. It was sort of a guy thing: We had to compete first, then we could connect.

We have kept up with the games, and with the beers, and with the connection for all these years. We are such good friends, we might as well be brothers.

Which brings me back to naked men.

There is a man who frequents the Mt. Auburn Club in Cambridge, where Peter and I have our Tuesday games, who I have come to know on a nodding basis. For the sake of this story, I'll call him Malcolm. Over the years we have spoken a few words, just passing chitchat on the way in or out of the locker room.

Malcolm is a pharmacist. The significance of that fact is that he has strong opinions about the use of medications. As a psychiatrist, I sometimes prescribe medications. Among the medications I sometimes prescribe is Ritalin, a medication often used to treat attention deficit disorder. Also, I have written books about the treatment of attention deficit disorder, a condition I both have myself and have been treating in children and adults for over twenty years.

It has been especially rewarding for me to treat people with ADD because, first of all, I understand the condition so well, and, second of all, I so often see people's lives dramatically improve once they begin treatment.

However, Malcolm, as I was to learn, doesn't see what I do as such a good thing. I learned this the day he spoke to me when we both were naked.

I was coming out of the shower, drying my hair with my towel, when I saw Malcolm walking toward me. He was wearing nothing but his bathing cap, which gave him an oddly jaunty look. An older man, Malcolm looks fit and trim, the picture of well-being. In just a moment, I was to learn what he was like underneath his skin.

"Well," he said, as he drew closer to me, "there is Dr. Ritalin."

This was not intended as a compliment. In fact, his words felt like a slap in the face. In that one instant, I knew how people felt when they encountered prejudice. Malcolm's few words taught me more about bigotry than any course I had ever taken. This wasn't racial bigotry, but it was bigotry, nonetheless. Malcolm had made up his mind without knowing all the facts.

In one short sentence, he insulted what I had trained many years to be able to do: offer expert assistance to children and adults with learning problems. He lumped me together with all the doctors who irresponsibly prescribe medications, and he did so with the most casual flick of his tongue. Just one stiletto sentence, as we stood naked next to each other in the locker room.

I wanted to say many, many words to him. But I replied with just a few. "I wish you wouldn't call me that," I said.

"Why not?" he went on. "You are a leading proponent of Ritalin."

"That's not true, Malcolm," I replied. "I am in favor of using Ritalin when it is indicated and appropriate, and I am opposed to using it when it is not."

"Oh, that sounds profound," Malcolm said in a mocking tone.

I try to build bridges, not burn them. But this man was really provoking me, as well as hurting my feelings. Until that moment, I had liked Malcolm, at least what little I knew

of him. I had no idea that he could be so gratuitously insult-
ing. I said to him, "Malcolm, I wish you wouldn't talk to me
like that."

He paused. I think he could see I was serious. His tone
became less aggressive and more conciliatory as he said, "It is
just that Ritalin is so abused by so many people!"

"Just because some people abuse it doesn't mean that we
should get rid of it, does it? And it sure doesn't mean you
should call me Dr. Ritalin, without knowing anything about
how I conduct my practice."

I don't mean to debate the relative merits of Ritalin here.
My point is to show how easily life can bring us into contro-
versial waters, often when we least expect it, such as when we
stand naked in the locker room. We are always vulnerable to
the secret angers, prejudices and misunderstandings of other
people. In one casual moment, a person can devastate
another person, with a glance or just a few words.

On my way out of the locker room, I said to Peter, "Did
you hear what that guy said to me?"

"Yes," Peter said. "I thought you handled it well."

"But why did he say that?" I asked.

"Because he doesn't know you. And he doesn't know what
you stand for. You have to let it go," Peter replied.

"But it's hard to let it go," I protested. "He was wrong. I
want to go back and tell him so."

"Ned, look," Peter said, sounding somewhat impatient,
"you have to get over it. What matters are the people who
know you. Listen to them. There will always be people like
that guy who take potshots. You just can't let it bother you."

"But it does," I insisted.

"Then get over it," Peter replied with a laugh. "Let's go have a beer."

We sat and talked, and I eventually forgot about Malcolm. I'm remembering him now as I write this, of course, but I remember him through the lenses Peter gave me.

This is what friends are for. There are Malcolms in all of our lives. There are moments when we get insulted, unfairly, when we least expect it, even when we are naked. The difference between being able to handle it well and falling apart is often made by a friend.

In fact, life involves many Malcolms, at least for most of us, and a ton of insults. The more we try to accomplish, the more likely it is we will encounter people who think what we are doing is stupid, dangerous or even immoral. Life does not come equipped with a safety net. We have to build our own. For me, friends like Peter are key parts of the safety net.

I am still thin-skinned. The Malcolms out there still bug me, and they always will. I doubt that at my age I will change in that regard. But people like Malcolm would make me seethe and stew much more were it not for friends like Peter and my wife, Sue. Even my daughter, Lucy, has learned how to spot me in a funk and tell me to snap out of it. Just the other day she said to me, as I was worrying about some Malcolm-type problem, "Dad, didn't you write a book about worry? Well, don't worry!"

I have learned that I can't do anything to prevent Malcolms from walking up to me, even naked in the locker room. But I have also learned that I do not have to live in fear of them. I have friends.

ECHOES . . .

Charlie

*The relationships we make with animals can be as intense
as any friendship with a human, and just as important. My
niece, Molly, was a world-class equestrian during her teens
and early twenties, tirelessly training, often getting up at
four in the morning, driving hundreds of miles to go to
events, cleaning out stalls, risking her neck as she and her
horse jumped obstacles no one in their right mind would
tackle—all while she attended school and kept up with
"normal" life. The following is her account of going back to
visit her horse, Charlie, after she had given up riding to pur-
sue a career as a doctor. When she wrote this she was a
fourth-year medical student at Brown, heading into a residency in emergency-room medicine. She is as brave a young
woman as I have ever met.*

—E. H.

As I stepped out of my little Budget rental car into the
baking North Carolina sun, I took a minute to survey
the expansive horse farm's idyllic beauty. It was here that my

best friend and partner of so many competitive seasons was retired. I had not seen Charlie since he had been led out of my family's Massachusetts barn several years before and taken off in a trailer to his eventual new life.

During this trip south, I had thought a lot about the many roles this generous liver-chestnut gelding had played in my life. We had bought the talented but wild runaway at a bargain price when I was sixteen and just starting to hit the highly competitive equestrian Three-Day Eventing scene. Charlie and I spent the next five years forging a once-in-a-lifetime partnership that eventually took us to the top of the sport and around the world representing the U.S. Equestrian Team.

During those tumultuous teenage years, Charlie was a rock of stability in my life. I could always count on him. I also shared more intense moments with him than with any person. He was my protector at the most terrifying jumps, someone who would soar to impossible heights, twisting his powerful body to safely carry me through imposing combinations of solid oxers and steep banks into water. He was the one who was there on the days when I fought back tears after particularly tough sessions with my difficult coach. He seemed to sense my mood and would slow his pace down as we walked back to the barn, allowing me time to get myself together. Charlie was the child that I could make myself sick worrying about, such as when he ruptured his front tendon and my parents and I spent the night in his stall icing his swollen leg, or during the many long nights I spent camped out in the barn watching over him when he had colic. Although the sight of blood normally did not faze me, seeing any of Charlie's would inevitably send me fainting to the floor.

Galloping along the different cross-country courses, it was as though we could read each other's minds. I could communicate so much to him with a slight squeeze of the reins or a shift of my weight. I just had to tickle his neck with my little finger to let him know I was proud of him, and he would flick his ear back and swish his tail once to let me know he agreed. We put up with each other's little quirks the way close family members do, he with my attempts to be overly controlling with the reins and me with his inexplicable fear of white towels. Charlie took me to the top and always did his best not to let me tumble to the ground. I could always count on him to try his hardest, simply because I asked him to. He was someone I could utterly, completely trust. This is why I will never fully forgive myself for breaking his trust in me.

I broke Charlie's trust by sending him away. For various reasons, I had decided to retire from competitive riding. I worked out a deal where Charlie would do some competing with my former coach and then, eventually, would move to North Carolina with a lovely woman who would just do dressage and ultimately retire him at her farm. The competing with my driven coach would be hard on him physically and mentally, but in the end he would have the best life I could give him. New England winters had always been too much for his delicate metabolism and would only become worse for him as he aged. Intellectually, I knew I was fortunate to find such a situation for him, but as I huddled sobbing in my bedroom and listened to the familiar clop-clopping of Charlie's hooves as he innocently walked to the waiting trailer below, my heart was torn out.

Charlie and my coach never did well competitively, and to my relief he had been retired within the first year. I had not wanted to visit him before now because I thought it would be too painful, and probably because of the guilt I felt, as well. Finally, my parents had talked me into going to see him.

So, there I was, five years later, going to visit Charlie for the first time. I walked into the manicured stable, my eyes fighting to adjust to the darker light. Would he recognize me? I doubted it. And what would he look like? Would he have aged much during that time? I quickly scanned each head that popped out from behind the stall doors.

I walked halfway down the long aisle before I saw him. A wave of emotion overtook my entire being, like a strange physical force. Tears instantly sprang from my eyes and a hoarse cry that seemed to come from the depths of my stomach leapt out of my mouth. Charlie was far more composed. In the same way as he had done a million times before, he gave me one of his familiar appraising looks, with his kind, liquid brown eyes and softly nickered a welcoming hello. As I hugged his warm neck, he arched his head around and let it rest gently on my shoulder. Charlie's new owner tactfully disappeared until I was finally able to stop crying.

I spent the next two hours hanging out with Charlie as he grazed in the sun. Later, when I sat down on the plane to go home, I felt emotionally drained, but somewhat more peaceful, too. Charlie was happy and safe and, even though I had given him up, I could see that it had been the right thing to do. Plus, seeing him again reminded me that although our competitive partnership was over, we shared a connection and a closeness that would last forever.

Herbie

This story (which, be forewarned, contains some off-color words) is one of my favorites in this book because it captures so perfectly the combination of hostility and affection that fills most close relationships, especially between men.

—*E. H.*

I had a friend named Sean who was diagnosed with cancer when he was fifty. He had put his affairs in order and was preparing to travel home to Ireland to die.

He asked me if I would drive him to the airport, but not to tell anyone when he was leaving. He didn't want any fanfare. On the appointed day, I arrived and found Sean sitting on a suitcase outside his building, dressed in a suit that fit both his body and his personality equally poorly, chin against a cane looking at his watch. I was a half hour early, but Sean was in a hurry to leave his home, so I started to help him get into the car. As I came around to the driver's side, I saw Herbie standing at the curb, about a hundred feet in front of us.

Herbie and Sean were inseparable friends up until they had a fight, and they had not talked to each other since.

"Sean, Herbie is standing up there," I said. Herbie had no way of knowing when we were leaving and was never home at that time of day.

"Oh, f--k Herbie. Herbie's an a--hole."

"I think he wants to talk to you, Sean."

"Drive on, me boy."

"Sean, I think we should stop," I said, and I pulled the car up to the curb where Herbie stood.

"Ahh, for fool's sake," Sean muttered. Herbie stood at the curb, leaned into the window and took Sean's hand, tears in his eyes.

"Sean, I will look after the boys. You were a good man and a good friend. You've been a brother to me, and you'll always be a part of me."

I could barely see, I was crying so hard. Herbie was, too, but he hadn't let go of Sean's hand yet.

"You, too, Herbie. You, too. Thanks for everything, and the boys know they can turn to you." Herbie leaned in and the two men hugged, and then Herbie turned and walked away.

I pulled away from the curb. Regaining control, I said, "Sean, that was wonderful to watch. I've missed seeing you two together, and I feel honored to have watched you say good-bye to Herbie."

"Ahh, f--k Herbie. Herbie's an a--hole!"

The subject was closed. I still laugh as I think of that painful day. Sean knew what Herbie needed that day, and he gave it to him. I guess I did the same.

Guys

During my surgery rotation in medical school, I ended up having the hardest time parting with, of all people, a chain-smoking chief resident named McCormick, who had called me a "useless dink" every day of the three-month rotation. Why did I like him? Why was it so hard to say good-bye to this person who insulted me and taunted me day after day? Because I knew he didn't mean it. Because, in fact, I knew it was his way of saying he liked me. "Useless dink" means "I like you"? Sometimes, it actually does. Especially with us guys.

There are some people, particularly men—and particularly men in macho fields like surgery, business, finance or sports—who just plain cannot say, "I like you." If they manage to spit the words out and they don't throw up as they do so, they come across as insincere, at best, and manipulative, at worst—like the man in the Bud Light commercial who says, "I love you, man," to his buddy as they're sitting on a dock, simply as a ruse to finagle his buddy's Bud Light away from him.

Some men have learned lately how to say, "I like you," or even, "I love you," without gagging. But most of us have not. So we use code words. "Hey, how ya doing, you fat old can of lard," can mean, "I'm really glad to see you." "Go Red Sox," can mean, "I love you." "Man, you are one ugly dude," can mean, "You're my best friend." It is strange, but true.

Men have deep feelings, just as deep as women, and they wish to make close relationships, as well. But closeness among men can be difficult, mainly because of competition. Sometimes, we fight rather than bond. And yet, we can be great team players. In the example that follows, we see a man who was close to his buddy on the football field, but only on the football field.

Since it is not likely that we guys are going to change fundamentally in the near future, maybe what we can concentrate on doing is keeping up with our friends—spending time with them—even if we have to use code to express our underlying feelings. The big lesson we men need to learn is that we can't wait forever to make our feelings known, even if they are in code.

The man in the story that follows speaks for millions of people, as he writes simply and plainly of his regret that he didn't stay in touch with a buddy from long ago.

Something about the spare, almost stark style of this piece reminds me of Aeschylus. Granted, this is not Greek tragedy. But, in its honesty and utter simplicity, this account depicts the tragic fate of so many friendships, great opportunities never fulfilled.

There is a happy ending. After he wrote this piece, Hank contacted Butch. Following a few lost telephone messages, they reunited and now, at last, are good friends.

—E. H.

I am fifty-seven years old, have many acquaintances, but almost no close friends with whom I have maintained contact.

During senior year of high school, on the football team, Butch and I were a team ourselves. I was tackle, and he was a linebacker. We worked the stunts on our own. The team had a 5–5 season, but both of us were on all-state at the end. However, we were not close off the field.

I moved away right after graduation.

I didn't return until our twenty-fifth reunion.

Butch's wife said that, before they came to the reunion, Butch kept saying, "I hope Hank is there!"

I had no idea that would be his reaction, even though I knew that I had thought about those days and what we had done many times. When I found out about his statement, I felt really moved. I vowed to maintain contact. But, I have not.

When I think of our connection, I feel both extremes of high and low. High about what we had. Low about what we haven't had.

Thursday-Night Poker

In the vignette that follows, a man tells of one way a group of guys can stay connected, without taking sensitivity training! A simple ritual—a Thursday-night poker game—kept these men connected for years. Important human moments need not contain any explicitly "deep" conversation. The fact is, we men want closeness; we just go about finding it differently. For a man, a poker game or a silent game of catch in the backyard can be as rich a human moment as a deep conversation might be for someone else.

—E. H.

For the last twenty years, I have played in a weekly Thursday-night poker game. Some of the members of the game have come and gone over the years, but all of us in the group, without ever saying so expressly, have committed ourselves to this weekly gathering.

I have missed games because of being out of town, on business or a family vacation, but, for the most part, the others and I have structured our lives to be available every Thursday. If we don't have a game, which happens occasionally, my week is disrupted. If I'm home on a Thursday night, I'm uncomfortable—I feel out of place. I miss the jokes, the laughter, the competition.

I sometimes have not participated in activities involving my wife or son, or cut them short, to make the game. But they both know how meaningful my weekly outing is, and they don't resent those times I've put them second because they ultimately benefit. Emotionally, I'm happier.

My son might find ten dollars on the kitchen table, if I won the night before. If I win on Thursday night, I'm happy spending those dollars for the weekend, going to dinner or the movies. If I lose, I'm anxious to get back the next week and get even. But, as far as I'm concerned, because of my weekly card game, I'm never a loser.

The chatter at our group is a reflection of our lives. At first, it was talk of our kids beginning school, or whose wife was pregnant. Then, it was bar/bat mitzvahs, and who was getting a car for their kid. Now it's college graduation, weddings and the results of our cholesterol and PSA tests.

Thursday night is an opportunity for me to mentally cleanse, forget all the other issues in my life, both good and bad, for four hours, and refresh myself for another week.

I know that soon this game will change. We will all move on as we retire, move away, and finish our lives and careers elsewhere. I just hope wherever I go, I'll find another Thursday-night game.

CREATING
CONNECTIONS . . .

Invitation to reflect: Is there a friend in your life, past or present, who influenced you as Tom Bliss or Peter Metz influenced me? What friends come to mind when you think of the people you'd like to invite to a perfect dinner? Do you have a Thursday-night poker game or the equivalent?

Common obstacles to connection: Time and competition: These are two of the biggest obstacles to adult friendship. Time these days is scarce for everyone. Time is so short, it is almost inevitable that friendship goes on the back burner, unless you deliberately make it a point not to let that happen. Also, competition, particularly among men, can make opening up difficult, as you don't want to show vulnerability.

Possible steps to take: In addition to my squash games with my friend Peter Metz, I have other games scheduled with other friends on Sunday mornings and Friday evenings. These have been going on for over ten years. This is the best way I know to overcome the obstacle of time: You put time with friends into your schedule, and you stay faithful to it.

As for competition, the squash games build competition right into the process. I do think that, among men especially, competition is an element that can't be avoided; better to acknowledge and allow for it than to avoid it or pretend it isn't there.

On the other hand, if the competition becomes alienating, or, if due to your competitive feelings, you find that you don't want to see a friend or you start avoiding that person, then you might consider the possibility that you are denying yourself something good—a friendship—for no good reason.

Most of the time, when competitive feelings get out of hand, we are blowing the competition out of proportion in our minds. We see the other person's victory or successes as a devaluation of ourselves, instead of being merely what they are: the other person's victory or successes. If we let the other person's victory or successes lead to the end of the friendship, then we are exaggerating the importance of the other person's victory or successes, and we are underestimating the importance of a friendship.

Chapter Six

FALLING IN LOVE

FIRST LOVE

Do you remember your first love? Of course, the person you think of depends on how you define "first love." I guess our mothers were the first love for most of us. But how about your first romantic love? Well, mine was a girl named Lauralee, in the first grade, in Chatham. I don't think she noticed me at all, but I sure noticed her. I was too young for much in the way of erotic desire, but I do know I thought Lauralee was pretty special.

How about your first more mature crush or love? For me, that would have been, unfortunately, a crush on the girlfriend of one of my friends when I was in high school. I never let either of them know what a crush I had; I just simmered in silence, longing for what never happened.

How about the first actual romance? You know, the first person where the love was requited, a kiss was completed and your heart went bang? For me, that was, well, let me change her name, in case she'd be embarrassed, and call her Annie. Annie, I have no idea why we broke up. I don't even remember *how* we broke up. *Did* we break up?

I was in college, so was Annie. Freshman year. Fred Tremallo had introduced us when Annie was a student at the Exeter summer session the summer before, and I had come up to visit. Fred thought we would like each other. How right he was.

Annie was beautiful and smart. She was also a little insecure, like me. She was talented and sensitive, and I fell in love with her with all the energy I had been saving up for years to fall in love with, ever since I fell in love with love, which I guess started with Lauralee, but really gathered steam when I started to read novels and entertain higher levels of hormones.

Annie, I know we must have broken up, because I'm here and you're there, but I'd really like to know what happened. I wish you could call me and tell me.

I hope your memories of me are as fond as mine are of you. I hope you don't look back and think I was some kind of a dweeb! I was a little bit of a dweeb, I guess, with my literary pretensions and serious silences.

But you were smooth as silk. I can tell you I look back and think you were right out of a fairy tale, full of beauty and New York sophistication and unpredictability. You taught me so much about love. I don't mean in the grand, tragic sense of that word. I mean it in the sense of what it feels like to have a big, thumping I-can't-get-you-off-my-mind-and-I-really-like-it feeling for a girl. You introduced me to that. You introduced me to looking forward to a phone call, to wondering what someone will be wearing, to wondering if you loved me as much as I loved you, to wondering when to say, "I love you."

I wrote you my first love letters. I wrote you my first love poems. I am sure the poetry was poor, but I can assure you the feelings were rich. You were the first person I made out with (okay, okay, I won't go into the details here), and I will be forever grateful to you for not rejecting me then.

Your smile was so engaging, but your reserve could be so impenetrable. Do you remember how you'd turn your head so your long blonde hair would cover my view of your face and I couldn't see your expression? Used to drive me nuts.

But then, your mood would change, and you would look at me and smile, and the whole wide world would feel good. At those moments, I knew bliss. There is no headier drug than romantic love, and the first time you feel it for some-one—and miracle of miracles the someone feels it back for you—life lifts up, as it never has before. Not until you have children do you ever feel such a rush again.

I felt that we were one, that you understood me and I understood you, that you loved me and I loved you, that you were attracted to me—and God knows I was attracted to you—that the rest of the world did not exist, just you and I out on the sea, with love as our snug boat.

Of course, things didn't "work out," in that we're not together now, but my goodness, they worked out great by any other reckoning. Sure, it was not perfect; or let's say it *was* perfect, but pain was part of the perfection. You hurt me when you stood me up one time, another time when you didn't appreciate some presents I had worked so hard on for you. I hurt you when I stood you up one time, and when I didn't like a friend of yours you introduced me to. We hurt each other, but that is part of the deal of first love, isn't it?

We had such fun. How did we break up? Or did we just fade away? Did we ever say good-bye? Did we have a last kiss? There was no tearful farewell that I can recall, no parting at the train station, or walking in opposite directions down a rainy Cambridge sidewalk late on a Sunday afternoon.

I don't think we ever did say good-bye. Now, we never will. You will live with me forever, my first love. I thank Fred Tremallo for introducing us. I thank you for being you, and for the time you spent with me.

I hope you are happy now. I really, really hope so.

Thank you, Annie, for being my first love.

I'll never forget you.

ECHOES . . .

A Man I Used to Know

Love sneaks into our lives when we least expect it. Sometimes, when you are looking for love, you don't find it; but, when you are not looking at all, it can find you. In this piece, we see a love develop out of nowhere. One year, they were friends, nothing more. The next year—for no apparent reason—they became, well, something more.

In my view, there are almost as many ways to love as there are people to meet. We do ourselves a disservice if we narrow what we are allowed to feel to such an extent that we extinguish unexpected feelings altogether. In this story, we see how one woman's life was enriched by such unexpected feelings.

—E. H.

Kevin and I met in college. He was married. I had been going steady with my boyfriend for two years. Kevin and I were just friends. We worked together on the campus newspaper, often long and late hours. No sparks, just sweat. But then, when we returned to campus for our senior year, something happened. He looked . . . different. And he looked at me differently. He and his wife had separated, he said. They'd "had" to get married while still in high school. Their daughter was now four years old. They would stay close friends for her sake, but neither of them felt they could remain together as husband and wife.

We continued working on the newspaper together. One night, as we were wrapping up, we were the only two left in the office. It was late, and we were tired. My hair was dirty, and I was in jeans and a sweatshirt. He had circles under his eyes. In addition to going to school, he was working in order to earn money for his daughter. Still, we sat and talked and talked, almost until the sun came up. My boyfriend started to joke that I was spending more time with Kevin than I was with him. It was true. That relationship, too, had overstayed its welcome. I wasn't surprised when my boyfriend broke it off shortly before Christmas. And, to tell the truth, I wasn't disappointed.

I went home for the holidays to see my family, but I found myself eager to return to campus, eager to see Kevin. It had been three weeks, and when we ran into one another in the newspaper office, we embraced in a hug that lasted forever, or so it seemed. From then on, we were inseparable. I knew it wasn't healthy. I knew that he had a wife—estranged, yes—and a young daughter. I knew that I was still young and immature and not ready for a messy relationship. But I knew that I was totally in love with this boy, and I knew he felt the same way. And, with chemistry like that, anything seemed possible.

It went on that way for the second semester of our senior year. We simply could not get enough of each other. At seminars with professors, we would sit playing footsie under the table, thinking we were pulling off something big. We covered stories together, pasted up pages together. We were still sweating over the newspaper, but it was more from making out than from overworking. Every time he kissed me, it was like he'd never kissed me before. It was a heady, romantic, whirlwind time. And it was deepened by the fact that we had first been buddies. There were no games, no pretense. It was the most intense relationship I'd ever known. I was twenty years old, and I thought we'd have all the time in the world.

What I didn't realize was that when college ends, so does one's old life. We exchange our jeans for suits, our dorm rooms for apartments, and, often, our old friends for new ones. We pay our own bills, fix our own schedules. Unemployment was sky-high the year I graduated from college, and Kevin and I went our separate ways to jobs in different states. He wanted and needed to be near his daughter, which I understood perfectly well. But that also meant he would be near his wife. The divorce wasn't final, and that made me nervous.

I jumped before I got pushed, or so I thought. I broke up with Kevin and, in doing so, broke my own heart. We both cried. He came once, unannounced, to my town. I wasn't there. He taped a note to my door, using a Band-Aid. "A love like ours comes along only once in a geophysical light-year," he wrote. I cried when I read it. I still have that note. It has been twenty-five years.

I heard later that Kevin did get back with his wife, but ten years later, they divorced. He called me once, when he passed through the city where I was now living. He sounded good. His daughter was now in college herself, and he had a serious girlfriend. He'd been angry at me for a long time, he said. I explained that I'd been freaked out by the intensity of the relationship—and by the fact that he was a married man with a child. At twenty, I simply was not emotionally equipped to handle such serious business.

When I met my husband five years after college, he reminded me a bit of Kevin. Handsome and dark, quiet but passionate. He didn't have the baggage that Kevin had; in fact, I was his first serious girlfriend, a job I took very seriously. We married two years later, and I sent Kevin an announcement. He wrote me back a note: "I'm jealous. It should have been me. Love always."

I still have that note, and sometimes, when I'm going through old boxes, I'll pull it out and read it—and, yes, press it against my cheek. I have a teenager myself now, and I hope her first love will be as sweet and as lasting as mine was, for a small part of my heart will always be reserved under the name "Kevin."

The Tide Turns

The author of this piece is now a psychologist. He is also my friend. He loves life as much as anyone I have ever met. You can sense that positivity in his story here.

— E. H

I should have numerous childhood memories of "The Cove" because I swam there almost every summer after-noon of my childhood. Yet, all my earlier images were washed away by the experiences of one day—actually, it was probably only two or three hours—when I was fourteen years old. The day I fell in love with Jenny Weller.

Now, at the age of fifty-three, I cannot help thinking of that August afternoon whenever I visit that tiny crescent of beach facing a huge granite rock across fifty yards of shallow water on a small Massachusetts lake. Of course, The Cove, like so many places from my childhood to which I have returned, looks much smaller than I remember it from childhood. But the feelings of first love were huge then, and they can be huge today, if I let them sweep back over me.

I discovered my own capacity for romance that day. I suddenly understood how beautiful a woman's smile could be and how desirable her body could be. I also discovered the feeling of wanting to stop time, to hold onto a moment. Throughout my growing up, I had always wanted to grow faster, to be bigger, to move on to the next adventure. But, suddenly, that afternoon I wanted to hold onto time as much as I wanted to hold Jenny. Because, even as I admitted to myself that I was in love with her, I knew that it was hopeless. Nothing could come of this. I couldn't tell anyone; it couldn't turn into anything; no one would take it seriously. Who would believe that I loved Jenny?

Jenny was twelve years old. Twelve! Impossible! I was fourteen. That was plausible. Fourteen was a lot more grown-up than twelve. She was still a little girl, or at least everyone would think of her that way (or so I thought). I had known her as a little girl. Her parents were my parents' dear friends. Her mother was my aunt's closest friend. She was my younger sister's baby-sitter. We had known each other for years. We had grown up together . . . in the summers, at least. There was no way to convert my love into something real that people would understand or respect. I wasn't even sure that I was supposed to be in love at my age.

But the worst part of it all, from my point of view, was that my sixteen-year-old brother, Luke, was totally smitten with Jenny's older sister, Nancy. Luke was sixteen. He was older and sophisticated. He was allowed to be in love. I knew that, because the adults thought their romance was enchanting. They gossiped about Luke and Nancy. She was beautiful and grown-up and very popular with boys in the town. I don't think Nancy loved Luke as much as he loved her, but he was dedicated to her. Everyone could see that. What he felt was the genuine article.

The idea that a second Johnson brother would fall in love with another Weller girl (Nancy's younger sister!) was ridiculous. Luke and Nancy were teenagers. People took them seriously. In the eyes of my family, the two of them had invented love for my generation. No one could ever imagine that I could love Jenny. The adults would consider me ridiculous if they knew. Anything I did or felt would be a cute and miniature version of Luke and Nancy's original creation. I was always extremely aware of what adults thought, which was probably why I hadn't admitted to myself how strongly I felt about Jenny. I saw myself through adult eyes too much of the time. It made me uptight and responsible: a good boy.

In the warm late-summer water of The Cove that day, all my inhibitions and reservations fell away. My mother was up on the beach, reading a book as she always did. Jenny was down at the edge of the water, playing with my sister, Debbie. Jenny was a gifted baby-sitter; everyone recognized her talent. She was always able to focus totally on the child. More than that, her optimism was magnetic. My sister loved her. I cannot remember what I was doing before we found ourselves in the water. Perhaps I was uncomfortable being with my mother at age fourteen; perhaps I felt out of place and was wishing I were with my friends. Maybe I was just watching Jenny, preparing to be in love with her in a few minutes. Perhaps I was studying Jenny's slender, athletic body. I don't remember.

All I remember is that at a certain point Debbie was back up the beach with my mother and Jenny was off-duty, free to swim with me. She dove into the lake, swam out some distance, turned around and swam back underwater, emerging suddenly with a big smile. And she looked at me with the same vivid attention she ordinarily gave to my sister or other small children.

Jenny had blue eyes and a sunny Midwestern face. Above all, she had an extraordinary smile, an irresistible smile, the smile of a profound optimist. (I've seen pictures of her as a middle-aged mother. She still has it.) When she smiled, you wanted to be near her. I had always known that. Suddenly, however, her smile was different. It wasn't a girl's smile—not really—it was a lover's smile. Not the smile of a flirt, not the kind of sexually self-conscious smirk that you see on the faces of so many girls of the MTV generation. It was the whole-hearted smile of a lover that I believed I saw, though I wouldn't have been able to articulate that at the time.

The effect on me was as sudden as a cartoon WHAM! Or BLAM! She changed instantly from a young girl into an extraordinarily beautiful creature. All of a sudden, I saw her breasts and her hips and the slight enlargement of her thighs that said "woman," not little girl. I stared at her smile. I looked at her body. I'd never stared at an actual girl's body before, not in person, not straight on when a girl was looking back at me.

Jenny smiled and then dove back into the water. There was nothing for me to do but go after her. A strong swimmer, she kicked away from me. I stroked as strongly as I could and caught up to her, grabbed her at both sides of her waist, picked her up and threw her up out of the water. She splashed back down and took off again. I went after her again. Swim, chase, lift and splash. Over and over and over. We played the game for a long time. Was it an hour?

I forgot about my mother and my little sister. I wonder what my mother thought. The game looked like a wrestling game, a boys' game that I might have played with my brother when he was twelve and I was ten. He might have grabbed me and thrown me like that. Here I was playing a boy's game with a girl, a beautiful girl with a strong, erotic body. I was aware that I was trying to make it look like a child's game, even while I was sure that it was not. I was in love for the first time. I wanted to wrap my arms around her waist, and I did, the young merman chasing the beautiful mermaid. She swam away from me, and I grabbed her ankles. I wanted to hold her in my arms. I settled for playing tag. I wanted to hold Jenny because I loved her. I wanted her to love me back.

I was having rapid-fire romantic thoughts. I imagined going to a movie with her. I imagined us being a couple. (I didn't think of anything frankly sexual. 1961 was a different time.) I thought we might even be a better couple than Luke and Nancy. Maybe our love would be stronger. Maybe I could be a boy—a young man—who could be a lover, that is, someone whom a girl could love. That was the first day that I ever had that thought.

Of course, it was impossible. It was August, she was twelve, I was only fourteen. I was headed for boarding school in a couple of weeks. I never did hold her again. Except in my mind. And I have gotten to do that for almost forty years.

CREATING
CONNECTIONS . . .

Invitation to reflect: Who was your first true love? Where is that person now? How do you feel when you think of him or her?

Obstacles to connection: There is no obstacle to past romance. Maybe that's why we all like to read about it. It is over; it is done. We can make of it what we want to. On the other hand, a lot of people carry heavy sadness from past loves. Or they carry anger, bitterness, guilt or resentment. These feelings can fester, and take up a lot of space in our minds. The mind does not have infinite space, any more than we have unlimited time. It is a bad idea to waste either space or time.

Possible steps to take: Bask in the past loves you fondly recall. The others? Is there a way to let go of the pain of a bitter divorce or a cruel relationship? The way I have dealt with Uncle Noble, who was not a lover, of course, but a cruel stepfather, is to talk about him with people close to me often enough that I sort of put him through a wash-cycle of conversation. Something in the process of talking about past pain, over time, helps detoxify the experience.

I also went back to Charleston, now as a successful adult, and I visited the house where I lived with Uncle Noble and my mother. I walked through the rooms, stood in the living room where he attacked Mom with a poker and where he mixed his martinis, and I discovered that it was all over now. I have had other relationships in which I have been hurt. I do find that soothing my wounds in conversations with others is the best remedy there is. Other suggestions include:

Every failed relationship can teach you something important about yourself. Ask yourself, *What can I learn here* (other than how to hate)?

Remember the old maxim, *No good deed goes unpunished.* Life is unfair. Often bad things do happen to good people. This relationship simply may have been your turn.

Also, remember the equally difficult but true saying that suffering leads to growth. Put differently, *What doesn't kill you makes you stronger.*

If none of those help, go back to step one, and talk to someone you trust. That always has been and still is the best cure for emotional pain.

Chapter Seven

MARRIAGE
AND
RELATIONSHIPS

THE ONE I STILL WAKE UP WITH

My wife, Sue, is my second wife. My first wife, Ellen, and I got married in our late twenties and divorced in our early thirties. She, like me, has remarried.

We fell in love in medical school. She had been a music major, and I had been an English major, so we shared a background in the humanities in the midst of all the scientists in medical school. But, more than that, we shared a huge amount of affection and warmth, in the midst of what could be the cold and unfeeling world of medical training.

We got married in our final year of medical school and lived in an apartment on St. Charles Avenue. We loved to cook. We really got into New Orleans cuisine, and Ellen and I took many trips after classes to Langostino's, a market near where we lived.

My dad died that year, and I will never forget how Ellen handled that. I got the news over the phone from the hospital. Then, I went into the study we shared in our small apartment, closed and locked the door, turned off the lights and lay down on the couch.

Ellen came to the door. She had heard my end of the phone call and knew what happened. She tried to come in but found the door was locked.

"Leave me alone," I said.

She said okay and went away.

After a half hour or so, she came back and asked, through the closed door, "Are you all right?"

"Just go away," I barked.

"Ned, I'm worried about you," she said gently.

"Don't worry about me. I'm fine. Just leave me alone. Let me deal with this the way I have dealt with everything else — alone."

Then, I heard Ellen start to cry. The door was paper-thin, so there really was no muffling of the sound. "Don't close me out," she said through her tears. "I want to be with you now. You shouldn't be alone."

"Just go away and leave me alone. Can you just do that much for me?" I snapped at her.

"No, I am not going away," she stated, still crying. "If I have to stand here all night, I will, but I am not going away."

"Damn it!" I grunted, stood up and opened the door.

There stood Ellen, all four feet, eleven inches of her, tears streaked down her cheeks, with her arms open. I moved toward her, and she embraced me. At last, I started to cry myself.

We went in and lay down on the couch together. (She was so small that there was always plenty of room to do this!) I told her stories about my dad, and she listened and commented and cried and sometimes laughed. I must have lain there with her for three or four hours, late into the night. I grieved the passing of my dad with Ellen.

I will never forget and I will always treasure how tenacious she was in not letting me push her away. Here she was, this slight woman with a heart as stout as a Sequoia, holding me back from giving up. Here she was, risking my anger and rejection, preventing me from hiding from what I needed to do.

Lying on the couch with her, remembering Dad, I grew closer than ever to Ellen.

So why did we split up? After we came up to Boston together to do our internships, we started to drift apart. We were both on call every third night, and usually these nights were not in synch, so we would go for days literally without seeing each other. In addition, the warmth that had brought us together in the first place seemed not enough to base a whole life on. We both sensed that we would be better off if we parted before we had children. So, we did.

If there was fault, it was my fault.

We divorced without rancor. In fact, we went to the notary together and we went to court together, and we stayed friends for quite a while after it was over. Ellen was—and, I am sure, still is, although we have lost touch now—a wonderful, brilliant, kind woman and doctor. I hope, with all my heart, that she is happy. But as sad as it was to say good-bye—and it was one of the saddest moments of my life—it was the right decision, as I am sure she would agree.

But we get more than one chance, sometimes. I know Ellen got a second chance and remarried. So did I.

For me, this second go-round has been all I could have hoped for. Sue and I got married in 1988, seven years after my divorce. The story I would like to tell is of the moment I decided to ask her to marry me.

We had been going together for about a year-and-a-half. I was skittish about getting married again, not only because getting divorced had been so sad for me, but also because I had seen the damage remarriage had done to my mother, as well as to many of my peers. It seemed people went from the frying pan straight into the fire, more often than not. I had decided that maybe I'd prefer to stay single.

But, then, there was Sue. I asked her out because, one day, I saw her wearing a straw hat with a red band around it. Oh, sure, more went into my asking her out than that, but, honestly, it was the straw hat with the red band that gave me the courage to think maybe we'd be a good match. And, sure enough, we hit it off right away.

As time went by, she wanted us to make The Decision. She didn't want to stay single. She wanted to have children, if not with me, then with someone who could make the commitment and get married. She told me she loved me very much, and would love for me to be the one for her, but she couldn't wait forever. Six months was the figure I believe she gave me.

Oh, the quandary I was in. I would go to sleep at night debating the issues and would wake up in the morning right where I left off. I would ask friends for advice, and I would ask senior colleagues for their sage points of view, (knowing full well that half of them were on marriage number three or four!). I looked to my closest relatives—my cousins—for help, and I looked up to heaven for a sign. I found that the problem with divine signs is, how do you know what is a sign, and what isn't? Is the black bird flying alone across the blue sky a sign from God that I should stay single, or is it a lost crow?

So, I tossed and I turned, and my six months became five, then four. Sue sweetly held her ground, soothing me with such words as, "It is best for us both to move on, if we can't decide." Kind of her to say "we," but that is the way she was, and is: kind.

The lists of pros and cons didn't work. Prayer didn't seem to work. My friends' advice was pretty clear: Sue is great, but you should follow your heart. In other words, we love her, but it's you who has to marry her, and we don't want you to blame us if it doesn't work out!

I didn't know what to do.

I thought The Decision was supposed to be clear; that you were supposed to *know*. Did it mean Sue was the wrong one for me if I didn't *know*? I knew I loved her, I knew she would be a *great* mom, and I knew she was smart and cute, and we had fun together and I respected her mind and liked her body. What else did I want?

Still, I didn't know what to do.

Then, one day I found out.

It happened in a moment. Truly, it did. I know it may be hard to believe, but I decided to throw away all my fears and worries and ask Sue to marry me . . . in a single moment.

The moment was this: I was at a school where I worked as a consultant, when Charlotte Dooling, one of the teachers there, came in to talk to me about a student of hers. After we concluded the discussion of the student, Charlotte off-handedly asked me, on her way out of my office, "By the way, when are you going to ask that wonderful girl you brought to the party to marry you?"

That was it. At that moment, it became clear what I should do.

You may not believe this, but when I left the school that afternoon I drove to Shreve, Crump, and Low at the Chestnut Hill Mall in Brookline, Massachusetts, and bought a sapphire-and-diamond engagement ring, using the money I had saved from the advance I received on my first book. Not more than two hours had passed from when Charlotte made her chance remark to when I picked out the ring.

What was it in what Charlotte said? Was her remark my divine sign? I don't know. All I know is that after she made her remark, I *knew*.

As a psychiatrist, I would go out of business if I couldn't give better advice than to say, "Wait until you hear the magic words," or "Wait until you know." So, I come up with fancier ways of saying basically just that. And I analyze the problem and empathically join my patients in their concerns. (Empathy comes easily to me on this issue!)

But, in spite of the value of analyzing and thinking, many of our biggest decisions come down to single moments of revelation, moments in which, for reasons we do not comprehend, it becomes clear what we should do.

Sue and I have been married since 1988. My life has changed dramatically for the better since we got married, but Sue and I do have our moments of great anger and irritation with one another. My goal in our marriage is to make room for conflict, not to avoid it. Particularly, given the troubled childhoods Sue and I came from, it is good for us to be able to fight and later discover that the bond between us remains as strong as ever.

I remember school vacation in 2000. We took the kids to Washington, D.C. We had a good time, but the city was clogged with protesters throughout our visit. I remember, as we were driving out of the city to return home, I remarked that it was too bad we had come when protesters (I can't even recall what the protested issue had been!) were in D.C., as it had made for horrendous traffic. Sue then quipped that she thought the protesters had added some spice to the trip.

Spice! That was not the word I wanted to hear. Suddenly, I felt like Sue was an adversary. I felt disappointed, even attacked, by what she said. This was clearly an overreaction on my part, but a strong reaction nonetheless. Often, in relationships—at least, in our relationship—a small incident will unexpectedly trigger intense feelings. "Wouldn't it be nice," I curtly said to Sue, "if you could just agree with me once in a while and not have to debate every point? Here I am hassling with this rotten traffic, and you have to tell me you think it adds *spice*? Give me a break!"

"I didn't say the traffic added spice, I said the protests did," Sue rejoined. "And if you wanted a woman who just agrees with everything you say, you shouldn't have married me."

I gripped the steering wheel and drove on in wounded, angry silence. Sue, who is as stubborn as I am, also sat in silence. The kids, who seemed to be oblivious to our exchange, began to ask about lunch.

My mind raced. Was our marriage a bad one? Why was Sue so withholding of simple support? Was I wrong in asking for sympathy? Was I too needy? Why did she have to be such a, such a what? Someone who always has to *consider* what she agrees to! Why couldn't she just *agree??!!* All I needed as I drove in the traffic was a little T.L.C., not reasoned opinions from Sue on the relative merits of visiting Washington when protesters jammed the streets. But she couldn't give that. Maybe she had a point, maybe I had married the wrong person. But I couldn't give full vent to my anger with the kids sitting right there. Were they picking up on my feelings anyway? Was I screwing them up, instead of being a good dad?

In time, my anger—and the traffic—subsided. "Sorry," I mumbled, taking the gargantuan step of being the first to apologize. Sue reached over and held my hand. We talked about where to stop for lunch. Harmony was restored.

But, not permanently. We do not have a permanently harmonious relationship. I love Sue and I love our kids—they matter to me more than anything in my life—but we do have conflict, and it does flare up from time to time. I think this is true of almost all close and honest relationships.

Sue is still the one I wake up with. Sometimes, if I wake up first or if she falls asleep before I do, I will look at her sleeping head and think to myself how almost arbitrary it all is. I might have married someone else so easily. So might have Sue. And we might well have been happy with our someone elses. I imagine Sue would like to have someone for a husband who is not quite as much of a worrier as I am, and she might wish she had married someone who had living parents who could be grandparents, and she might wish she had married someone rich. She might also wish she had a husband who was better at doing laundry and who did more work around the house—and, oh, I'm sure her list could go on and on. I, too, could post up a list, if I tried.

But that's not what I think about most when I see her sleeping head. What I think, when I see that head, is, *There's my life raft.*

When you think about it, it is amazing that two adult human beings can live together for a few days, let alone for years, not to mention raise children in the bargain! When you look at all the compromises and sacrifices you have to make, a rational person might ask, "Why bother?"

For me, the answer is not abstract or philosophical. The answer is concrete and practical. I am happier, healthier, more productive and more satisfied in life since I married Sue than I was before I married Sue. Marriage—and children—are not for everyone. But, for me, nothing ever has made my life better.

Thank you, red band on straw hat; thank you, Charlotte Dooling; thank you, whoever sent you both.

ECHOES . . .

The Big Valentine

One of the strangest facts about romantic love is that as much as we want it, it can also embarrass us. We sometimes run as fast as we can to get away from it. In fact, I think people are much more afraid of love than they are of any other feelings, including anger and aggression. The reason is that love opens us up much more than other feelings do. Love makes us vulnerable, while aggression keeps us safe. In love, we open our arms; in anger, we put up our fists. One leaves us open, the other puts up a wall.

We learn early on how vulnerable our yearning for love can make us feel. And we often discover, at a very young age, as did the author of this piece, that when we find the love we yearn for we don't always accept it. But, if we are lucky, one of those times we stop and say, Okay, let's give this a try.

—E. H.

The basement in my mother's Denver home is filled with years of mementos: my baby crib, Girl Scout uniform,

and nearly every art project and writing exercise I ever created. While home on vacation, I decided to weed through
some of this buried treasure. As I sifted through the "junk," I
stumbled upon something long forgotten: a beautiful valentine card with my name scrawled in a child's handwriting on
the envelope. Suddenly, I was transported back to 1970 and
into my little desk at Carson Elementary School.

Brring! The bell screeched that the school day had
begun. I obediently took my seat in Mr. Riddle's fifth-grade
classroom. Today was no ordinary day: It was Valentine's
Day. In the afternoon, we would have a party and place the
tiny cards declaring our love and friendship into the crisp
white paper bags we had so diligently decorated earlier in
the week.

As a ten-year-old, I was closer to childhood innocence than
adolescence with its raging hormones. Even so, my interest
in boys had begun to sprout. I had a small bud of passion
ready to open—his name was Jimmy. A flaxen-haired boy
with brilliant green eyes and a rather wide but endearing
nose, Jimmy had come to Carson during second grade. I
decided that Jimmy was far worldlier than the other boys in
my East Denver neighborhood when he treated our class to
a slide show of his family's vacation in India. Though the
startling images of poverty and the sludge-brown waters of the
Ganges River did not inspire me to visit there, I figured that
anyone who had traveled to this strange and distant land must
be someone special.

Over the years, my interest in Jimmy developed into a
secret crush. I had an inkling that the pitter-patter in my
small heart was echoed in Jimmy's. It was Jimmy, after all,

who nominated me for the Best Citizen award in our fourth-grade class—a move that had elicited the *oohs* and *aahs* of inquisitive boys and girls.

When party time arrived, I sifted through my bag of valentine goodies and discovered something no one else had: a big adult-sized card. The card was a brilliant scarlet, festooned with a raised pink-foil Cupid flying through a bouquet of hearts and emblazoned with the words "To My Sweetheart." Inside, the machine-imprinted script declared "I love you." Conspicuously absent was a signature. My face flushed. The din of the classroom was drowned out by my pounding heart. A crowd of girls clustered around me to get a closer look, their giggles punctuated only with the question I, too, asked, "I wonder who sent it?"

I floated out of school that afternoon. Could my secret admirer be Jimmy?

Halfway down the steps outside the building, I heard someone call my name. I turned around to find Jimmy standing at the top of the stairs, his body silhouetted in the soft afternoon sun. This was usually a crowded place after school but, at this moment, we were the only two people in sight.

"Did you like the big valentine I sent you?" he asked, wide-eyed.

Feelings of shock and embarrassment gripped me. My tongue was frozen with shyness. I stood with my mouth agape before mumbling, "Uh, oh, I don't know!"

Jimmy looked perplexed, scuffing the cement with the toe of his dirty tennis shoe. Not knowing what else to do, I turned and ran home, clutching my valentine bag in my small fist.

Tears rolled down my cheeks and evaporated quickly in the brisk rushing air. I stumbled into my house, pretending nothing was wrong.

Although Jimmy and I went to junior high and high school together, we never spoke a word about that day. We were friendly—but not friends.

Time eventually dulled the pain of that embarrassing memory, but for years I replayed the scene over and over again. The images of Jimmy's hurt and bewilderment and my fear and shyness were burned into my mind. There was no opportunity to explain how I really felt. I had sealed my fate and my feelings when I ran away—sealed them up like the big Valentine's Day card.

As an adult, I continued the trend of pushing away the nice guys with the big hearts, preferring to isolate myself in the safety of love from a distance. It took years before I finally realized that real intimacy can only come by acknowledging your feelings and opening yourself up to another person. The risk of rejection is far less painful than the chronic ache of regret.

I saw Jimmy again at our ten-year high-school reunion. He greeted me at the door with a friendly kiss on the cheek. He was lean, tan, nattily attired and sported a slim, surgically enhanced nose, looking quite different from the yearbook photo on his name badge. His warm smile, however, was still the same. My heart did a flip-flop as Jimmy stepped back to get a closer look at me. We chatted briefly about what we were doing now—he had graduated from an Ivy League school and was working as a psychotherapist in Denver— before other old classmates interrupted our conversation.

Later in the evening, Jimmy approached me. "You know, Christine, when we were in elementary school I was hopelessly in love with you," he said, swirling the ice in his mixed drink. "So, I took a chance and sent you that big valentine. You probably don't even remember it," he mused.

"Of course, I remember it," I said, glad that he'd brought up the subject.

"You obviously didn't feel the same way I did," he continued, raising his eyebrows. "I was crushed."

After all these years, I finally had the chance to be honest. "Oh, no," I assured him, "I had a big crush on you, too. I was just so shy I didn't know what to do, so when you told me *you* were my secret admirer, all I could think of was running away."

We stood in silence for a while. "Really?" Jimmy asked, with a gleam in his eye. "Thanks for sharing," he said, in good psychotherapist language.

It felt wonderful to have reconciled my feelings after so long. We talked, we laughed, we danced. We caught up on the lost years. But neither of us harbored any fantasies of rekindling that old flame. For, just as I had lost my shyness and found boyfriends, so, it turned out, had Jimmy.

My Heart Still Stops

This account, from a woman in Virginia, captures in just a few paragraphs the passions of a lifetime. Married twenty-six years, this woman writes, "My heart still stops when I see him across a room." It is heady enough for your heart to stand still when your eyes meet for the first time, but for that still to happen after twenty-six years of marriage . . . well, as the character in the movie said, "I'll have some of whatever she is having."

When I called up the author to ask permission to use her story, I could hear the smile in her voice as she told me how deeply she still loved her husband, and I could feel the electricity she felt when she told me how passionate they still were to this day.

Not all marriages stay this passionate, of course, and that is all right. Don't think that because your heart no longer skips a beat when you see your spouse across a room at a party that that means you are out of love. We all express and feel our love in different ways. Some of us are more like the ocean than the sun. But this couple's love from the very beginning seemed fiery and hot. It has never cooled off.

It is interesting, as this author shows, that passion like theirs and conflict often go hand in hand. Having someone to argue and spar with can vitalize a relationship like a tonic of youth.

—E. H.

My strongest feeling of love is the same as it has been for over twenty-six years. I connect physically, emotionally and spiritually with my chosen life partner, my husband, Jerry.

Our first meeting was one of very mixed emotions. He was a well-dressed, confident, upper-middle-class fraternity member at Florida State. I was a liberal, jeans-wearing, anti-establishment daughter of a struggling, small-town blue-collar worker. The electricity between us was strong and immediate. We were attracted to each other and repulsed by each other. That was 1975.

We married in 1978 and continue our strange but wonderful relationship. We taught each other so much. He taught me to dress well, and he built up my confidence. I taught him to be compassionate and to make himself more vulnerable to love and other emotions. He became my soul mate.

He was with me through the birth of our three daughters and the realization of one of our daughter's severe handicaps: cerebral palsy and autism. I stood by him as he watched a business he built crumble and fail. He stood by me as I watched my mother die of cancer, and we cried together. He has helped me be able to laugh at myself and to recognize my strengths.

We have watched our daughters grow into exceptionally well-balanced people, partly because he and I are so different and have brought different viewpoints to our family life. With him, I can face each day knowing I am never alone. I always have a friend and a confidant, and also an opponent. I have someone to love, to hate, to touch, to hold and to argue with.

Now, we work in the insurance business together. When we go to meetings or conventions or parties, even when I'm not nearby, I am with him.

My heart still stops when I see him across the room. That look in his eyes is still enticing and exciting. It always has been, and always will be.

Better Late . . .

Do you know people who married the wrong person, after letting the one they really should have married get away? I know several. Sometimes, when we are young, the kind of love that will last bores us. Instead, we often are drawn to tempestuous relationships, and we fall in love with people who treat us badly. The "nice person," the person who treats us well, leaves us yawning, while we pine away for the one who rejects us at every other turn.

Sometimes, though, the early relationship that doesn't pan out isn't boring, it is just not meant to last, for reasons no one understands. For the woman who wrote this account, that early love, amazingly enough, came back later on.

—E. H.

I am experiencing a transforming, joyous new relationship in my life. Actually, it is the revival of an old relationship. This is my second chance.

When I was sixteen, a wonderful young man asked me to marry him. We had known each other for a number of years, shared many common interests and respected our different talents. We loved foreign movies, jazz, ballet, and rock and roll. He admired my academic accomplishments; I, his talent for writing poetry and short fiction.

We did not marry at that time. Instead, we each entered into unsuccessful and, ultimately, unhappy and destructive relationships. We simply endured as we reared families. Then, we both divorced. I remained single for twenty years, he for eight.

His mother, however, was determined to see us together. People who think you should always just mind your own business should take a lesson from this woman. She knew we had missed something special by parting, all those years ago. But, she did not just sit and wistfully stare out the window, musing on what might have been. Not her!

Instead, she sought me out and reunited me with her son about a year ago. We finally married—forty years after originally breaking up—on Valentine's Day of 1999.

My life is now so enriched and really transformed by this man. Before this marriage, I rarely let myself get close to any man, and I had no dates at all in ten years. I worked constantly, twelve to fourteen hours a day, and I never sat down to eat at home. I was always on the go. I couldn't find time to entertain or socialize in any but the most superficial of ways.

Now, I find time for human connections of all kinds. My husband is teaching me how to connect with myself and others.

It is never too late to find love. It is never too late to learn how to enjoy other people. I am learning. This relationship is the rarest of treasures and yet, it cost me only the willingness to open up to it. It is transforming all the aspects of my life—and, yes, I tell my husband about these feelings every day.

Happily Ever After

As children we see our grandparents in a light that all but excludes their ever having felt romantic love. Can you imagine your grandmother falling in love with your grandfather? I can't. This author gives us the unusual glimpse of one great-grandmother explaining to her little great-granddaughter how she fell in love with Great-Granddad, all those years ago.

—E. H.

My fondest early-childhood memories are of the summer afternoons I spent at my grandparents' house in Brooklyn.

One Saturday, when I was about five, I sat beneath the great sycamore tree reading *Cinderella* with my grandmother. My grandfather and his friends' laughter echoed from the yard, where they were playing a spirited game of pinochle, and my grandmother smiled at my grandfather adoringly, as she read the end of the fairy tale to me, pronouncing, "and they lived happily ever after."

"Grandpa was my Prince Charming. He still is," she assured me.

"I know. Since you were eleven years old," I informed her, as if she didn't know.

"That's right," her eyes glowed, as always, when she thought of my grandfather, the love of her life.

At five, I still wondered how he had afforded the expensive-looking glass slipper in the midst of their immigrant poverty in the tenements of Manhattan's Lower East Side, but I imagined that my wily grandfather had managed a way, somehow, in much the same way as he had gone from cleaning filthy bedsprings to earn pennies at age seven, to being a self-made millionaire at sixty—all in one lifetime. And my grandmother had loved him through the making of two fortunes and the loss of one, as she had told me many times. I wondered whether that was what "happily ever after" really meant.

"Are you and Grandpa in happily ever after yet?" I asked, deciding that this was too important to be left to wondering.

"Yes, sweetheart, I suppose we are," my grandmother answered, smiling at me, but keeping her voice serious so I wouldn't think she thought the question was silly.

"Vat's dis 'heppily efer offter'?" came the voice of my great-grandmother, ruler of the roost, from several feet away, where she was snipping some of her prized peonies.

My grandmother and I exchanged a glance. The romance of fairy tales, after all, was not easily explained to the five-feet-high, by four-feet-wide figure of my great-grandmother, who still stoked the coal bins in the basement, emptied their ashes, and played poker and pinochle for money with the men of the neighborhood.

My grandmother briefly explained what it meant, as I sat wide-eyed, watching my great-grandmother's stern face yield unmistakably. Could it be that she had known a Prince Charming of her own once? I was incredulous. My angelically beautiful grandmother, yes; but the universally acknowledged Terror of East Second Street? I didn't think so.

My great-grandmother set down her garden shears beside the peonies, and came and sat next to us on the bench beneath the tree. "I can say about *det*," she said, with a short chuckle, "det," being her pronunciation of "that." I looked at her in absolute wonder, atingle with delighted anticipation of the story about to come. She reached over and patted my head, in a gesture of uncharacteristic affection.

The breeze picked up then, wafting to us the fragrance of the nearby peonies, mixed with that of the roses, lilacs and hydrangeas a bit farther away. My great-grandmother seemed lost in her own memories for a few seconds. Her face, which had softened even a few minutes before, now appeared almost young and pretty to me, suffused with a sweetness I never guessed lay buried deep inside her. When, at last, she spoke, I couldn't even discern her accent. It was as if her memories had transported her back in time, and transformed her, once again, into the girl she had been when she had fallen in love.

I listened raptly as she told the tale of the most beautiful love story I have ever heard:

"When I was fifteen years old, I went to work as a barmaid in the tavern in our village. One night, as I was filling a jug with wine to go serve the men at one of the tables, there was a knock at the back door. I was surprised, because it was so late, so I only opened the door a crack, just enough to see who it was. There in the moonlight stood a young man. So handsome he was! I never saw a man so handsome yet.

"I opened the door and asked what did he want, and he said he grew grapes and made wine. Did we need any? He spoke Yiddish, but not the same as we did. I understood him, but he sounded strange. It was a good kind of strange, though; it made me smile. And he didn't look like the men in our village, or even in the big city of Krakow, where I had been once. He was tall and strong, with big shoulders and arms, and beautiful, thick, curly black hair." *Hair like Mom's and Grandpa's?* I wondered to myself, delighted by my great-grandmother's dramatic sweep of her arms as she measured the unbelievable span of the handsome stranger's physique.

"He took my hand and led me outside into the moonlight. Just looking at each other we stood like that, for how long I don't know. I knew right then that I would be his wife or never marry. He knew it, too. He was promised to another girl—an arranged marriage by the matchmaker and the parents, that's how it was in those days—but he said he couldn't marry any girl but me. I was the most beautiful girl he had ever seen," she said proudly. I stretched my imagination beyond her barrel-like form and wiry white hair, seeing her as she'd likely been then, girlishly rounded, her dark hair wavy but not yet coarse. Her eyes glowed now with such brightness that I didn't need to imagine how she'd gazed upon her love.

"What happened?" I asked, interrupting her reverie.

"We got married. You know the rest of the story." She patted my head again.

That was true. Mine was a family of storytellers. By the tender age of five, there weren't too many stories—if any at all—that I hadn't heard and memorized, although certain of the more colorful details of some of them had yet to be repeated within my hearing.

"The handsomest-ever man was Grandpa Yidah?" I gasped aloud, thinking of my mother's stories of the ailing tailor she had adored for his gentleness. Grandpa Yidah was not a strapping handsome stranger who flew in the face of convention and swept barmaids off their very feet. Of course, until a few moments before, my great-grandmother had not been a beautiful barmaid, either.

"When did you start happily-ever-aftering?" I asked, remembering all the travail I had heard about: the perilous transatlantic crossing in steerage, the death of an infant daughter, poverty and sickness in the tenements, and countless other hardships.

"Right offter det," she laughed, her accent in place again, the moment returned to memory, still cherished but long past. My grandmother was smiling, too, waving to my grandfather across the yard.

I sat in silence now, in deference to the deeper meaning I had discovered about happily ever after: There are no glass slippers, no pumpkins-cum-coaches, no fairy godmothers—there is only love, ever new and ever beautiful.

CREATING
CONNECTIONS . . .

Invitation to reflect: Think of someone you love. Imagine being with that person now. Hold the person in mind for a few moments. Linger and laugh together in your mind.

Common obstacles to connection: One of the greatest obstacles to love is also one of love's great catalysts: namely, familiarity. On the one hand, feeling at ease is essential to letting your guard down and allowing love to flow back and forth between you and another person. But, as a person grows more and more familiar, and you feel more and more at ease around that person, the next thing you know, if you are not careful, you are taking that person for granted and treating him or her as part of the backdrop of your life, instead of as a living and changing human being.

Possible steps to take: First of all, don't think you are above all this, or that you are so smart you've already done all you can do, or that nothing works. Push aside your cynicism for a minute. Now, try to remember the first time you saw the person you love. Recall how the relationship grew. Tap into the wellsprings of passion and desire and newness and excitement you felt.

Next, fueled by these images and memories, set up a celebration, just the two of you. For example, you might go out on a date. Take separate cars. Arrive independently, as you might have done years ago. Maybe sit across the bar from each other and flirt, just with your eyes. Play the game. Then, one of you make the first move. End up having dinner together. Ask questions, as if you didn't know the answer, like "What is your favorite music?" or "Where would you most like to go on vacation?" or "What have you never done before that you'd really like to do?"

Essentially, you are playing with each other, setting up conditions that encourage taking a fresh look at someone you know and love.

Chapter Eight

OUR CHILDREN

NO GREATER
RESPONSIBILITY,
NO GREATER JOY

It was the middle of the night—or should I say early in the
morning, whatever you call 3 A.M.—on July 16, 1989. Sue
lay on an operating table, I sat gowned in surgical scrubs at
her head, and Dr. Campbell had his hands in her womb.
Suddenly, I heard him proclaim, "It's a girl!"

Sue, who was awake but groggy, let out a faint, but given
her state of consciousness, resounding, "Yay!"

I chimed in with a much louder whoop, as our daughter
was lifted up into my vision. "She's beautiful," I told Sue,
who, lying flat, could not see much of anything. "I'm going
for a closer look," I told her, and I went over to the warmed
table, where this bewildered member of our family was sput-
tering and choking, clearing her pipes and stretching her
limbs, as she greeted her new home, the world.

"We're going to name her Lucretia Mott Hallowell," I told
the nurse who was suctioning her everywhere, it seemed. The

nurse looked up at me. "But we'll call her Lucy," I quickly added, as if to offer reassurance that we wouldn't burden this child with too strange a first name. "That's a nice name," the nurse said and went back to work, saying, "She weighs eight pounds, twelve ounces. Pink and healthy."

We didn't have children until I was thirty-nine and Sue was thirty-three. Then, we had Lucy.

Years ago, my friend Peter Metz, who started to have his kids well before I did, said to me, "Ned, when you have your first child it will change you like nothing ever has. Trust me, you won't believe how great it feels."

When he said that, I wondered exactly what he meant. Was having kids like taking a drug? That early morning of July 16, 1989, I started to find out. It was sort of like taking a drug and, indeed, certain drugs that occur naturally in our systems, the hormones vasopressin and oxytocin, do contribute to the surge of nurturing, cuddling feelings most of us experience around babies.

But when that baby is your own, feelings beyond any drug-induced state begin to remake you. A kind of devotion soon takes over your whole soul.

The process is like a miraculous revelation. Suddenly, the world is never again the same. Suddenly, your inner life changes for good. Suddenly, you become altruistic in ways you never thought you could. Suddenly, your life means something more than you ever thought it would. Suddenly, you see life in a way you never knew it could be.

After Lucy was spruced up, Sue, still groggy, went off to recovery. Lucy was having a little trouble breathing, but the doctor assured me this was nothing to worry about and told me to go home. First, I called a slew of relatives of mine and Sue's and we whooped it up.

At about five o'clock, I walked into our condominium in Cambridge. Early-morning light filled the rooms, as if nothing had changed. But I knew different. I went to the refrigerator and opened a bottle of beer. Taking it to the bedroom, I sat down on the bed where Sue and I slept, and I drank my beer of celebration. We had a baby! I wanted to go back to the hospital, but I was awfully tired. And the beer started to make me feel even more tired. Still dressed, I lay down on the bed, kicked off my shoes and looked up at the ceiling. "Now I'm a dad," I said out loud and patted the bed, where Sue would have been. "Good for us, Suzie." Gradually, my eyes closed. "God bless you, Sue and Lucy," I murmured. Soon, I was asleep.

The next day I found out that Lucy might not be fine. She had a heart problem, called situs inversus, in which her heart lay on the right side of her chest instead of the left. Sometimes, this condition signifies nothing other than an anatomic variant. But, other times, it is associated with heart problems that can lead to death. Lucy would have to have a cardiac ultrasound test to find out which kind of situs inversus she had. Sue, thank goodness, was still groggy and unaware.

I went over to the place where they did the heart test and waited. It took hours to transport Lucy, have her wait her turn, and find the expert to do the test. I sat in a waiting area for what seemed like forever.

Just as I was about to crumble in worry, my friend Alan Brown walked into the waiting area. To this day, I have no idea how he knew I was there. He just showed up. He came and sat down next to me and told me he heard Lucy was having a cardiac ultrasound. I explained to him what the reason was, and he stayed and waited with me.

After a while the cardiology fellow walked into the waiting area and asked, "Is Mr. Hallowell here?" I jumped up as if shot from an ejector seat.

"That's me," I barked.

"Your baby is fine," the cardiology fellow said.

Never in my life, before or since, have any words thrilled me more. Without thinking, I hugged the cardiology fellow, and even fell to the floor and kissed the poor man's feet. He must have thought I was some kind of a nut. Alan Brown gently pulled me away, and we embraced.

The ordeal was over but, of course, as all parents know, the worry had just begun.

Lucy is my first child and my only daughter. If you had told me, before she was born, how much I would love her, I would have said that was only in fairy tales. Humans just don't have it in them to love that much. But Lucy showed me otherwise. This is one of the great gifts children give us: Children bring out more love in their parents than the parents ever knew they had.

Lucy and I have had many moments together that make me glow inside when I think of them. Then, there are others that make me wince with guilt, like the moment when she was three and I yelled at her for dropping a glass bottle of grape juice on the kitchen floor. She didn't mean to do it. Why did I yell at her? I can still see her anxious little face, and her frightened little body backing up, trying to put distance between herself and her yelling dad. Oh, that hurts me to remember!

But, then, there are other moments—so many of them—like the one when she learned to ride her bike. We had been going down the street after dinner to the huge parking lot by the Catholic church, where she tried to learn to ride. The first couple of times Lucy rode with training wheels. Then, one night, I asked, "Lucy, wanna try it without the extra wheels?"

She paused and looked scared for a moment. But her fear couldn't stop her. At the next moment, she said, "Sure, Dad." She is as spunky as her mom, and just as stubborn, too.

I took the screwdriver I'd brought with me and took off the training wheels. Then, I held the bike as Lucy climbed on. We stood still, me holding the bike, Lucy trying to balance. Then, I started to push, and Lucy started to pedal. Once we got moving, I said, "Okay, ready for me to let go?" Lucy was concentrating so hard that I don't think she even heard me. I let go, first one hand, then the other. Lucy teetered like a drunk, did a half turn, and fell.

"Let's try again," she said. We did. Same result. "Let's try again." And again. Same results. "One more time," she said, with determination. Once again, she fell. She was collecting quite a few bruises. But, each time, she'd go just a little bit farther.

Once again, she got on the bike, I gave a push, and she started to teeter. Then, something amazing happened. This must happen every day, on bicycles all around the world. But it seemed miraculous to me. As Lucy started to teeter, she righted herself. Then, she teetered again and righted herself once more. Suddenly, this ride, whose predecessors had been no more than 20 yards, became 50 yards, 100 yards, 150 yards, 200 yards. She teetered and righted herself yet again.

Three hundred yards. Lucy was riding a bike! I looked at the Catholic church next to us and figured this must have been an act of God! I could hardly believe what I was seeing.

What's so amazing about a kid learning to ride a bike? Nothing, unless that kid happens to be your first child, the love of your life, and the proof of all you ever hoped might come true. Then, a kid learning to ride a bike is tantamount to the parting of the Red Sea.

It was not only that she learned to ride that night, it was also that I passed the test of being able to teach her how to ride. It was not only that we both mastered something we had never mastered before, it was that we knew we'd be riding together forever, and that we could ride well.

A few years later, Lucy wrote a poem, which I have on the wall in my office at home. Like her bicycle ride, to someone else it wouldn't matter that much. But, to me, it is Shakespearean. Here it is:

Dreams

As I look up at the stars at night
I feel a feeling oh so bright
My eyelids are getting heavy,
My thoughts are going wild.
Suddenly I'm asleep with my lazy head
On my pillows, my thoughts still going wild.
I dream about cats, I dream about dogs,
I dream about my house, what if it were made of logs?
Oh the wonderful things you can do in your dreams,
Oh the wonderful things you can do in your dreams.

Something happens to everything Lucy does, whether it is riding a bike or writing a poem or just sitting and waiting for dinner, that makes it matter to me. I tell her this, but she gets bored hearing it and says, "Yeah, Dad, I know." All this that is magic to me is mundane to her.

But the wonderful things she does are not in her dreams or in mine. They are in real life every day.

Three years after Lucy was born, Jack followed through the door in my heart that Lucy had opened and, three years after that, Tucker joined us, too. Jack spent ten days in the intensive-care unit, because he aspirated meconium and had to have a course of antibiotics. He was big—nine pounds, ten ounces—but Sue managed to deliver him vaginally. Tucker was also big, and this time the doctors went back to a C-section, as his heart was slowing each time Sue pushed. He weighed nine pounds, five ounces. Tucker was our only child who did not have to start off life in intensive care.

Not to say that he hasn't required intensive care since. All three of our kids are spirited and strong-willed. But their spiritedness has been like a prod to me to stay young, and their strong wills a revelation to me of how a good childhood can create confident children. Sue and I lacked confidence growing up because our childhoods were not so good. But our kids are developing into confident, secure children.

To give you an idea of what I mean, one morning in the summer of 2000, Lucy walked into the kitchen, a towel wrapped around her head, as she had just come out of the bath. She was wearing a T-shirt with a cartoon of a woman giving a speech and the caption, *First Woman President!* I looked at the T-shirt, which I hadn't seen before, and I read the words out loud, "First Woman President!" As she walked past me, Lucy said, in a low voice directed my way, "Yeah, and it's gonna be me!"

She wasn't born confident; she's acquired it through experience. Genetically, she inherited my attention deficit disorder, so, during her first years in school, she held back a little bit, as she was not aware of everything that was going on. But, once that condition was diagnosed and treated—she now takes the medication Concerta—she improved dramatically and developed more confidence than Sue or I ever had.

Sue and I revel in this. It more than makes up for all the bad times we each went through.

Just as Lucy started to give me life and love in ways I had never known until July 16, 1989, Jack and Tucker have also come to me like messengers from the Land of Positivity.

Not long ago, Tucker, age five, and I were playing on a dock by a lake. He slid down a little ramp toward the water. "This is fun, Dad," he said. Then he added, "I mean this is fun for a child. Do you think you would have thought this was fun when you were a child?" *Oh, Tucker,* I thought, *yes, I do, but not nearly as much fun as watching you, or hearing you say what you just said.* "Yes, Tuckie," I answered, "I think I would have thought it was fun when I was a child. In fact, I think it is fun now!" At that, I slid down the ramp, but, being less agile than Tucker, I slipped and fell into the water, which left both Tucker and me laughing and splashing.

Not a day passes without one of my children providing me with a human moment, one of those moments in which we feel connected with what is best in life.

When Jack was about five, I was out of town and I called home. Jack answered.

"Hello, Jack," I said.

Jack gave an answer I'll never forget. "Hell-ooo," he began, then paused two beats before adding, rhythmically, "my good friend!" Ever since then, one of my nicknames for Jack has been "my good friend."

A few years later, Sue, the kids, and I drove to Washington, D.C., over spring break. We left later than we had planned—as usual, it was hard to get everyone organized to leave early—so, we drove late into the night. Around midnight, we stopped at a Best Western motel on the New Jersey Turnpike. All five of us packed into one room and fell asleep almost as soon as our heads hit the pillows.

At six o'clock, Jack woke up. He came over to me and tapped my shoulder. "Daddy," he whispered, "I'm awake."

"I can see that, Jack," I said, my eyes half-open.

"Daddy," he asked, "can I turn on the TV?"

"No," I replied, "all the rest of us are still sleeping. Why don't you try and go back to sleep?"

"I can't," Jack replied.

"Well, then, why don't you read one of your books or just play quietly?"

Jack walked away, and I fell back to sleep in an instant.

An hour later, Jack tapped my shoulder again.

"Daddy," he said, "can I show you something?"

"What, Jack?" I asked, a little annoyed at being awakened again.

"Look what I made," he announced.

I anxiously peered up over my covers. To my relief, I did not see any obvious disaster. "What did you make?" I asked.

"Look!" Jack said, pointing at the door.

In the haze of the morning light, I could make out something tied to the door handle. As I followed it, I could see it extended clear across the room and ended up tied to the handle on the window opposite the door.

"It's a clothes line!" Jack proudly announced. Looking more closely, I could see the line was made of all the clothes that had been strewn around our room. Jack had tied each piece of clothing to another piece, making a kind of rope or, as he put it, a "clothes line."

He looked at me, waiting for my response. I could tell he wasn't sure how I'd react. "Wow!" I exclaimed, in genuine appreciation, "that is really clever." Sure, I could have been annoyed that he had perhaps slightly damaged some of the clothes. But, truly, what I felt, and what Sue felt when I woke her up and showed her, was pride over what Jack had done with this single hour of his life between six and seven in the morning, at a Best Western on the New Jersey Turnpike.

I didn't make too big a deal of it with Jack, other than to let him know that I thought his project was really cool. After all, I didn't want "clothes lines" adorning various parts of our house every day. But it seems to me that what was going on in Jack's brain between six and seven that morning was what makes life extraordinary. Whatever force it is that advances civilization was guiding Jack's construction of his "clothes line." Whether we call it play, or creative thought, or independent study, or just fiddling around, the process of mind that led to the production of that "clothes line" is the same process of mind that leads to the birth of every new idea.

How do we keep it alive, not only in our children but in us all? For me, as a parent, nourishing that fearless curiosity is one of my most important goals. The best way I know how is to help them feel safe, and make sure they know that they are loved unconditionally.

But making sure of that isn't always easy.

Lucy, now eleven, rolls her eyes when I tell her that I love her, which I do a few hundred times a month, and she angrily folds her arms and looks cross when she's told she can't have yet a third sleepover in a certain week, but she always comes back to cocking her head and asking, "When can we go shopping at Limited Too?"

But they know we love them, no matter what. It is the greatest gift Sue and I give them, this unconditional love. I don't know exactly how we transmit the feeling, but I know they feel it. It isn't the presents we give them or the trips to Limited Too that do it (although Lucy might disagree!). It isn't the endless declarations of love that I keep spouting to them all the time. It isn't the money we spend or the words we speak. It isn't even in the time we invest or the deeds that we do (although they matter a lot).

They know we love them because the love is in our hearts and they can feel it, no matter what. I always knew my mother loved me, even though she invested little time with me, spent little money on me, and sometimes forgot where I was. She had problems, problems that kept her from showing her love as much as she wanted to. But I always knew that she loved me, and loved me unconditionally. How did I know that? Because it was in her heart. If love is in a parent's heart, the child will feel it, no matter how great the obstacles might be. And, if love is not there, the child will know that, too, no matter how much money or how many disclaimers he receives.

If ever I wonder about the existence of God, all I have to do is think of Lucy, Jack or Tucker. They are all the proof of God I need.

When Sue and I were lucky enough to have children, my life began to turn—and has continued to turn ever since— toward its happiest phase. Who knows what problems lie down the road? But, I can tell you, ever since Lucy, Jack and Tucker arrived, I've never had to wonder what I live for.

A PENGUIN-FAMILY STORY

When he was seven, my son Jack wrote the following story about a family of penguins. I add to this chapter about children this story by a child.

I saw the story for the first time when it was posted to the wall of Jack's second-grade classroom, along with stories his classmates had written. As I stood and read the story, I couldn't quite believe my eyes. Here was a wonderful tale, with a plot and a moral and a hefty dose of humor, all composed by Jack, entirely on his own. I felt so proud, so amazed, and so enthralled that I stood and contemplated the story, with its accompanying illustrations, as if it were a masterpiece in a museum. Come to think of it, my children's classrooms, along with our refrigerator door, constitute my favorite of all museums.

The moments when we behold what our children have managed to create delight us each day, much as a magical garden might, a garden that every morning brings forth flowers we've never seen before, unique new species that surprise us and show us how talented and unpredictable Mother Nature can be. If you had such a garden, you'd wake up each morning and wonder what might have appeared in your garden overnight. That's how I feel every day with my kids. What will they make? What will they do? What will they show me and teach me today? How will they make me smile inside?

Before you read the following story, imagine you have just had a really long and hard day, during which people acted at their worst and summoned up all your most cynical and nasty feelings. Then ask yourself, *Is there any better antidote to such dreary feelings than a story written by a child?*

I present the story just as Jack wrote it, with all his peculiar spellings intact. I have inserted only a few punctuation marks. Unfortunately, I can't reproduce Jack's handwriting, with its occasional backwards *r*s and *j*s, twice-written letters, and different-sized words. Nor can I reproduce the green-colored penguin Jack drew as an illustration to accompany his story. But, what I can reproduce is enough to show what this seven-year-old boy had learned about friendship and differences. It is a helpful story, especially if you know any green penguins living in a purple world.

> *Once upon a time there was a world of purple penguins and a family of nice penguins but the youngest was green. Every day he went to school he got teased. So one day he went home and his parents had a big bucket of purple paint. And he said, why do you have those buckets of paints?*
>
> *We're gonna paint you purple. And so they did. The next day he came home and took a bath. When he got out*

he was green again. What are we gonna do? The next day he came back from school and his parents had a purple marker and he said why do you have that purple marker? Because we're gonna color you purple, and so they did. But the next day he went swimming and the marker came off. Now what are we gonna do?

The next day it was his birthday. They had a fish feast and fish cake. He and his friends went swimming and cout some fish and avoided seals. Then they jumped out and played games and then it was time to go to miniger golf. They all tied, then they ran to ice cream. They all got chocolate and vanilla swirl! And everybody left.

The next day he went to school and came back and opened presents and these are some of the things he got: a fishtex; penbaseball; penfootball; petbat; stuffed animals like fish, frog, bear, seal, lizard, raccoon and more. Books and more.

The next day he said it does not matter if I'm green. I was just born like that. And he never got teased again.

THE END

LOANERS

Nothing changes us like having children. Suddenly, we serve—and, boy oh boy, do parents serve—a greater purpose than our own pleasures.

But the reward is like nothing we ever imagined we'd ever find.

I think of a time when I was in New York City for a few days just before Christmas with Sue and our three kids. It was a special trip, a treat. We went to see the tree at Rockefeller Center and the skaters and the flags there; we went to the top of the Empire State Building; we went to see the Rockettes at Radio City Music Hall; we walked the sidewalks, stopping to see the fantastic Christmas displays in the store windows, like the one at Lord & Taylor and the one at Saks. We ate at a little deli and had smoked salmon. We bought a Nathan's hot dog. We watched people. We rode elevators and escalators and took some taxis. We walked by many tall buildings and looked up and up and up.

We also got tired and grumpy at times. Tucker had a few colossal Tucker meltdowns, and Mom and Dad had a few Mom-and-Dad meltdowns, as well. We spent too much money and ate too much food. But none of that mattered. The snow in New York was magic dust, and the lights lit up not just the streets but a play we all had parts in. The whole trip was a great production. Courtesy of the Big Apple and our imaginations, it became a three-day spectacle, a show we would treasure when we got back to the workaday world of our everyday lives.

On the last night we were there, we ate in the hotel restaurant. As we waited for dinner (that can be a prime meltdown time, the time between when you have ordered and when the food arrives), I tried to think of some question that would catch the kids' imagination. I asked them to describe what they thought heaven looked like. Lucy replied, immediately, "It is like a big, huge shopping mall, with lots of Limited Toos."

Sue groaned. I then asked Jack the same question. He said he imagined heaven was a big white palace with a golden fence around it.

Then I looked at Tucker, who was four at the time. He looked back at me, blankly. "Heaven, Tucker. What do you think heaven looks like?"

He shook his head. "I just don't know, Dad," he replied. "Can you help me with this one?"

Could I help him with this one? Where did he get these phrases? Anyway, I could help. I sure could. "Yes, Tucker, I can help you with this one. I do know what heaven looks like, at least for me. It looks like the five of us, sitting right here at this table. Nothing could be better than this, if you ask me."

"Not even Limited Too?" Sue asked, with a wink.

"Not even Limited Too," I replied, as happy as I could possibly be. Children make us happy—so very happy—in such ordinary ways.

They are not mine, these kids. They are not Sue's. They are on loan from heaven. They are given to us to care for, to learn from, to nurture and to enjoy. Before long, they cross over that invisible divide that separates childhood from adulthood and, then, they perhaps get some loaners of their own.

But how blessed are we to have them now? How much love is in a child? To answer that, I think of a little boy named Ronnie who was in my care when I was a medical student in pediatrics at Charity Hospital in New Orleans.

Ronnie was seven years old, and he was dying of cancer. He knew he was dying, but he tried to stay upbeat. He always smiled when I came in to check him over. He was so upbeat, you would have thought he was the doctor and I was the patient, sometimes.

One day, not long before he did die, he motioned me to bend down so he could whisper in my ear. "You are a gooooood doctor," he said. "Will you please do me a favor, and make sure my mom and dad don't get too sad after I die?"

ECHOES . . .

Catching a Recruit

One of the rites of childhood is learning how to fish. This story captures some of the ordinary magic in an early morning trip to catch stripers and blues—and pass on a tradition.

—*E. H.*

It was still dark when I rolled out of bed, went next door to my nephew's room and shook him lightly on the shoulder. "Sam, wake up. It's time to go get some big fish."

Instantly, Sam was rubbing his eyes, rolling out of bed and looking for his clothes. Hardly the response one would expect if this was a school day. Sam is my nine-year-old nephew, who was visiting with his family at our summer place in Provincetown, Massachusetts, for a "say good-bye to summer" Labor Day Weekend.

Sam has an older sister, who had no interest in "smelly" fish, and a younger brother, who was a little too young for the trip. So, this was a great time for Sam to go out alone with his uncle on a real "grown-up" adventure. The two of us tiptoed down the stairs and into the kitchen.

"Now, Sam," I said, "you've got to eat some cereal quickly so that you'll have the strength to pull in a big one." Sam, who can be particular as to what he eats, gobbled down the cereal I gave him in no time and was putting on his jacket before I was half finished with mine. We left the house just as the first hint of light was coming over the sand dunes to the east.

First, we had to row our small dinghy out to our boat, which was anchored about fifty yards off shore. As was usually the case, the cool night had calmed the winds and Cape Cod Bay was as still as a bathtub. "Aren't the fish still sleeping, Uncle Frank?" Sam whispered. Certainly a reasonable question, since every other creature except us seemed to be tucked in their beds.

"No, Sam," I replied. "The big striped bass have great eyesight and like to eat at night and sleep all day. Sort of like your older cousins, Ned and Jake. And bluefish eat both day and night."

At that moment, a small striper broke the water just ahead of Sam. Sam grabbed the edge of the dinghy and, with wide eyes, said, "What was that, Uncle Frank?"

"Oh, just a small fish chasing a smaller fish, Sam."

"Well, let's catch him!" was Sam's reply.

"No, Sam, we're after the big ones. After all, we've got to feed everyone for dinner."

Soon, we reached our boat and, after getting out of earshot of the shore, I opened up the throttle halfway and headed for Race Point, where there's often good fishing. "Here, Sam, you hold the wheel and steer us straight for that lighthouse, but look out for lobster pots."

Well, no one has ever taken any job more seriously. Sam

put both hands on the wheel, stuck his jaw out a fraction and we just flew across the bay. Before long, we had reached Race Point, and I got the lure I wanted from my tackle box. "Now, Sam, watch out for these big hooks. Your cousin Eddie and I were fishing once, and Eddie caught a nice striper. But, when he was landing the fish, the fish shook its head and put the hook deep into Eddie's hand." Sam proceeded to step back three steps from the lure. "But, see these barbs on the hook? Watch. We'll crush them with these pliers. That will make it easier to get the hook out of the fish—or out of you!" Again, Sam's eyes were as wide as saucers. "Okay, Sam, let's catch some fish."

We began to troll slowly up and down the shoreline. The sun was just beginning to come up, and the sky had turned a beautiful splash of deep red and purple. "Uncle Frank, how will I know when a fish has taken the lure?"

"Oh, you'll know, Sam. The fish will pull so hard, you'll almost fall out of the boat." Sam sat a little deeper in his chair and held the rod a little tighter.

Watching Sam wait for that fish, all excited, being so good and so serious, I couldn't help but remember myself at about his age. Mr. Koshibu—or Mr. K. as we called him—was my seventh-grade science teacher. He was the person who introduced me to fishing. Mr. K. taught the natural sciences and was a born conservationist. He often held our attention in class by telling adventure stories from his own experiences, a sort of "and I survived to tell the tale" type of character.

One of the tricks he used to get us to study was to offer to take anyone who did well on his test out for a Saturday morning of trout fishing. Only later did I find out that he was happy to take anyone fishing no matter how they had done on the test. The drive to the trout stream took almost two hours, so he would tell nature story after nature story as we drove in the dark, eating donuts and drinking half-and-half coffee. I learned so much on those trips about the beauty and power of nature that, even now, nearly forty-five years later, I search out natural wonders when I want to feel right with myself.

Now, Sam was out here to catch fish, not watch me lose myself in my memories, and nothing was happening. The sun was well up, the sky a deep blue, and the wind was crisp. I spotted a flock of terns diving into the water far up ahead. "Reel in, Sam. I see fish," I yelled. Soon, we were flying over the water, and Sam was hanging on tightly but with an ear-to-ear grin. As we got closer, we could see the bluefish coming right out of the water as they chomped their way through a school of baitfish. "Sam, we'll circle the school and drift down into it so we won't spook the fish," I shouted. As I cut the motor, we could hear the terns yelling, while the sound of the jumping bluefish was almost like the roar of a waterfall. I quickly put on a surface lure and cast into the school. "Here, Sam, you take the rod, reel in and make the lure pop." Sam's hands were shaking, but he grabbed the rod and began to reel in. He barely had turned the reel once, when his rod bent in half. Sam yelled out, "I got one, Uncle Frank!"

Well, he sure did, and that bluefish was heading for England. I don't think there's any other fish that pulls harder than a blue. I wrapped my arms around Sam, and together we gradually leaned back to gain line, and, then, we would reel in together as we bent forward.

That worked for a while, until the blue saw the boat and,

with a burst of speed, was off again, to Spain this time. Every time the fish would make a run, Sam and I would both yell in appreciation and laugh for the sheer fun of it all. With the light tackle we were using, Sam could feel every pull of the fish, and he was linked to the fish's power by the line. I was worried that the line might break and Sam would be crest-fallen, but he did a great job.

Finally, I grabbed the leader and pulled the fish aboard. I had warned Sam about the razor-sharp teeth on a blue, and this was an eighteen-pounder with plenty of teeth, so I wasn't surprised that Sam was very quickly standing on his seat while his fish thrashed about on the deck. "Watch, Sam," I said, "how I can grab the fish here and get the hook out with these pliers. What a beautiful fish! I'm so proud of you. Now let's go home and show everyone what you caught and have some breakfast." I put the fish in a bucket, started the engine and we headed home.

Sam, who had been so anxious to steer coming out, now just sat and held onto the bucket that held his fish.

As we motored home, I felt that Mr. K. would have been proud of me for passing along his secret to another boy.

The Time of Day

I think, as a parent, one of the hardest decisions I have to make each day is when to put what I need or want to do ahead of what my kids need or want me to do. In the following vignette, a mom wrestles with this issue and finds a surprisingly great reward.

—E. H.

Yesterday, at about five-thirty in the afternoon, I was trying to mow the lawn—quickly—before my husband got home from work. I knew he would want to mow it when he got home, and I thought it would be a nice surprise to have the job done.

My son, Elliot, had been inside watching a movie. It was a nice break for me. Soon, however, Elliot came out—with two games in hand—and shouted for me to stop mowing. I told him to wait a few more minutes, as I completed three more rows. I actually snuck in six more, knowing he wouldn't keep track. Then, he yelled again. I said, "You know, if I finish the lawn, then we can all play when Dad gets home." I continued to mow.

A minute later, I looked over and saw him sitting at the picnic table—looking straight ahead with the games stacked up in front of him. It was pathetic. He looked lifeless.

I turned off the mower and yelled across the yard, "Hey, Elliot, I just finished. Want to sit on the porch and play a game?" I hadn't actually finished and, in fact, still had one-quarter of the yard left to do but, when I called him, Elliot lit up like a Christmas tree. He grabbed the games and ran toward me, with a smile worth a million bucks. It was HUGE! He looked more alive than I had seen him look in a week.

We played the game and both enjoyed it as we never had before. It was human connectedness and a simple decision that had an *invaluable* payoff. I'll never forget the pleasure that showed in his smile and in his spirit. It was the greatest thank-you I have ever received.

Baby's Breath

When you bring your first child home from the hospital, your skill level is low and the challenge is great. Psychologists will tell you this is a recipe for anxiety. However, nature has built into babies and their parents a special protection against this anxiety, which I call the "Ooooooooooo" response. When you hold any baby, but particularly your own baby, you experience a special kind of human moment characterized by a feeling of "Oooooooooooo." Translated into English, "Ooooooooooo" roughly means, "You are so incredibly adorable and cute and lovable and so divinely cuddle-able that I would like to simply rock you in my arms forever, and I just do not have the words to describe the transcendent feeling that you give me."

The author of the following short piece gives an excellent example of "Ooooooooooo."

—E. H.

Eleven years ago, I was a new mother. I'd always wanted to have a child but, like most new parents, I was somewhat surprised at how overwhelming it was to keep my baby happy twenty-four hours a day. One particular evening, my little son had been overly fussy, and both of us were worn out from his crying. Finally, exhausted, I lay down on the couch with the baby stretched across my chest. Both baby and I fell fast asleep.

A while later, I awoke to the bright glow of the moon shining through the window. I opened my eyes to find this tiny body still sprawled across me, his little hands tightly clutching the sides of my shirt. His bow-shaped mouth was slightly open and his sweet baby breath caressed my face with each rise and fall of his chest. His skin was translucent, and his dear face was the picture of innocence bathed in the moonlight. Tears came to my eyes, as I realized that this delicate child nestled close to my heart had truly stolen my heart. I felt wondrously blessed to have this precious son.

From that moment on, whenever I grew frustrated with my attempts to keep my child satisfied, I'd transport myself back to that perfect night, to feel again the soft weight of his warm body on mine and his light breath blowing across my face.

Letting Go

Taking my kids to their first day of school was hard enough. What this woman describes—dropping her son off at college—seems almost unbearable. I know I will have to do it in a few years—Lucy is in sixth grade now and the other two are not far behind. I try to get ready. Sue and I talk about how difficult it will be.

—E. H.

R.I.T. in Rochester, New York, is about 360 miles from our home in Madison. This meant we had about six hours door-to-door with Curt, before saying good-bye for what will probably be—if not the next three years of school and co-op internships—forever. His room here at home will become a guest room, except when he returns for a week at Thanksgiving and Christmas, or for a week in March or August. Then, the room will have that sweaty adolescent smell and be virtually unnavigable, due to the piles of dirty clothes and debris that seem to follow him about. Even Daisy, our thirteen-year-old cat, will wander into his room, look around and leave, finding no sleeping boy-man to settle in and sleep against.

Curt slept for most of the six-hour ride as he was, typically, up late the night before (in this case, packing), and we had left in the early morning. Peter did most of the driving, and I read a book about family and children. I began to feel that, perhaps, I had lost, or was about to lose, my final chance at the one role that I have, for the last twenty-four years, identified myself with: that of Mom.

The letting-go process is difficult, at best, but I am constantly questioning both sides of a series of panic-driven questions. Did I tell them enough? Did I encourage them enough? Will they be strong, smart, sensible? More important, do they know, really know, how much they have brought to my life? Do they know, really know, how much I love them? Will they remember all the close moments and special occasions? Or, will they remember a harried working mom, grumpy and crazed as I raced from car pool to scouts to getting dinner on the table? Will they remember that I always cooked their favorite meal on any and every special occasion? Or will they will remember a bleary-eyed mother who waited for them to come in past curfew and went crazy with worry and anger at their apparent disregard for my concern? All these things clawed at me and rattled my brain as we sped along the New York State Thruway.

When I hugged and kissed Curt good-bye that night, I couldn't help but feel I had "unfinished business." Cori, my twenty-three-year-old, will be moving into an apartment next month. Carly, my seventeen-year-old, will be leaving for college next fall. I think my worry and self-doubt associated with

letting them go is a big, fat question of my abilities and success as a parent. I think the letting-go process is, in my case,
a sense of self-doubt as to how well—or not so well—I prepared them for life in the world . . . out there. Letting go is
also a signal that one part—possibly the best part?—of my life
is over.

I have many things to work on: inhaling and exhaling are
two of them; letting go is another.

The Children's Ward

Everybody has heard about cancer in children, but it is a topic that is so overwhelmingly sad that we tend not to dwell on it. However, being around these children can inspire you as few other experiences can.

If you have ever been to a children's cancer ward, you know what I mean. I don't think there is any place on Earth that brings together in one setting such extremes of sadness and hope.

You see these kids and their families and the doctors and nurses and other staff; you see the balloons and the bald heads and the stuffed animals and the I.V.s; and you don't know whether to cry or pray or jump for joy. You see the nurses carrying around juice and medicine; you see the doctors studying a chart or listening to a little girl's heart; you see a mom sleeping in a cot next to the bed of her son; you see a dad playing catch with a Nerf ball with his son who barely has the strength to throw the ball; and then you know the meaning of the word humble.

We are humbled by the example of these people—the children, their families and those who care for them. We

*are humbled by the disease that sometimes takes the lives
of these children, and we are humbled by the cures that,
sometimes—now more than ever—take these children out
of death's grip.*

*Where on Earth is there greater courage than in a chil-
dren's cancer ward? Where is there greater sadness, worse
defeat? Where is there greater joy, greater triumph? Such is
the intensity that most of those who work there have to steel
themselves so they can continue to think critically and ratio-
nally. For most who work there, it is work. But a very special
kind of work. A work for which no salary could ever be
enough, nor any compensation match that of a healthy
child, teddy bear in hand, leaving the ward for a regular life.*

*Here is a story by one of life's heroes, a woman who
worked on such a ward, about some of life's other heroes,
the people she met there.*

—E. H.

As a young nurse, age twenty-one, I became interested in
spending an extended time with my young pediatric
patients. When an opening in the pediatric oncology unit at
Children's Hospital became available, I applied and received
the assignment.

The learning curve for treatments was steep in 1980:
autologous bone-marrow transplants, new chemotherapies,
hyperalimentation, and care for the whole family, not just the
affected child. All that was exciting, but I was unprepared for
the profound effect that these terminally ill children, their
parents and siblings would have on my life and my beliefs.

I bonded closely with many of these families who spent up to months in our unit each year. I learned through giving my time and talents—and just by listening—what these families at least appeared to be going through.

I saw the miraculous speed and maturity that three- to eight-year-olds used to face their mortality. I learned the sorrow and grief of seeing a beautiful, small child—destroyed by chemo, meds, surgery and radiation—still be willing to try once more for a new treatment in order to live—for life itself, and for his family.

I believe I loved many of these children as I would one day love my own children. However, I gained far more than I gave, from the honesty, grit and determination of these incredible children.

They asked me easy questions, such as: "Do you have an innie or an outie?" referring to my belly button, while trying to raise my scrub shirt. And hard ones, like, "Why doesn't my hepatoblastoma hurt unless it bumps into something else inside my tummy?"

I thank God we have made such tremendous strides in treating and curing some common pediatric cancers, like acute lymphocytic leukemia, osteosarcoma, hepatoblastoma and neurologic tumors.

I look forward to one day seeing each of these children—Joshua, Norton, Christopher and others—in heaven.

My approach to life was forever changed. Now, I see life as a time of giving, loving and accepting our stay on this Earth as merely a visit.

CREATING
CONNECTIONS . . .

Invitation to reflect: Think of the most enjoyable time you have spent with a child in the past few weeks or months. Savor it for a while.

Common obstacles to connection: Children are the world's greatest connectors. They also provide us with some of the most memorable human moments. The greatest obstacle to an adult's participating in this unbelievable feast of life is finding the time for it. If you don't make time for your kids, they will be grown up before you know it, and it will be too late. Make the time. Whatever you do, make the time.

Possible steps to take: One way to make sure that you make time for kids is to schedule it in. Have routines and rituals that ensure you will spend a good amount of time with children—your children and/or other people's. Obvious routines include having breakfast together or a family dinner. Maybe you all go to church or some other religious ceremony on weekends, and follow that with a special meal at a restaurant or at home, or an outing to a park or a ballgame or whatever you all like to do. The Orthodox Jews have a wonderful observance that protects time for family: From sundown Friday to sundown Saturday they can do no work, not even drive. All that's permitted is reading the Torah or spending time with family and friends.

Think of what would work in your life. Make sure you don't fall into the trap of just ferrying your kids from one "enriching" activity to the next, from violin lessons to soccer to karate. Instead, make sure you have downtime together, play time, time for hanging out and doing nothing. Some of the best stuff happens when you are "doing nothing" with your kids.

Chapter Nine

WORK, SUCCESS AND FRUSTRATION

THE NERVE
TO DO IT

The day I started my medical internship, I almost quit.

Four years of medical school had brought me to my first day as an intern at the West Roxbury V. A. Hospital, one of the teaching hospitals affiliated with Harvard Medical School and what then was called the Peter Bent Brigham Hospital.

The day I started work was a sunny July morning, promising all the warmth of a summer day. That warmth would be delivered at about the same hour I would almost quit. As I pulled into the parking lot and walked across the grassy lawn toward the hospital, it occurred to me that this red-brick edifice looked innocently comfy, like a high school embedded in a residential neighborhood. In fact, it was a national referral center for veterans with spinal-cord injuries, as well as a major center for cardiology and surgery, fields I knew very little about, but was supposed to be expert in as of today.

I had been at the hospital twenty-four hours earlier to sign papers, get my beeper, name tag, white coats and find the ward to which I was assigned, so I knew how to get where I was going. I was just terrified of getting there, even though all I had to do was show up for rounds.

And start taking care of patients.

That was what froze me, in spite of the heat: I didn't know how to take care of patients! I couldn't tell someone throwing a pulmonary embolus from someone throwing up. I didn't know what to do if someone collapsed on the floor in front of me. I was shaky reading EKGs under pressure and I had never once inserted a chest tube. Sure, I had seen other people handle these situations in medical school, and I had answered questions on written exams about what I was supposed to do, but I had never actually done it before — let alone in the middle of the night, with nobody helping me and with someone's life at stake. What if I screwed up?

In addition, ultimately, I was headed into psychiatry, while everyone else who would be working with me was heading into internal medicine. The Brigham was one of the most competitive programs in the country. Everyone who was accepted was at the top of their medical-school class and had EKGs and chest tubes down pat, or so I imagined. I, on the other hand, was an outsider. I had been accepted just to do the first year, then go into psychiatry. Would my peers look down on me?

As I was walking toward my ward, I caught a glimpse of one of the senior residents fixing his gaze intently on a man sleeping in a bed about ten yards away from him. Suddenly, he raced over to him, held his wrist, called his name, thumped his chest, then yelled to a nurse I couldn't see to call a Code Blue. In seconds, the man's bed was surrounded by people in various kinds of white and blue garb, all working together to save the old gentleman. So many people surrounded the bed that, soon, I couldn't see a thing. I was thrilled I wasn't needed. I realized that was not the proper attitude; I should have been so eager to assist at my first Code Blue that I would climb over the others to join in on the action.

I found my ward, joined the senior resident and started to make rounds with the other new interns. They all seemed very pleasant, but nervous, like me. The senior resident was organized, helpful and thorough. I took index cards from the pocket of my white coat and marked down pertinent information on each patient as we "rounded" (as it is called) from room to room. I had learned about using index cards in fifth grade, and continued to use them in medical school. I was relieved to see that some of my colleagues also used index cards. Most, however, used clipboards. As I frantically took dismal stock of such discrepancies—all the while praying we would not come upon a patient who needed an emergency rescue, while believing my peers were praying for just the opposite—I began to tilt, like a crooked scarecrow. *Breathe deep*, I told myself. *Straighten up. Fly right.*

After we finished rounding, we were supposed to go off and do the work of the day: whatever procedures needed to be done, from taking someone to X ray to doing a spinal tap; write progress notes based upon what was said on rounds; and be ready for a Code Blue, which would give us the chance to go save a person's life right away.

With the thought of the Code Blue, I lost hold.

While the other interns headed off in various directions to do their work, I bolted for the men's room.

I can remember the mirror in that men's room now, some twenty-five years later, as if I were staring into it right this minute. I put both my hands on the sink and I leaned forward, looking into the glass. I said to my reflection, "What are *you* doing *here?*" I was as white as the porcelain of the bathroom fixtures—and as covered with moisture.

As my thoughts raced and my legs went rubbery, I struggled to regain control. Waves of fear coursed through me, like shocks. My vision thinned, as if the air were getting rare in the room, and I gripped the sink to steady my legs. I had played out this become-a-doctor string as far as it would go, and now I had to make good. But I didn't think I could.

Suddenly, I had an idea. I was saved. I could apply to law school! It couldn't be too late. It was only July 1; there must be some law schools in the Boston area that had openings for September. I could tell the senior resident that I had a change of heart, medicine was not for me, and I could go home and do the sensible thing, which was to become a lawyer. As I imagined law school, with its nice, safe books and no Code Blues, I calmed down. Ah, yes, a solution: Get out; become a lawyer.

I was still holding onto the sink. I was still looking at my reflection in the mirror, but not really seeing my face, as my mind was occupied poring over law tomes, playing out my future in a field I was desperate to love.

If ever there was a turning point in my life, this was one. I truly was ready to quit my internship. I was scared stiff, I had formulated my Plan B, and the only force keeping me in medicine at that point was the grip of my hands on the sink.

It is said that many people who commit suicide wouldn't have, if they had just waited a few minutes. This is because suicide is often impulsive. One of the reasons we put people who want to commit suicide into hospitals against their wishes is that most of them change their minds after a short while. Hospitalization simply buys time. Time, in turn, buys life. Standing at the sink, I needed time.

Something—Who knows what? The same something that prompted Charlotte Dooling to tell me to marry Sue?— secured my hands to that sink, until hope entered my heart. Thank God, no one came into the men's room during the time I was there. I am sure I would have felt so embarrassed that I would have exited, probably leaving the hospital, and my life as a doctor, in the process. But no one came in to interrupt my private panic.

It felt as if I were there a long time, but that could not be, as people came in and out of that men's room frequently and, as I said, no one came in. I don't know how long I was there, but I was there long enough to change my mind—twice, in fact, first to quit medicine, then, finally, to go back.

I went back because, as much as I didn't have the stomach to stay, even more, I didn't have the stomach to leave.

What kept me there, though, was more than just the fear of leaving. What kept me there was hope. I looked away from the mirror, out the half-open window and, in the sunshine outside, I saw a white-coated intern helping an old vet walk down the front steps. I wanted to be doing that, not poring over legal tomes. I heard the voice of my friend, Tom, now an orthopedic surgeon, telling me I could handle internship just fine, piece o' cake. I remembered successfully starting IVs as a medical student, and helping out at Code Blues without botching up too much, and I remembered delivering babies. I imagined me with my friends sitting in the cafeteria at three in the morning while on-call, and I no longer felt alone. I remembered the old advice to interns: Whenever you don't know what to do, ask one of the nurses—they know, they've been around. Gradually, the waves of fear abated, and I let go of the sink. I splashed some water on my face and opened the window even wider to take in the wonderful, hope-filled sunshine. It was now a hot day.

When I left that bathroom and headed off to collect lab values—and to remain a doctor to this day—I wonder if a guardian angel somewhere didn't dust off his hands and say, "Whew, that was close!"

Looking back now, I shudder at how close I came to leaving the hospital and changing my life forever. Certain moments of mastery and success in my past kept my hands on the sink long enough for me to find the strength to stay.

I remember one day in particular when I surpassed even the expectations medicine would place upon me. It was in seventh grade. I played soccer, but not well. I wanted to play well, but I just did not have the athletic skills of my peers, sort of how I felt when I started my medical internship. I made the junior varsity (the school only went through eighth grade) by the skin of my teeth, mainly because I was willing to do whatever I had to do, like carry ball bags (we didn't have the luxury of an equipment manager or anything fancy like that), the water cooler and whatever else was lying around.

The coach of the varsity, who for some reason had his eye on me, was a legend at the school. His name was Harry

Boyadjian, and he came from Jerusalem. He'd had eight straight years of undefeated teams. This was back in the 1960s when soccer was just getting started in the United States, and it was still news to most American kids that you weren't supposed to kick with your toe, but with your instep. Mr. Boyadjian was the kind of coach who looked out for kids, even those who were not on his team but on J.V., as I was.

Often, as I would be walking back in after practice, Coach Boyadjian would jog past me and say something encouraging. Just a few words, like, "Hey, Hallowell, work hard, you'll make my team." To this day, I do not know why he did that. I was a nobody in soccer at the school, just a runt on J.V. But, every week, I would get a nod, a look or a word from the legendary coach. I watched for him every day.

His encouragement didn't go to my head. How could it? I could barely kick with my instep, let alone think I was on my way to stardom on the varsity. And yet, these brief moments of being noticed by the Main Man stoked my thirteen-year-old confidence-furnace like a blessing from Pelé might have done.

Then one day, my coach, Coach Fitts, came and told me I was starting in a game at what was then called center forward. This was the key position on the front line. The regular center was hurt, and I was to take his place. No matter that I had never played the position before. No matter that I barely knew how to kick the ball. No matter that my teammates looked at me like, "*Who* is playing center????"

Something momentous in my life happened during that game; it changed me forever.

Some people contend that there are no moments of truth in life, moments in which a life heads this way or that, moments that make all the difference. But they are wrong. We all have experienced moments that changed us forever, whether we know it or not. I had one that day.

You can get ready for a certain moment for a long time and, then—*presto!*—in that moment, you change, and your world changes with you. The moment you conceive of a brilliant idea, for example, can change you forever, but you took years preparing for that moment. Or the moment you see a certain face across a room can change you forever.

Or the moment you score three goals in a soccer game, as I did that afternoon in October 1963 at the age of thirteen.

When the game started, I felt nervous. But, as I started to run, I forgot about the fact that I wasn't supposed to be a very good player, and I just fell into the flow of the game. Coach Fitts always stressed playing your position, so I stayed in my lane, running up and down the field.

My first goal came as the ball squirted out of a group near our goal, and one of the defenders passed it on up to me. I took the ball in stride and carried it down the field, passing it off when a defender came up to tackle me. My teammate took the ball and saw me racing toward the goal. At just the right moment, he passed it back to me, and I kicked it without even looking for an open spot. I just wanted to shoot before the goalie could get ready—and before I would have to do anything fancy.

The ball shot along the ground—not more than an inch above it—heading straight toward the goalie. I closed in, hoping for a rebound, but, as the goalie bent down to field my shot, it squirted right between his legs and into the net. I couldn't believe what had just happened: The ball was in the net, behind the disgruntled goalie. That meant I had scored a goal. Me. This was an entirely new feeling, one that, up until that moment, I had only watched others experience.

But, before I had time to exult in what I had done, the game was back on, and I was running up and down the field again. Once more, I picked up a ball on a pass from one of our defenders and raced toward the opponents' goal. This time, I outran the other team's players and broke in on the goalie all by myself. But, in my enthusiasm, I stumbled as I got close. Desperately, as I was falling, I stretched out my left leg and managed to nudge the ball away from the grasp of the goalie. It trickled over the goal line and into the net. A second goal. Could this be? Now, we were ahead, 2–0.

My last goal came toward the end of the game. Back then, in American soccer, you kicked the ball in from the sideline, rather than throw it in as you do nowadays. We had a sideline kick deep into the other team's territory. I stood my ground in the center of the field, and, when my teammate launched a beautiful, high, arching kick-in that was headed right toward me, I realized I was supposed to do something I was very bad at doing. I was supposed to jump up, higher than any defender, and strike the ball toward the goal with my head. In practice games, I never did this well. I would miss the ball completely, or hit it in the wrong direction. Thank goodness, in this game, I didn't have time to think very much about what I was supposed to do. In an instant, the ball was above me. I can see it now, thirty-eight years later, as that ball has stayed right there in my memory all this time, like a beacon marking a turning point in my life. I took aim and jumped up, looking right into the center of the ball, as I had been coached to do, and, what do you know, I managed to head that ball sharp and clean into the upper-left corner of the opponents' goal, well beyond the leap of the now thoroughly frustrated goalie.

We won that game, 6–1.

Jogging back toward the locker room, I couldn't believe what had just happened. Teammates ran by me, patting me on the back, saying, "Great game," and I said stuff like, "Thanks, you, too," and whatever else I could think of in my daze. For a few spinning, golden moments, I was the hero of a game. I might as well have been Julius Caesar, returning in glory from a conquest, for how on top of the world I felt.

I remember that game and those goals quite clearly. And the feeling. Oh, yes, I remember that, too. Such a feeling never dies.

Harry Boyadjian had prepared me for it. The regular starting center who couldn't play had opened the door. Coach Fitts, who, I learned later, was acting on a suggestion from Coach Boyadjian, gave me the chance.

I have never scored as improbable a victory in my whole life as I did that afternoon. I never went on to star in soccer, or in any sport. That day was my moment of sports glory, my only taste of what some kids taste on a regular basis, and some adults as well.

But that one taste, those few drops of victory over my own fears, has lasted my whole life. That one taste proved to me that what I had been told was not just a line of blarney. I had been told, for as long as I had been told anything about life, that the little engine that could, can; that where there's a will, there's a way; that David can slay Goliath; and so forth. But, as a thirteen-year-old, I was also learning some of life's cold, hard facts, and I was becoming quite the little cynic. The little engine that could, thought I, was just another one of those lines they feed you, like Santa Claus, to keep your hopes up. But anyone with a brain can see that most engines just plain can't. If everybody *could* be rich and famous, everybody *would* be. If all it took to succeed was the desire to succeed, then there'd be a whole lot more successful people than there are. I was developing a cogent, cynical argument that life is a deck that's stacked against you.

So, when Harry Boyadjian, having prepped me with nods and glances, then saw to it that I was put in the center of the field on game day, and, when I came through, not just with my pride intact, but with what had to be called, on that level, a miraculous performance, well, I had to start to believe in miracles. The little cynic had to rethink his position. He gave way to the dreamer, who resides within me to this day.

Since that afternoon in October, no dream quite as astonishing as that one has come true for me. Better dreams have come true—like finding my wife and having our children—but no dream quite as unlikely as that one.

Sometimes, it only takes one miracle—one moment—to make you a believer forever.

Who knows, maybe if I hadn't had that moment in 1963, I would have taken my hands off the sink and left the hospital—and my medical career—in 1978. Who knows?

THE CHOICE

A woman named Carolyn told me the following story about her father. It contains some of the simplest, yet most powerful, advice I have ever heard:

> I remember my dad playing word games with me as a little girl. One time, he made me cry over such a game: "My grandmother loves coffee but not tea, daffodils but not flowers," etc. He went on and on, urging me to guess some secret he was trying to clue me toward. Finally, I got so frustrated, I started to cry. He held my hand and said, "Carolyn, you have a choice, always a choice. It takes courage to choose to keep trying. You can give in when you're stuck or you can ask questions. You can see being stuck as a signal to try a new way." I don't remember what I did at the time, or if I figured out the secret, but I have thought about his advice often. Although I miss the feel of his hand in mine, I know that everything I am about is connected to him and what he stood for.

What Carolyn's dad said can be applied to so much. "You have a choice, always a choice. It takes courage to choose to keep trying. You can give in when you're stuck or you can ask questions. You can see being stuck as a signal to try a new way."

How many jobs could be saved if we followed the advice of Carolyn's dad? How many businesses? How many relationships? How many projects?

You have a choice, always a choice. We often choose to give up, to walk away, to get angry, to withdraw but, at other times, we hang in there, persist and look for a new way.

Don Chiofaro, a man who worked himself up from being the son of a cop to a major Boston businessman, once told me, "No is just the first step on the way to yes."

I wonder why we choose to stop at no, sometimes, but persist at other times. I wonder why, sometimes, we find the strength to keep trying but, at other times, we just can't do it.

I think the answer might lie in Carolyn's dad's advice. Carolyn's dad was saying more than "just keep trying." He was saying that you can find the reason to go on by learning from the moment. If you can think of a moment of frustration — in a relationship, or at work, or in the midst of a project you are trying to complete, or even in improving your golf swing! — as a signal to try a different approach, rather than as a reason to quit, then you might just take a deep breath, maybe walk away for a minute or two, and come back with renewed hope, or at least a willingness to try again, this time in a different way.

You have a choice, always a choice. I have started saying those words to myself, and to my kids. *Yeah, right,* the cynic inside me replies, *like this person is going to change?* "Yeah, right," my kids say back to me, "like my teacher is going to change? Yeah, right. Not!"

It is so tempting to give up, to be cynical, to assume that

you just can't win with this guy, or with that project, or with this teacher or with that boss.

And yet, and yet, we do have a choice, always a choice.

Sure, sometimes, the best choice is to get out. Sometimes, divorce is the best choice, or quitting the job or abandoning the project. But each of those options is still a choice. I tell myself to make sure what I am doing is my deliberate choice, not just an angry reaction born out of frustration.

It is hard to keep on trying. I have learned that I do much better when I can find an ally, rather than when I try to tough it out alone. I can keep on plugging if I have someone else with me.

Here is where the deal gets tricky. It is hard—especially as an adult—to ask for help. It takes a special strength to reach out to others. I have worked on developing that strength in my life, rather than trying to be a stoic soldier.

To the man who has given up drinking and craves another drink, to the woman who has divorced and swears never to date again, to the child who thinks math is so impossible she'll just not bother to try anymore, to the people who believe they just can't trust anyone anymore—to all these people, and to myself, I would say, *We have a choice, always a choice. . . .*

I say to myself, *Make this moment count.*

Every day. Every moment. We have a choice. Always a choice. Make this moment count.

ECHOES . . .

Early Work

Do you remember your first real job, the first job you took seriously and, more to the point, the first job that took you seriously, the first job that actually expected you to work hard for eight hours, the job in which you first discovered how hard it really is to work for a living, and how much you have to do that you don't like doing to earn a day's wages? Do you remember thinking to yourself (as I do) after your first day, You mean I have to go back and do that again tomorrow? And the next day, and the next? *My first job like that was working the midnight-to-eight-o'clock shift as a short-order cook at a greasy spoon called Donuts Please near Fresh Pond Circle in Cambridge. I will never forget that job.*

When I got paid for the first time at that job, I tasted the sour pleasure of being paid very little for doing and putting up with what seemed to me to be very much. When I looked at that first paycheck, minus those seemingly irrational and gargantuan deductions, my heart sank. So this is what I have to look forward to for the rest of my life? *I trudged on down to the bus stop in the morning sun of Cambridge, duly initiated. In spite of myself, I also felt rather proud.*

> *The woman who writes of a similar moment of initiation to her work life in the following piece is as fresh and enthusiastic today as she was the few decades ago when she started out. I know, because she is my dear friend.*
>
> —E. H.

When I was a teenager, it was a given that I would work every summer to help contribute to family costs— chiefly to my college education that loomed ahead. At fifteen, I cleaned house for a little old lady; at sixteen, I was a waitress; and at seventeen, I sold hardware. But all these, done in a resort town on Cape Cod, seemed like dress rehearsals for my first *real* job—a job in the Big Apple. I would live at home with my father, in the same two-person household I had grown up in, a beautiful little carriage house in Brooklyn. Eighteen years old and just back from my freshman year, I was ready to throw my book bag aside and show the world, at last, what a true sophisticate I was.

Tottering in on Monday morning to the Metropolitan Life Insurance Company's branch office at Union Square, in my high heels and nylons, my blue linen sheath and matching gloves, I was startled to discover a dreary room full of other file clerks, where my big task was to slit open an endless number of envelopes, remove the checks inside and, taking in hand an ink pad and a mechanical date stamp that I carefully set to the current day's date, open one of the hundreds of tiny file drawers, find a dog-eared file card that corresponded to the person whose payment I held in hand, and stamp the date in a tiny square. Lest the high heels and gloves had been put on in vain, I wobbled down one day for lunch by myself at a famous old restaurant on Fourteenth Street, where a kindly waiter winked at me, and I sighed with relief at being recognized as a woman of the world.

When Friday came, marking the conclusion of my first week, I was ready to reevaluate the meaning (or meaningless-ness) of work, at least as I had imagined it, when, at about four o'clock, the office manager pressed a tiny brown envelope into my hand. I found it stuffed with cash—*cash!*—my whole week's pay, in coins and bills. It actually amounted to sixty-five dollars and change, but there seemed to be an enormous number of bills in there, far more money than I had ever held in my hand before. So *this* was the meaning of work!

Clutching my purse with its precious cargo, I raced home on the subway, hoping I would reach the house before my father did. The door was locked—I was in luck! I burst in to our cozy living room with its overstuffed sofa and chairs and let out a whoop. Then I shook out the contents of the heavy little envelope onto the dining table. Ten, twenty, thirty, forty, forty-five, fifty, fifty-five, sixty, sixty-one, sixty-two, sixty-three, sixty-four, sixty-five dollars and forty-seven cents! I smoothed out every one of those bills till it was perfectly flat. Then, I took the whole bundle of them—and every nickel, dime and penny besides—and, one by one, I laid them out along the arms and the backs of all the living-room furniture, till the place looked like a carnival of money.

Finally, I stepped back to admire the whole effect, kicked off those wobbly high heels, and went into the tiny kitchen to mix a perfect dry martini, for the moment when my father walked through the door to congratulate me.

Out Cold

I know the man who wrote the following piece. He is one of the most creative people I have ever met. One of his greatest gifts, which shows in this story, is his capacity to be surprised by life and to take notice of what he hadn't expected to see. After I read this, I wondered to myself at the coincidence of it all. I think what made the moment so powerful for this man was not that what happened happened, but that he was prepared to react as he did. This is often the case with human moments: They are not necessarily extraordinary in and of themselves, but our reactions make them so.

—E. H.

I work in an advertising agency-like office. The details of what I do are difficult to explain, but, fortunately, I don't need to because they are irrelevant to the point of this story. I only mention the advertising thing to help establish the mood and atmosphere of where I go every day to earn my daily bread. It's high stress and full of tight deadlines, where we all are trained to be total slaves to our clients' whims, and where we will often be expected to work all night to accommodate a last-minute request from an executive who simply forgot to tell us the whole story at the project's start-up.

I had just finished one of these all-nighters. The clients came in for a review at ten in the morning, and it turned out that they loved what I showed them. I took some satisfaction at having pulled this off, with the odds having been so heavily stacked against me. The hysterical and tightly wound project manager had actually given me the wrong script, and, when I discovered this only five days before the project was due, instead of being thanked for discovering the mistake while there was still barely enough time to fix it, I was officially blamed for the error. So, while I was pleased to have successfully pulled off another high-profile project, I wasn't exactly basking in glory. With what's typical Orwellian post-project hindsight in my company, praise was awarded to those most at fault, and blame was assigned to all the non-squeaking wheels.

After the client review, my adrenaline rush started to subside, and I began to feel spacey and exhausted. To clear my head and mentally prepare for the unpleasant project aftermath, I decided to go outdoors for a walk around the block. It was around noon, on a chilly but sunny day in autumn, and I was walking along a sidewalk in the heart of Boston's tony Back Bay neighborhood.

Deep into my brain cleansing, I was suddenly jolted back into reality by the sight of an attractive, well-dressed, elderly woman lying on the sidewalk in front of me, her head surrounded by a pool of blood. It was surreal. People were just walking by as if she weren't there. I guessed that she had only just fallen; otherwise, there certainly would have been some sort of crowd with police and paramedics. But here we were, just squeamish, klutzy me and this woman, who seemed quite conscious and alert, despite the horrifying image of her lying on that cold sidewalk in the midst of all that blood.

Once I realized that she was alive and able to communicate, I put my jacket under her head and went running into a nearby bank to call an ambulance. By the time I came back, others had gathered to help out, and the woman was now standing, saying, "I don't know what happened. I just fell."

It was very cold outside, so I suggested that we walk into the lobby of the bank and wait for the ambulance. Once inside, I realized that all the blood had come from a fairly superficial head wound, and she had managed to stop the bleeding with a handkerchief that another passerby had given her. We chatted a bit, and, at that point, she seemed calm enough for me to be able to give her some totally uninformed reassurance that she would be fine, and even to offer some humor, suggesting that her biggest problem would be a hell of a dry-cleaning bill. She was obviously still very frightened and putting on a good front, and so was I.

The ambulance was slow in arriving (and I had to go into the bank to phone two more times) but, eventually, it showed up. I walked my new friend over to one of the paramedics and gave a brief description of what had happened. As the paramedics began lifting the woman into the ambulance, she paused and said, "Wait a minute." She then leaned forward and gave me a huge hug, whispering in my ear, "Thank you for your thoughtfulness."

I don't know whether it was my exhausted state, the timing in my life or simply the recent bout with bad office politics, but this quite unremarkable good deed on my part became one of those life epiphanies. I suddenly realized that the amount of satisfaction, self-worth, good feeling and pride I felt on receiving that simple hug meant much more to me than the collected worth of anything I had ever achieved in my twenty-year career as a video producer. With that simple heartfelt hug, my life's priorities went swirling into place. I went back to the office—the tears I had shed having dried—feeling strengthened and enlightened.

When You Hate Your Work

I am going to tell this man's story myself, because he can't tell it in his own words. He died in 1978. I knew him well, and we had many conversations prior to his dying. He taught me a lot about work and about life.

—E. H.

Ben was raised to be a banker or a lawyer or an investor or some other kind of businessman. However, he was not cut out for that kind of work.

"Every time I tried one of those jobs," he told me, "I would get bored. I didn't like having to wear a suit and tie and look like everybody else. I would start to make mistakes, and, sooner or later, I'd get fired."

"Why would you get fired?" I asked.

"Because I wanted to get fired, to tell you the truth. When I worked for Morton Salt, for example, and I had to travel from city to city, I was going crazy inside. I knew the family wanted me to hold a responsible job like this, but I hated it. I learned that one of the hardest things in the world to do is go to a job you hate, day after day after day."

"But they make kids who hate school do that," I countered. "Didn't you feel like you had to?"

"Sure I did. That's why I kept slugging it out. I'd get a job because I scored high on the tests they gave, and I would give a good interview. But I always knew I was a square peg in a round hole. The job I liked best was the one I had at the boatyard. I could be outdoors working on boats, which I loved. But, then, they moved me indoors, which was a promotion. They were grooming me for management. I was supposed to be honored. I got a raise, and my prospects were improving, or so they told me.

"But that promotion was the kiss of death. I got completely bored looking over the numbers and telling other people what to do. I hated it. I got fired pretty soon after that."

Ben was a good-looking man, an athlete and a Harvard graduate, class of 1936. He was brilliant, creative and intense. He also had a mental illness—bipolar disorder—which could make him erratic and undependable. Holding down a job was nearly impossible in his younger years.

He married and had three children, but, because of his mental illness, his wife divorced him. He bumped around for a while, not quite knowing how or where to fit in. He knew he had talent, but he didn't know where to plug it in.

He loved to teach sailing. He could always find work in the summers on Cape Cod teaching young people how to sail and to race. His temperament was perfect for that. He had a real gift for connecting with young people, and for giving others confidence.

One winter, a private school took a chance and gave this

man with a history of mental illness a job teaching seventh grade.

"That changed my life," Ben told me. "At last, I found a job I loved. Teaching came naturally to me. No matter what subject, I could teach it. History, English, math, geography. I could teach them all. And you know what I liked the best? Teaching the stupid kids."

"What do you mean, 'the stupid kids'?" I asked.

"The kids labeled slow. I saw them as a challenge. They also were usually the nicest ones. Gentle giants. They could be big oafs off the farm, and some teachers would even be afraid of them. When they got frustrated they could be known to get a little feisty, maybe even punch a wall. But I understood them. And I wanted them to go back to the farm at least able to read. I really liked them. And you know what? They liked me."

"What did you do with them that worked?" I asked.

"Just kept at it. I didn't give up, and I didn't let them give up. I always treated them with respect, too. I knew they were dumb, and they knew they were dumb, but that didn't mean I didn't respect them."

"Jeez, how could you respect them if you thought they were dumb?" I asked.

"What a question for you to ask, you an aspiring young doctor. I respected them because they were trying to do something that was hard for them to do. I respect that in a person, don't you?"

"Yes," I said, duly chastened. I liked the image of Ben, surrounded by these students no one else thought could learn, doing his best to teach them, doing what turned out to be his life's work.

"After that first year, I knew I had found my career. That's when I moved up to New Hampshire. My first job in the Derry public schools paid twelve hundred dollars a year. But I loved it anyway. I made lots more at Morton Salt, but I was miserable there. I learned that what counts is finding the job you like."

"And, you've taught up there for how many years now?" I asked.

"Going on twenty," Ben said. "I still like the dummies the best."

"You're not supposed to call students that, are you?" I asked with a wince.

"Why not? They're dumb. I don't care, they don't care. They're going to be damn good people. And, you know, lots of great people are dumb. And lots of really bad people are smart. Being smart is overrated. And being a good person is underrated."

Ben taught right up until his death from cancer in 1978. A busload of teachers and students came to his funeral. There is a plaque at the public school where he taught, honoring him as one of the best teachers ever to teach there.

For the first part of his life, he hated his jobs. Work was torture for him. But, for the rest of his life, once he found his calling, he loved his work. He helped others, applying his special talent as a teacher. He gave an education to a legion of kids who, otherwise, would have languished and left school with no skills and no self-respect.

I knew Ben well. He was my father.

CREATING
CONNECTIONS . . .

Invitation to reflect: What do you consider the greatest obstacles you've had to overcome in your work? Of which of your achievements are you the most proud?

Obstacles to connection: In my own personal life, and in my work with patients, I have observed that, by far, the greatest obstacle to success—in anything—is lack of confidence. Most people are more talented than they believe. But they— we—sell ourselves short. I do it in my life all the time. Do you do it in yours? Instead of taking action, I brood and think of all the things that could go wrong, or dwell on how I am not up to the task at hand.

Possible steps to take: Connect. Never worry alone. This is what works for me, and I have found it works for most people. The great virtue of groups—like families, teams or closely knit organizations—is that individual members give strength to each other. People buck each other up. Just as Coach Boyadjian saw more in me than I knew was there and, a few years later, my teacher, Fred Tremallo, saw more than I knew was there, other people can help us discover within ourselves more than we ever knew existed. All you have to be willing to do is take the coaching, be open to the teaching, and respond to the challenge. Never give up. And the best way to develop the strength not to give up is to lead a richly connected life.

Chapter Ten

SELF-DISCOVERY

TURNING FIFTY

I turned fifty on December 2, 1999. I never anticipated what that easy-to-anticipate, merely chronological fact would do to me emotionally.

I felt I'd hit the final phase of life. Maybe because my dad died at the age of sixty-three, turning fifty made me think I was close to my own death. For the first time ever, I realized I would never do all that I had hoped to do.

When I was in the twelfth grade and eighteen years old (just writing those words makes me wince, as it feels like only a summer or two ago that I was in the twelfth grade and eighteen years old), I had big plans. I wanted to become a great novelist. I was reading Dostoyevsky and writing tortured stories of my own. I envisioned a life of books.

Well, I have lived a life of books, but I never became a great novelist. Instead, I became a psychiatrist and a writer of other kinds of books. The books I was destined to write turned out to be books aimed at reaching people in a different way than novels do. But, nevertheless, I am not the great novelist I once hoped I'd become, and I will go to my grave with no Nobel

Prize. My twelfth-grade dreams will not come true.

When I was in twelfth grade, I thought of my life in terms of *someday*. Someday, I will do this; someday, I will do that. I wondered what I would become. I dreamed big dreams.

When I turned fifty, it hit me that *someday* had come. Someday was now. My life was no longer one of dreams and potential. I had become what I was going to become.

I didn't care that I hadn't become a great novelist. That surprised me, as I had always thought I would deeply regret not reaching that goal. But what I realized when I turned fifty— what surprised me like a warm day in December—was that the goals I had set were not at all what mattered in my life now. Whether or not I was a great novelist didn't matter. Whether or not I was famous or rich or powerful didn't matter. What I once had thought would matter so much didn't matter at all.

What mattered was love.

That fact was so simple. It had been there, like the back of my head, all along the way, but I rarely saw it. I had actually intimated to myself, ever since I was a little boy, that love was what mattered most. But I became distracted. I became caught up in the need to shine, to excel, to achieve, and I was seduced into judging myself along those lines. I never let myself enjoy to the fullest the best of life, because I thought I hadn't *achieved* enough.

When I turned fifty, I looked at Sue and I looked at my kids, and I looked at my work and my friends, and I thought to myself, *Thank you, God.*

My ambition now, if you can call it an ambition, is to open my life up to love in as many ways as I can, and to help others do this, too.

I want to love my family, my friends, my patients and my work as a writer, teacher and doctor as fully and completely as I can. I want to love my garden, my pets, my church and God as fully and completely as I can. I want to love my neighbor as myself. I know I won't always succeed in that, but I want to try. I want love to be my keel as well as my measuring stick. If I try to love well, I will continue to grow and be of use. The rest takes care of itself.

What was the allure of becoming the great novelist? I think it was, in part, the joy of making something, a complex kind of play. I was a pretty good writer, so I had the experience now and then of taking pleasure in having written a good sentence. But my drive to become a great novelist was mainly my drive simply to be great. It really didn't matter great at what, just be great. It was my attempt to get noticed. It was my ticket out— out of an ordinary life and into the big time.

I grew up wanting to make it big. I guess a lot of people do. It's the American Dream. My most realistic shot to the top was to become a great writer. I went to Harvard, a school where there are a lot of people who also want to make it big. Looking back now, I don't know that I actually wanted to make it big; I just thought I had to, in order to become happy. I thought I had to *achieve* happiness. I now know I only have to allow it to grow. I have to stay out of its way.

I want to do what I've loved all along, while I still can. I want to play, in the broadest sense of that word. For the happiest people, work is play. What I've really loved, all along, what I've liked to play at, is a combination of talking, writing, hanging out with people and thinking. I've always loved words and stories about people. That was what I lived for, even in school and college when I was quite shy. Even then, I wanted to know: What's going on with him, with her? What's new? I remember staying up late into the night with many different people, talking about life, about the latest controversy, or just gossiping about everyone and everything.

When I turned fifty, it hit me that I might not have much time left with all these people to sit up into the night and talk.

As you read this, you might think, *What is he saying? When he turned fifty, he realized he should just sit around all the time and talk?*

No. What I am saying is that I realized my life was unnecessarily burdened by my need to achieve and my feeling that I would be a nobody if I didn't become a somebody.

I hope I don't raise my children to believe that. I am quite sure that Sue and I are not visiting that curse upon them.

The summer after I turned fifty, I went into the cold Atlantic Ocean off Cape Cod with Lucy, Jack, Tucker and Sue. Tucker could swim but he was a little scared, so I held him in my arms. Accustomed to the fresh water of lakes, he smacked his lips in astonishment and said, "This water tastes salty, Dad!" Jack tried climbing up onto my shoulders. Lucy wrestled with an inflatable float, trying to balance it so she could hoist herself up and recline upon it. Even Sue waded in, despite her abhorrence of cold water. As soon as the water reached above her ankles, she shrieked and held her fists up, forearms trembling, as if she were carrying a heavy load over her head, but still she waded onward into the icy water so she could join us.

There we all were, in sight of the Provincetown monument, swimming in the same ocean I used to swim in when I was the ages of Tucker, Jack and Lucy.

Here I had come these fifty years, from a stormy family marked by alcoholism and mental illness, to a safe cove. Here I was, swimming with the woman I loved and the three children I adored. And, although I was not a great novelist, I was doing some good in the world and enjoying it, too.

The adolescent who wanted to be a great novelist actually wanted, if he had been wise enough to realize it, exactly what the fifty-year-old man, in fact, had found: love in his life, joy and usefulness in the world.

Do I still feel a pang or two when I realize I won't make it to the ranks of the immortal in literature? Yes, I suppose I do. A pang or two. That ambition is like a woman I courted but never married. I know some people who married the likes of her. I'm glad I didn't, but I still feel a pang or two.

I am grateful I didn't lash myself to ambition at the expense of everything else. I have seen many people destroy their lives, and the lives of others, in pursuit of great goals, of the Big Time. Even some of those who Make It turn monstrous along the way.

Now, at age fifty, I see so clearly what really matters that I can commit myself to it more and more.

How do you commit yourself to love? There are many different ways. You decide for yourself what works for you. Living a life based on love may mean, for you, working at General Motors and seeing to it that the company benefits as many people as possible. Or it may mean helping the neighbor you really don't like. I will tell you what it means for me: It means I try to follow the best in my heart. It means I try to open myself up to others as much as is useful. It means I try (often unsuccessfully) to understand rather than judge, and to forgive rather than resent. It means I try, judiciously, to deepen my connections to other people, to the groups I care about, to nature and to all that captures my heart. It means I allow my heart to be captured.

I am not going to quit my job and become a missionary. In fact, I will continue to work the same as ever. I will simply try to be even more clear with myself and with others about what matters—and what doesn't.

These feelings about the primacy of love—in the broadest sense of that word—have actually guided me throughout my whole life, whether I knew it or not. When I was growing up, my search for the security I wasn't getting at home led me to the many teachers and friends who basically saved my life. When I was at Harvard—surrounded by the smartest people I'd ever met—I saw firsthand how much more important love was than brainpower. As the founder of my high school, Exeter, said, "Though goodness without knowledge is weak and feeble, knowledge without goodness is dangerous." At Harvard, I discovered that intelligence alone was not enough to lead a fulfilling and useful life. I also discovered that being smart was pretty easy; what was difficult was to be loving and smart at the same time.

When I turned fifty, I decided, from that point forward, to devote as much of my energy as I could to translating the abstract message of love into concrete, doable deeds.

Now, I am trying to center myself back in that cove on Cape Cod, and bathe in all that it represents: harmony, balance and joy. In that salty water, with Tucker in my arms, Jack on my shoulders, Lucy before my eyes and Sue on her way out to meet us, I see myself, at last, at peace. I have done enough. If I do more, fine and good. But, I feel and know now that life is not a matter of how much and how well you achieve, but rather, how much and how well you love.

ECHOES . . .

Breast Cancer

This essay, about a woman's bout with breast cancer, captures not just one, but a series of many human moments: moments of love, and moments of discovery about life and about what helps people most in times of need.

In just a few paragraphs, this author teaches us a great deal. Her humble and almost offhand account is full of tenderness, as well as insight. When I read this piece for the first time, I felt instant admiration, not only for the author but for all the people she brings into this story of hope. Were this passage not true, you would almost think it was made up by a great storyteller, as it includes so many timeless elements: the steadfast husband; the mother trying to protect her children by shielding them from what she is going through; the great network of other breast-cancer victims; the legion of friends and senders of cards; the anonymous nun who offers a prayer; the elderly roommate, who, in just a few hours, becomes someone the author will never forget. All these characters and more combine—in words so simple and clear that the story unfolds like a flag—to show us what lies at the center of life.

—E. H.

I've always been blessed with a wonderful family and many friends. I thought I appreciated them, but I found out that I didn't really know the depth and meaning of that appreciation until I got sick. I certainly know now.

I was as healthy as a horse until age fifty-two. Then, the dreaded call came: "Mrs. Seaman, I'm sorry to tell you this, but you have breast cancer—lobular carcinoma—and my recommendation is a bilateral mastectomy."

My first reaction was shock; my second was, "Dear God, how am I going to tell my children and my parents?" I knew my husband would be strong and supportive, but my children were twenty-one and twenty-six, and their mettle had never been tested. My parents, ages eighty-three and eighty-seven, are part of our extremely close family, but my mother, especially, is getting fragile.

I called my husband first, and like the Rock of Gibraltar that he is, he said, "Don't worry, Honey. We'll get through this. Nothing will change. If anything, I'll only love you more because it'll make us both realize how precious our life together really is." (His words turned out to be true.) He gave me the strength I needed to make my dreaded phone calls.

My kids and parents fell apart. I could tell my mother lost a year of her life just hearing the words. My father shows his emotions less, but I could tell he was equally upset. My kids' reaction was somewhat unexpected. My daughter had just begun a new job in California, but she was ready to hop on the next plane home. Her boyfriend, whom I love like my own son, was ready to join her. My son, then a junior in college, is the rather quiet, seemingly unemotional member of the family, but he, too, was ready to head for home. My daughter and my parents called me every day, which meant the world to me.

The weeks before the surgery were the longest and most difficult. During that time, I had all I could do to deal with my own emotions, so I begged the kids to stay away until after my surgery. I didn't want them to see me in a disabled state. In hindsight, this was a selfish mistake, since they needed that physical connection, even if I didn't at the moment. Also, I was never disabled in a way that they would have seen. They ended up suffering and worrying a lot more than they would have had they seen me face-to-face. It also made them feel unwanted and unappreciated. My son ended up missing two weeks of classes, I found out a month later.

I began taking hour-long walks in our neighborhood to have some quiet thinking time and to build myself physically for the impending surgery. I suddenly realized that the natural inclination for a pity party was probably not my best choice, or I might end up losing my parents, too. So, I made a conscious decision to "buck up and make this no big deal." I made the effort to take the worry from my parents and kids, but it ended up helping me. Even though the days before the surgery were long at times, by telling myself it was "no big deal," it became less and less of one.

At this point, love and compassion poured in from many friends and even strangers, via phone, e-mail and visits. One person, in particular, helped to make those long days before surgery bearable. My Italian friend, Anna, called or e-mailed me every day—sometimes two or three times a day—comforting me, encouraging me, distracting me and making me laugh. I really don't think I would have made it through nearly that easily without her. I'll be forever grateful to her, and to my husband and my daughter and my parents, for their daily support.

The sisterhood of breast-cancer victims is an incredibly strong one. As the word got out, I got calls from women I'd never met. One such lady, my principal's wife, spent time with me sharing her experience and expertise, allaying my fears and concerns, answering questions and inviting me to a seminar given by physicians who treat breast cancer. Another lady from the American Cancer Society called to offer her assistance and sent me a package of things that are very helpful to a woman having a mastectomy. The nurse at my pre-op exam was also especially kind. She sensed my fear and spent an inordinate amount of time answering my questions. She came to see me in the hospital and had a fellow nurse call to tell me about her own breast cancer, about the choices of reconstruction and prostheses. People came out of the woodwork to be kind and share information that's so vitally needed at that time. Reading about such things is valuable, but hearing about personal experiences is priceless.

The night before surgery, my husband's retired veterinarian partner, whom I call my "spiritual confidant," called me to give me words of hope and inner strength that I so needed at that moment. He soothed and comforted me, encouraging me to have faith in my God, that He would give me what I needed to get well. I slept like a baby that night, thanks to his phone call. The morning of surgery finally arrived. I had held myself together pretty well up to that point, getting by with a LOT of help from my friends, family and strangers. I also have a strong belief in God and had done quite a bit of talking to Him up to that point, too. But, at six o'clock, I was surprised how suddenly anxious I felt when the anesthesiologist came in to tell me that the doctor had given him instructions not to give me any of the usual quieting drugs he was used to giving. (This was my surgeon's first surgery in a new hospital, and she liked her mastectomy patients awake in case they changed their mind at the last minute.)

The minute he left, a sweet, tiny, old nun crept into my room. She bore a striking resemblance to my grandmother, who was my hero, the sweetest, kindest person I've ever met. It was almost as though my grandma's angel had swooped down from heaven to comfort me in my time of need. The nun leaned over the bed, took my hand and said, "Honey, do you mind if I say a prayer for you?" My reaction surprised me. I broke down in a puddle of tears and finally regained my composure enough to say, "No, in fact, I'd appreciate it." I'm not Catholic but, at that point, any and every prayer was greatly appreciated.

When she finished, she moved up the bed and gave me a hug. She said, "Honey, I'm glad you cried. I've been getting up at five-thirty for over fifty years to pray with people before their surgeries, and I've noticed that people who cry do better!" With that, she quietly slipped out of my room like a stranger in the night. Suddenly, I was at peace. A calm settled over me, and I was back in my "no big deal" frame of mind. The nun was right: I did come out of the surgery well, partly because of her.

I woke up in my hospital room with my husband steadfastly at my side. There were gifts waiting for me—a basket full of surprises from a sweet, young teacher at the school where I tutor, and various other gifts—their timeliness just perfect. So many people were invaluable to me during that hospital stay that it's impossible to recall them all: my amazing surgeon, certainly a saint sent from heaven; the kind, caring nurses, so attentive all day and night; one anesthesia nurse who literally took over my breathing for me while I was in surgery; Mary, my dear little seventy-nine-year-old black roommate and mother of twelve, who, every so often, said, "Baby, you all right?" I would answer, "I'm doing fine, Mary, how about you?" It sounds silly, but that was very comforting throughout that day and night in the hospital, and it lightened my burden. We shared stories of pain and happiness, and I felt close to her, even though I was with her for such a short time. Twenty-seven hours after my surgery, I was home washing and drying my hair and typing e-mails!

What greeted me at home was literally overwhelming: thirty-five bouquets of flowers arrived over the next few days, and over seventy-five cards and notes. I had sent get-well cards to ill people before, but never did I realize the importance and the value of such a simple act. I've spoken to many breast-cancer survivors, and we all say that, for some reason, we can't part with those cards and notes.

Colleagues, organizations my husband and I belong to, even friends I hadn't heard from in years, remembered me. I can't begin to say what that meant to me. A high-school friend, whose mother had died three days before, came to visit me because she said she learned the hard way, too, how much the support of friends meant to her. She brought me healing vegetable soup, which my body craved at that moment. Other friends also seemed to know just what I needed at the time. Two weeks later, I was boarding a plane to Italy! My doctor asked me what I felt was responsible for my rapid recovery and positive attitude. (She calls me her "poster child.") I said that it might sound corny, but I have no doubt that the many connections I was blessed with were the reason. She said she didn't doubt that for a moment either, and that research, as well as her own experience, has shown that those who don't have that support system don't do as well. I'm forever grateful to each and every person who turned a dreaded situation into such a positive one.

I must tell you that a day doesn't go by now that I don't appreciate my life and the people I know at an entirely new depth. I only pray that I can be there for others as they were there for me.

Bunny LoMinto

Some of the most important moments of self-discovery occur during childhood. Often, we do not appreciate their impact until years later.

For example, when I was in the tenth grade, one afternoon as I was walking back into the locker room from soccer practice, a twelfth-grader ran up to me and put his finger in my face. "You are UGLY!" he shouted at me. "UGLY, UGLY, UGLY! DO YOU KNOW THAT? YOU ARE SO UGLY!" I knew this kid's name—I'll call him Buck Camillo—because he was the older brother of one of my classmates, Frank Camillo. Frank and I liked each other, so I couldn't imagine why Buck would want to taunt me. Back then, it was common for older kids to haze younger kids, so maybe that was all he was doing.

Still, I was stunned by what Buck did. After he dropped his little message on me, he just kept on running, laughing as he went. It was no big deal to him. But his words were so visceral and so intense that I have never forgotten the words or the moment. I can recall where the sun was in the sky, what uniforms we were wearing, even the glint off the ring Buck had on one of his hairy fingers.

I learned, in that moment, that I was naive. Up until then, I hadn't known how naive I was. I knew bad things could happen—Uncle Noble had taught me that—but I hadn't known they could happen out of the blue, literally, as you were just walking along, minding your own business.

The funny thing is, I still am naive. Even though I have had the equivalent of Buck's finger poked in my face many times since then, to this day that hairy finger shocks and surprises me, almost as much as it did back then in the tenth grade. I still do not anticipate gratuitous cruelty, and it still stuns me, whether it happens to me or to someone else. Even when I read about it in the paper, I am amazed.

The author of this story learned about it young, as well. I love her brave response.

—E. H.

One day during the autumn of 1949, I was walking home from school with my younger brother. I was in sixth grade, my brother in second, and I was responsible for his welfare during the walk to and from school every day. Suffice it to say that I took this responsibility *very* seriously. Usually, one of our cousins who was the same age as my brother accompanied us, and I was responsible for her, too. But, that day she was home ill, so my brother and I walked by ourselves.

It had rained earlier that day, and I carried a large men's umbrella at my side. My brother, Joey, chattered happily as he walked beside me. I was about to answer one of Joey's many questions, when, from out of nowhere, the neighborhood bully,

Bunny LoMinto, appeared in front of us, barring our way.

I was big for eleven, but Bunny, who was also a sixth-grader, was much bigger than I, because he'd been left back a few times. It took a lot to scare me, though, especially when my big-sister protectiveness took over.

"Whaddya gotta say to my face, runt?" asked Bunny, looming over my seven-year-old brother, who had frozen in his tracks, in a very rare moment of absolute silence.

Joey stole a terrified sidelong glance at me as he opened his mouth to answer, but no sound escaped.

"Huh?" demanded Bunny, jabbing Joey in the shoulder with a grimy paw, and knocking him to the ground. Leering at us maliciously, Bunny turned to be on his way.

"Why don't you pick on someone your own size, you big bully!" I shouted, pulling Joey to his feet with my free hand.

"Mind your own business, girlie," warned Bunny, menacingly, as he took a step back toward us.

"My brother *is* my business," I stood my ground, shoulders squared.

"Oh, yeah?" Bunny clenched a mammoth fist.

"I'm warning you, Bunny, stay away from us," I declared, brandishing the umbrella in one hand, and scooting Joey behind me with the other.

Bunny lunged toward us, moving more for Joey than for me. With a leap and a sweep of my arm more mighty than I'd ever dreamed, I crashed the umbrella down on Bunny's head. In a split second, a lump began to swell, and Bunny looked at me in utter shock as he rubbed his head.

"Jeez . . . ," he mumbled.

"I warned you," I said. "Get away from us."

Bunny backed away slowly, then turned and took off like a shot.

Joey peeked out from behind me. "He bent the umbrella!" was all he could muster, in his wide-eyed amazement.

Adrenaline still coursing through my veins in fight-or-flight mode, I realized what I'd just done. I looked at the mangled umbrella, which truly looked much worse off than Bunny had, and sighed. Even though Bunny had deserved it, picking on a little kid not even half his size, I hadn't meant to hurt him, just to scare him. What if I'd given him a concussion, or worse? I hurried Joey the short rest of the way home, visions of Bunny, unconscious on a side-street curb, passing through my mind.

Our grandmother met us at the kitchen door when we arrived home, taking in the bent umbrella and my worried expression in a single glance. Before she could even ask, out spilled the story, complete with Joey's awe and my guilt.

According to my immigrant grandmother's code of ethics, I had done the right thing, protecting my vulnerable little brother at all costs. Love and safety first, as far as she was concerned. Much as I basked in the glory of her approval, my conscience, nonetheless, pricked me. After all, Bunny might really be hurt. His family was poor, with countless children, and no father to support them. True, the rest of the neighborhood scoffed at the children as hooligans, and Bunny himself as worse, but all I could think of was the eternally weary and pale Mrs. LoMinto, sobbing uncontrollably as she wrung her hands over an unconscious Bunny.

At last, I told my grandmother I was going to the LoMintos to make sure Bunny was all right. My grandmother assured me I'd done nothing I needed to apologize for, but if I wanted to see if Bunny was okay, I could do so. However, if I wasn't back in fifteen minutes she was coming over there herself, and if anything had happened to me, she'd do to Mrs. LoMinto what I'd done to Bunny—or worse. The only person more feared than Bunny in our neighborhood was my grandmother.

I walked the short distance to the LoMintos, where I found Bunny sitting on the front steps. We held each other's gaze for a few moments.

"I wanted to make sure you were okay," I began hesitantly.

"Ya didn't hafta bother," he said gruffly. "Ya didn't really hurt me, girlie."

I resisted a smart retort, pretending to ignore his last comment, and mumbled, "I'm glad."

I was about to turn and go back home, when the beleaguered Mrs. LoMinto came outside. "You did this to my boy!" she accused, pointing to the now egg-sized lump on Bunny's head.

I nodded. "He was going to beat up my brother," I explained, adding heatedly, "and he's only seven years old!"

Mrs. LoMinto sighed, looking at Bunny with a mixture of exasperation, tenderness and worry. I wouldn't completely understand that look until I became a mother myself, but my innate protectiveness toward Joey gave me a pretty good frame of reference. "I'm sorry if I hurt him," I told her sincerely. "Even though Bunny's really rotten to everybody, you probably love him because he's your son."

She looked at me, all the fierceness gone from her initial expression, and nodded. "He'll be all right," she assured me.

"His skull's too hard to crack. He's just like his father," she added glumly, the comparison seeming to harden the tenderness she'd shown just a few seconds before.

Bunny looked sheepishly at his mother, then at me, and turned to go into the house. His mother followed, but first looked back at me over her shoulder and said, "I hope you never have a son like mine."

I turned and headed for home, wondering why I felt as if I would break down and weep. My conscience felt clear now; Bunny was fine, by his own mother's admission. Then, thinking about Mrs. LoMinto's parting words, I realized what was bothering me: I had regretted hurting Bunny because, to me, inflicting pain seemed an awful thing; but, unfortunately for Mrs. LoMinto, pain inflicted on Bunny was inevitable, and a lump on the head was by no means the worst she could expect.

I grew up, married and had children of my own; thankfully, none like Bunny LoMinto. In the course of motherhood, I had to protect my children many times, and never questioned the methods I employed—though brute force by means of umbrellas or otherwise never again proved necessary.

Part of me became a mother that autumn afternoon, not just because I had to protect my brother, but also because I witnessed the despair of the mother of a son whom she held beyond hope. I was always grateful to Mrs. LoMinto for her wish for me, and I thought of her often. It was by observing her, after all, that I came to recognize the role I was destined for in this life, that of mother and protectress. And I've never regretted a single moment of it.

The Pocket Incident

Sometimes, years have to pass before you find out an important bit of truth. As children, we often misinterpret the reactions of adults, or we imagine disapproval that the adult never felt. We can spend years laboring under some misconception, or spend years not basking in the glow we should have felt. This little episode offers a small example.

—E. H.

When I was in third grade, I had a best friend named Lori Beth. We had been friends since kindergarten, and we always did everything together. Lori Beth had long brown hair down to her waist, which I envied because mine was just a mousy tan color and very wispy. She also had five brothers and sisters to play with. I only had one sister and we liked to fight. Lori Beth's older sister, Sue, was our baby-sitter, so Lori Beth got to come to our house whenever Sue did. We were very close.

That's why I was devastated when a dark-eyed vixen named Tina transferred to our school. Tina decided it was time to get her *own* best friend, and guess who she wanted . . . Lori Beth! She would try to tempt Lori Beth away from me by giving her presents and inviting her over to her house. It was hard for Lori Beth to resist, and I felt we were growing further and further apart.

Finally, one day, I reached the boiling point. I stomped up to Tina on the playground and confronted her. "How dare you try to steal my best friend!" I yelled. Of course, Tina didn't accept that meekly and, before you know it, we were in a full-blown shouting match. Tina got in my face and I grabbed her dress to push her away. Her body went in one direction, but the pocket on her dress went in another! I looked down to find Tina's pocket clutched in my hand. "You're gonna pay for this!" Tina shrieked, and she ran away.

Sure enough, that night, I got a call from Tina's mother. I knew I was in the right, but I meekly followed Tina's mom's directions to apologize. It almost killed me! When I hung up the phone, I turned around to find that my dad had been listening to the whole conversation. He was kind but firm. The bottom line was, he said, if we hadn't been fighting, this never would have happened.

Years later, as an adult, I was talking with my dad about old times, and the "Pocket Incident" came up. My dad remembered it as vividly as I did, but his interpretation surprised me. "You know," he said. "It was so hard for me to keep a straight face when I had to tell you that you shouldn't have been fighting. The truth is," he continued, "I thought you were one gutsy girl for sticking up for yourself like that! It took all my control not to shake my fist in the air and say, 'That's my girl!' I was really proud of you."

Even after all these years, it felt wonderful to hear this praise from my father and to know that he was on my side! That tiny little show of support really meant a lot to me. And, if I ever run into Tina again, she'd better hope her pockets are sewn on tightly! Whatever happens, I know Daddy would approve.

Doing the Right Thing

There is a hymn we sometimes sing in my church that has a line in it that always makes me pause. "Once to every man and nation comes the moment to decide," it goes, continuing on to praise choosing the right side, siding with truth over falsehood, doing the right thing. The line that haunts me, though, is that first line: "Once to every man and nation comes the moment to decide." The reason why it haunts me is that it makes me wonder when my moment will come, and how I will decide.

It isn't as easy to do the right thing as an adult as we thought it would be when we were kids. Do you remember siding with the good guys and hating the bad guys on TV or in the comics? But that was before life got complicated and you had done enough bad things yourself to know you had a little of the bad guy in you, so it wasn't so easy to hate the bad guys anymore. And there were enough times when you had done the wrong thing for you to realize that doing the right thing wasn't all that easy, either.

We don't stand up and trumpet the moments when we didn't do what we knew we should have. We don't brag

*about the times when we joined in scapegoating somebody,
or when we beat up on the little guy, or when we took something because no one was watching, or when we simply
looked the other way while other people did what we knew
was wrong, wrong, wrong.*

*Those moments make the moment in this story all the
more impressive. Heroism is possible, for all of us. Anybody
can be great.*

The hymn, in fact, is wrong. It says once *to every man
and nation. It should say the moment to decide comes
every day.*

—E. H.

When I was in high school, I volunteered at the
Community Center for Holocaust Studies. This was in
a suburb of New York City, and the community had many
Holocaust survivors who had funded the opening of the
Center and subsidized it ongoing. Volunteering at the Center
was an indescribable experience, never more so than on one
unforgettable Sunday afternoon in February.

It was bitter cold, too cold even for snow, and I sat at the
front reception desk affixing labels for a fund-raising mailing.
When I heard the door chimes, I looked up in surprise; the
cold had been keeping people away all day. In with the rush
of frigid air, came an elderly lady. She was tiny and white-
haired, but she had a dignified air that made her seem imposing. I came around from behind the desk to greet her.

She told me that she had lived through the events and
needed no introduction. Her voice held no rancor, only the

resigned sadness of a long-since acceptance of tragedy.

I assumed that, since she was a survivor, she'd come to record her story; many survivors came to do just that. I didn't want to pry by asking why she'd come, but she held my fascination in the same way that all Holocaust survivors did. The surviving of such unspeakable horror was quite beyond my comprehension.

After a few moments, the woman said, "I've come to tell my story," just as I had suspected.

"Of course," I said, leading her to the recording room, noticing that she dragged her left leg when she walked.

"You limp a bit, too," she remarked.

"A childhood accident," I replied self-consciously. The two years of physical therapy I had undergone, and considered suffering, were nothing compared to the torture I knew she had endured.

"So young to know about aching bones," she said softly, patting me on the cheek. "I was, too."

I felt too guilty to speak. *But yours was a horror, deliberately inflicted,* I wanted to cry. *Mine was only an accident.*

As if she could read my mind, she said, "What happened to me is not what you think. Will you sit with me while I tell the story?" I nodded, seating her comfortably and setting up the tape recorder. I sat beside her and listened, transfixed, as she told her tale:

"I was fourteen years old when Hitler came to power in Germany. My father was a history professor at the University of Heidelberg. We were Christian, but many of my father's colleagues, as well as my parents' closest friends, were Jewish. My father and some of the other Christian professors did their best to convince their Jewish friends to leave Germany, but it's not so easy to make anyone believe that the land that they—and their ancestors for as many generations as they can recall—call home is no longer safe for them.

"By the time I was eighteen, no Jew in Germany was safe. My parents agreed to hide the daughter of their closest friends, knowing that their friends would soon be going to certain death. This daughter, Lili, was my best friend. I loved her like a sister. We hid her in a tiny closet concealed behind a staircase. It was hardly big enough for a five-year-old child, but it was the best we could do. It was too dangerous for Lili and I to speak to one another above a whisper, so we wrote notes to each other. I burned them in the fireplace when we finished reading them.

"One afternoon, I was alone in the house—save, of course, for Lili in her hiding place. I'll never forget how lovely it was that day; almost lovely enough to forget the evil that had descended on Germany. That's what I was thinking to myself when I heard a pounding at the door loud enough to wake the dead. Only the SS would pound that way, I knew. A dread the likes of which I had never known before—or since—gripped me like a vise. In a split second, I decided that, no matter what they did to me, I was not giving up Lili to them.

"I opened the door, and one of them rushed in, sticking his rifle in my face. Two others stood outside in the street.

"'Your father is a professor at the university,' said the soldier who'd come inside, and I nodded.

"'You know any Jews?' he spat.

"'Not anymore,' I replied, instantly regretting my defiant tone.

"'You sound like you're sorry. Are you sorry that the Führer has cleaned up the Fatherland for good Germans?' he demanded, his self-righteous fury rising.

"I shook my head, furious at my own unthinking stupidity, and terrified besides. I quickly mumbled an apology, but the damage was done. He roughly pushed past me, heading straight for the staircase where Lili was hiding, even more terrified than I. Knowing that if I moved toward—or even looked in the direction of—those stairs, Lili would be discovered in an instant, I held my breath and silently prayed to God to keep Lili safe, to send these SS away . . . and keep them away. I promised fervently that whatever God asked of me, I would do. I was willing to endure anything for my friend's sake.

"Suddenly, like a miracle, one of the SS outside opened the door and called for the one who was nearing Lili's hiding place. I was shaking so with relief and fear that I never heard why he told him they had to leave. I only remember the first one's evil leer at me as he pushed me to the floor and kicked me savagely, then crushed his rifle butt into my hip, shattering the bones. Then, they were gone as quickly as they had come. I lay there for a long time, in agony, but mindful of my promise to God.

"The crushed bones never healed properly. I refused to go to the hospital, knowing we would be asked why I had angered the SS. Then, we—and Lili—would be in the gravest danger. A doctor friend who my parents trusted did his best to splint and tape my hip, but it didn't do much good.

"We lived through the rest of the war uneventfully,

telling people that I had fallen ice skating, but hadn't told my parents because they'd forbidden my skating. Lili was never discovered. After the war, she and I came to America with my parents, and lived next door to each other after we each married. We were never apart a day of our lives. She died of cancer yesterday. She would have been sixty-five years old today."

The woman looked up at me, her face serene, without even a trace of tears, though I was weeping openly. I turned off the tape recorder and pressed her hand.

"Don't cry," she whispered. "Ours was one of the few stories of that horrible time to have any good in it."

I reflected that was true, but only in comparison to horror.

"Lili was blessed to have such a friend," I told her.

"We both were blessed. Without Lili, I never would have discovered myself. I found a kind of courage I never would have known I had if not for her. So, you see, she saved me as much as I saved her. Through her, I became the kind of person I'm proud of being." She smiled at me beatifically. "Will you take the advice of an old lady?" she asked, almost rhetorically. "Life is short. Don't waste a moment worrying what you might do—just ask God to grant you the courage to do what's right at every moment, and to do what's right *for* you when you're too afraid to do it yourself."

I have never forgotten her, or her wise words, which have served me well, and helped me, too, to become the kind of person I'm proud of being.

Hope

Where do you find hope?
You can't go down to the corner store (if you even have a corner store!) and buy some. Doctors like me can't write a prescription for it. You don't find "Hope" listed in the Yellow Pages, and, if there is such a Web site as Hope.com, you can't rely on that to supply hope when you need it.

For such a necessity—and hope most surely is a vital necessity—we don't always know exactly where to turn when we run out. It's odd that we keep emergency stores of all kinds of things, but we don't usually keep an emergency store of hope.

Many of the people who come to see me professionally are low on hope. Restoring hope is one of the most valuable interventions I can make. But it can be difficult to do.

Some people have little formulas or slogans for supplying hope, like "Tomorrow is another day," or "This, too, shall pass," or "The dark of night precedes the day." But, usually, those sayings are only helpful when you already have some hope to begin with.

When you have run out of hope, or when you are nearly on empty, you usually need something stronger than a slogan.

At those times, I, myself, find hope by looking into the eyes of my children. When I am low on hope, I look at one of them or all three at once, and I feel hope instantly start to pump, like a medically shocked heart. If my kids are not around, I try to bring their little faces into my mind. Or the face of my wife, Sue.

There are other ways, too. I might say a prayer. Or go for a walk. Or both. I might read letters people have sent me telling me I have helped them in their lives. Don't ever think your doctor doesn't take strength from being thanked. He, or she, does. I save such letters for times when I am low on hope. They serve as a concrete reminder that I can be useful.

Often, that's what we need when we lose hope: a reminder. We have forgotten the good things in our lives; they have vanished from our awareness.

Here's a brief story of how one person found such a reminder.

—E. H.

Following two or three years of helping my son through a difficult time (and working, wife-ing and mothering my girls, as well), I slipped into an inexplicable depression that winter. I was disgusted with myself for feeling as I did because I felt that there was no real reason for it.

I went to Florida by myself to visit my parents for a week and wondered if I would be able to get on the plane to return home. I would go out for a walk in the morning and then sit by myself at the beach all day, feeling more and more afraid of how I was feeling.

One morning, I set out early on my walk and passed a little boy, no more than five years old, fishing in a little pond near my parents' condo. He was so excited, and he smiled and waved at me. His smile was full of anticipation and hope. When I returned, hours later, he was still there. He waved and smiled again. I walked over to him. He had not caught a fish yet, but he was still there . . . smiling and hopeful.

It was as if a light turned on in front of me: hope. I try to see that little boy's face in my mind whenever things look bleak.

CREATING
CONNECTIONS . . .

Invitation to reflect: Can you think of a moment in your life when you discovered something about yourself or about life in general that you hadn't known before?

Obstacles to connection: When it comes to seeing ourselves as we truly are, we all have our blind spots. Oddly enough, it is not just our foibles we have trouble seeing. Many people see their weaknesses all too clearly, but are blind to their strengths. They will accept criticism from others and heap it on themselves, as well. But they can't accept compliments and they can't comfort themselves with kind words.

On the other hand, there are some people whose lives become tragic because of just one flaw they are unable to recognize. They get angry and defensive rather than recognize and change the flaw, so they never accept the insight that actually could help them. This is a major theme in world literature, as well. The most famous example of this in English is the opening scene of Shakespeare's *King Lear*, in which Lear angrily rebuffs his daughter, Cordelia, for speaking the truth, while warming to the false flattery of her two sisters, Regan and Goneril. The tragic irony in this play—as so often happens in real life—is that the only daughter who truly loves Lear is Cordelia, the one who speaks the unwelcome truth.

Possible steps to take: If you dare, you might try the following exercise. Think of the three or four people who know you best and whom you also trust. Make sure these are people who genuinely like you, and do not have any reason to hurt you. Then, over the course of a few weeks, make it a point to have a private conversation with each of these people. In the conversation, explain that you are looking for some honest feedback. Then, ask the person to tell you if there is any one quality or trait about you that that person thinks you might consider trying to change.

It takes courage to seek such feedback; it also takes courage to give it. So, make sure you choose the other people carefully, and also prepare them by letting them know you haven't gone nuts, you aren't depressed, you are simply—believe it or not—wanting to grow, even at your advanced age. You don't want to be like King Lear.

Most of us have a quality or two that all our friends know about but don't bring up with us because they don't want to upset us, or because they think you can't teach a grown person new tricks. These qualities are usually blatant, not subtle. There is an elephant in the room, but no one talks about it.

For example, you may be notoriously bossy and controlling, but no one dares talk to you about it, so they just keep a distance. Or you may be famous for your rash temper, but no one mentions it for fear of incurring your wrath. Or you may be unduly meek and subservient, but no one brings it up because they think doing so might hurt your feelings and you can't change it anyway.

However, many of these qualities can be changed. Not dramatically, perhaps, but enough to make a big difference. Lots of people simply do not know about their negative qualities. If only they knew, they could work on making a change.

Self-discovery can also stem from periods of reflection and introspection. Be careful of introspection, however, because without another person to bounce your conclusions off of, you can grow sour on yourself. Many people think they are introspecting—taking a hard look at themselves—when all they really are doing is attacking themselves in an unfair and self-destructive fashion. One of the great ironies of human nature is that the people who really ought to take a "cold, hard look" at themselves never do; and the ones who ought to go easier on themselves are the most self-critical.

Don't mistake self-criticism for self-discovery. A good way to combat self-criticism is to maintain close connections with the people who truly do like you. Not the people you think you ought to keep up with, not the people who demand your time, not the people who make you feel guilty when you haven't spoken to them in a while, but the people who really like you for who you are. Their feelings about you can be contagious.

Chapter Eleven

SPIRITUALITY

WHAT TUCKER
TAUGHT ME

Containing my two young boys in a pew in church is like trying to pop corn in an open frying pan: Not much stays where you want it to.

I learned this for the umpteenth time one Memorial Day weekend. Many families were out of town. What few kids were left had to go into the main church since no one was available to teach the Sunday school. Lucy was off with a friend, but Tucker and Jack were with Sue and me.

As the service began and we heard the readings from the Bible, I hoped my boys were listening, because the readings on this day just happened to contain the heart of my religious belief and the reason why I am a Christian. I couldn't have picked readings that were more central to my faith had I tried. But were the boys listening? I didn't think so.

As the reading proceeded, "If we love one another, God lives in us, and his love is perfected in us . . . ," Jack and Tucker poked each other with pencils. As the reading went on, "God is love, and those who abide in love abide in God, and God abides in them," Jack and Tucker wrestled each other to the floor of our pew, as parishioners looked over at us in annoyance. As Sue and I pulled them to their feet and sternly told them to sit still and listen, the next reading began. "Jesus said to his disciples, 'As the father has loved me, so I have loved you; abide in my love.'" Jack and Tucker looked at each other and puffed out their cheeks, trying to make each other laugh. The reading proceeded, "I have said these things to you so that my joy may be in you, and that your joy may be complete." At that point, Tucker's mouth burst open, expelling a jet of air and pent-up laughter that made the whole congregation jump. I exited quickly, Tucker in tow.

This is the moment when children in previous generations would have been taken home and spanked, or told to go to their rooms for the rest of the day. For better or worse, that is not the approach Sue and I take. We don't strike our kids. We set limits in other ways. On this day, I sat Tucker down outside the church and told him that he could not behave that way in church.

To give him his due, he was usually not expected to sit through Bible readings in the main church. And the message I have wanted Tucker to get in going to church is not a message of stern discipline, boring readings and solemn looks from sad-eyed grown-ups. I have wanted him to get a message of security and joy from church.

So, sitting outside, I held Tucker and talked to him about love. I told him that was what the readings had been about. Tucker looked at the grass and thought about who-knows-what.

Just at that moment, around a corner of the church where we could see what was going on but could not be seen ourselves, a ragged street person, dressed in various torn garments of black, hobbled into the churchyard. In a loud voice, he asked John, a member of the congregation who happened to be outside sneaking a cigarette, if this was a church. John put his finger to his lips to say, *shhhh*, and then nodded that, yes, this was a church. "Where's the bathroom?" asked the hobbling stranger. John started to point, then dropped his cigarette, stepped on it and escorted the man to a back building, away from where the service was being held. Tucker was wide-eyed, because the street person looked mean and dangerous, as if he might cause trouble.

In a few minutes, John and the stranger emerged from the back building. They both were smiling now, and the man off the street no longer looked menacing in the least. I saw John take out his wallet and give the other guy a few bills, then put up his hand, as if to say, "No need to thank me." The two gave each other pats on the shoulder and parted company, the other guy off to the streets of Cambridge, John back inside for what was left of the sermon.

I asked Tucker if he understood what had just happened. Tucker shook his head, no. As I tried to explain it to him, I realized, as I so often do, that it would be much easier just to let it pass. After all, who knew what the man would do with the money, or if you should always give money to those who need it, or if it was a good idea to be smoking a cigarette during church.

But I made the most of this human moment. I didn't know John much at all, but I told Tucker he was one of the good guys in life. John had just helped a man he didn't know, a man who was down on his luck. I told Tucker this was what God was doing for all of us, all the time, and that all God asked in return was that we try to do this for one another.

Tucker smiled up at me. "That's what Mommy does for me," he said. I stifled my desire to say, "How about Dad?" Instead, I just gave Tucker a little hug. "That's right," I agreed.

At that point, Tucker looked up at me, his little eyes sparkling. If you have a child, or you know young children, you know how their eyes can sparkle, like sunlight glinting off a lake in the early morning, the light never still but flitting here and there.

The sermon was over. I could tell because the congregation was now singing a hymn. We could hear it from outside, slightly muffled, but this particular hymn was unmistakable: They were singing "Amazing Grace" inside. And Tucker's eyes were sparkling outside.

How is it we were here? Me, the son of a psychotic father, an alcoholic, abusive stepfather and a sweet, alcoholic mother? How is it I was here, with my son, this little pup with the sparkling eyes? *Damn*, I thought to myself, *what more proof do you need that there's a God?* A verse of the hymn being sung inside then proceeded, as if on cue, to answer my question of how I had reached this morning intact. "Through many dangers, toils, and snares I have already come; 'Tis Grace that brought me safe this far, And Grace will lead me home."

John, the parishioner I hardly knew, had joined with the anonymous street person to show Tucker and me how the spirit can work in this world and, just in case I had not gotten the message, an angel had wired up Tucker's eyes to beam me one of his unforgettable glances. The angel had even sent down one of my favorite hymns to accompany Tucker's glance, just to let me know this glance was sent by Very Special Delivery.

May that angel never leave us, come what may. And may we always sing.

ECHOES . . .

The Power of Love

Have you ever felt that a spirit visited you? I don't mean necessarily that you conjured up a vision, although you might have, but I mean have you ever felt that a spirit was contacting you from the world beyond ours? Maybe you laugh at such stuff. Or maybe you see it happen all the time. I fall somewhere in between. I certainly don't laugh at it, but neither do I see it happen every day. My hunch is, however, that it does happen every day. We simply haven't learned yet how to detect these visitors on a more regular basis.

I believe my Aunt Duckie's spirit visited me not long after her earthly self died. Were she alive, she would scoff at such an idea, but I am certain it happened.

This is how it came about: A few weeks after Duckie died, I took Jack, Tucker and one of Jack's friends on a weekend trip to a New York Giants football game. This trip was extra special because one of the Giants' assistant coaches, a friend of mine named Mike Pope, had arranged for us to get field passes so we actually could walk onto the field before the game and mingle with the players as they were going through their warm-ups.

The night before the game, we drove from Boston to a motel near Giants Stadium. On the morning of the game, we prepared to go to the stadium, and the boys piled into the car as if they were on their way to the most exciting adventure of their lives.

I paid my bill at the motel, bought some drinks for the kids, and was about to get into the car when I checked my pockets for the tickets and field passes: They were missing.

I checked every one of my pockets twice before I started to panic. This would be worse than bad—this would be a disaster of immense proportions. I couldn't reach Mike Pope to replace the tickets and field passes, because he was holed up with the team. The boys would be so crushed, and there would be no Plan B that could even remotely measure up.

I ran to the checkout counter of the motel to see if I had dropped the tickets there. No luck. I asked the cashier to check around on the floor. Again, no luck. I ran to the gift shop, where I had bought the drinks. Still, no luck. I asked the doorman if he had seen any tickets or if anyone had turned them in. He shook his head, no. Then, I explained to him that there were field passes with the tickets, and that three boys would be heartbroken if the tickets and field passes were lost. I guess I thought my sob story might somehow induce the doorman miraculously to find what I had misplaced! But he just sadly shook his head again, no.

In desperation, I looked up at the sky and pleaded, "Please, please, help me find those tickets."

When I looked down, the tickets and field passes lay right at my feet.

The doorman blinked. "Those are tickets?" he asked. I nodded, yes. "Your tickets?" I nodded again. "With the field passes?" Yes. "Man, you are one lucky dude," he said, slapping me on the back. "Those are like gold around here. They don't lie on the floor for a second before they get scooped up!"

In my heart, I knew where they had come from: Duckie had sent them. It was her way of telling me she had arrived where she was going and everything was okay. I felt her presence just as sure as if she had been standing right there next to me.

The funny thing is, if I had told her a story like that before she died, she would have laughed and said, "Fiddle-dee-dee. Don't be silly. Those tickets were there on the floor all along. You just didn't see them."

I think we reject all kinds of messages from beyond, day in and day out, year after year. We cling to disbelief out of respect for scientific evidence, and when we do get evidence, as I found on the floor in the form of those tickets, we reject it as flawed, insufficient or even delusionary. The more educated we are, the more we do this.

But that day, for some reason, I didn't do it. Instead, I accepted the message. I got it. Duckie sent me those tickets.

In the following story, a woman receives another kind of message. Like Duckie's message to me, it came in response to a prayer.

—E. H.

I lay quietly in the darkened hospital room, feeling unequivocally that this would be my last night on Earth. Just a few hours before, the doctor had told my parents and me that the emergency CAT scan results had shown an enormous mass in my left kidney. They weren't sure what the mass was; only an ultrasound of the kidney would prove that conclusively. But, it was Christmastime, and no technician would be available to run the test until six o'clock the following morning.

The travel alarm clock next to my bed glowed an incandescent-green 11:45. A little more than six hours until I could have the test that would let the doctors know how to proceed. Sighing, I wondered whether I could last that long. The only thing that was keeping me going—that had kept me going these last few awful days since I had lost consciousness from a stabbing pain in my left flank—was knowing how horrible it would be for my parents to go on without me. With each passing minute, though, I felt sicker, weaker and in more pain.

I guess all I can do is pray, I thought to myself. Feeling too weak to even muster a whisper, I prayed silently: *Dear God, if I'm meant to live through this, help me. Send me a sign that You want me to fight. I'm too sick and too scared to get through this by myself. Please send me an angel to help me.* Then, too exhausted to continue, I closed my eyes and waited for six o'clock to come.

After a time—I'll never know how long—I felt a shift in myself that I can't quite explain, except to say that the pain was different, somehow. Not that it was gone; it was still there, but before it had felt larger than I was—so large, in fact, that it seemed to consume me. Now, the pain felt like just a part of me, not the other way around. I breathed a bit more easily, settling into the pain without fear.

Suddenly, the air around me turned velvety soft, as if someone had gently covered me with a veil of spun silk. The fragrance of lavender wafted through the air and, through my closed eyelids, I saw a pale-purple color all around me. *I'm probably delirious from the fever*, I decided, willing my eyes open.

Yet, the lavender persisted, both in color and scent, to fill the room.

"Grandma . . . ," I barely heard my own amazed whisper. The air shimmered in an all-but-imperceptible response. I knew this was the answer to my earlier desperate prayer. My grandmother, who had died almost twenty-five years before, had come, so I wouldn't be alone. I closed my eyes again, feeling the tears course down my cheeks. I lay there suspended in time, feeling only that magical velvety air, glowing with light and redolent of my grandmother—filled with her love. Gradually, the scent disappeared and the light faded, but the feeling of being loved and protected remained. Without knowing how I knew, I was certain I would survive, and, slowly, the strength to fight stole through me. *Grandma, please tell Mom that I'm going to be okay*, I prayed silently. Then, at last, I fell asleep.

The next morning, I had the renal ultrasound, which isolated an abscess so huge, I was rushed for emergency surgery to drain it. Had this happened a few months earlier, prior to the refinement of a new surgical technique, the entire kidney would have had to have been removed. And the surgeon assured me in the most solemn of tones, as I lay beneath the CAT scan machine that allowed him to surgically drain the abscess, that, with a few more minutes of jostling on the gurney in transit, the sac of infection would have burst, draining into my bloodstream and killing me for sure.

I murmured my gratitude sincerely, but all I could think of was the supernatural connection I had experienced the night before.

When the procedure was finished, I was brought back to my hospital room, connected to massive IV doses of antibiotics to clear up any stray cells of infection that might have wandered through my system, and made as comfortable as possible. The nurses fussed over me, clearly concerned for how ill I still, in fact, was. But, I remained beyond worry and fear, completely secure in my grandmother's delivery of the divine message of my complete recovery.

Shortly thereafter, my mother came into the room, with a smile as wide as the sky. Her face showed concern, but not the intense worry I had expected to see. In an instant, I realized that my grandmother had heard my final request of her.

"I dreamed about Grandma last night," my mother said. "She told me you would be fine," she assured me, with a tender kiss on my forehead.

"I know. She was here," I whispered in reply.

I had a long and exhausting recuperation, and, many times, I wondered whether I would ever regain my normal level of energy. But then, I would hearken back to that wondrous night, and remember how my grandmother had traveled across time and space to let me know that I would live and be well. And that was all I needed to know.

Invisible Forces

Whether or not you believe in God, you probably have experienced, at least once or twice, moments of inexplicable goodness, moments some people call miracles and others call really good luck. This anecdote, from Claudia Crawford, a woman in Maine, contains such events.

— E. H.

I feel very connected to my husband, to whom I was married for just six days, but dated for a year and a half, and was engaged to for another year and a half. We were coming back from our honeymoon when we were involved in a car accident. He was killed. Miraculously, I was thrown out of the car onto the highway. I had an out-of-body experience, saw a bright light and the outline of a figure that said, "Go back, go back." I awoke on the side of the road to find my husband clinging to life. He died in the ambulance, holding my hand.

One year later, a woman came to me and told me I had saved her life. I did not know her, but she said she knew of me, and of the terrible tragedy I had gone through at the age of twenty. One day, she was in the bathroom ready to slash her wrists because her husband, a minister, had embezzled thirty thousand dollars and run away with the church secretary. As she was about to slash her wrist, she felt God intervened and had her think of me. She thought, *If Claudia can pull through her horrible tragedy, so can I, because what happened to her was worse than what happened to me.*

I was overwhelmed that just knowing about me had saved this woman, whom I had never met. It was then that I decided how I could be helpful to others. I decided to become a therapist.

My tragedy has helped me empathize more with others and understand, firsthand, deep human pain. I continue to feel the presence of my husband. I feel his influence, like a "guardian angel," in my life every day.

What a Garden Can Grow

Here a man tells of what he finds in his garden. How often we forget our place in nature. Through the image of his garden, this man beautifully reminds us where we all stand. He reminds us that we are never alone, even if we are by ourselves, our hands in the earth, helping the flowers to grow. This man believes in God, but even if he did not believe in God, he still could have felt the same connection to something beyond, through his garden. You don't have to believe in God, or participate in any organized religion, to feel a deep spiritual connection to forces beyond yourself.

—E. H.

My soul grows strong in my flower garden. My garden allows me to see life as it is—from birth to death—with all the elements of life, from the warmth of sunshine to the changing of colors in the fall.

When I work in my garden, I can understand the problems that my clients and their family members are having. I can also let go of my stress in my garden, because I can communicate with this changing, flowering life with my hands.

My pride in life comes alive in my time in the garden. I know that I am contributing to this world, in my own small way, by making the Earth a prettier, more beautiful place with my various flowers. I take great joy in seeing the flowers bloom.

But my biggest joy is that I understand more of God's plan and the way of all life. We are never alone. My garden connects me to all of life. Each flower is different, with its own weaknesses and vulnerabilities; yet, each flower also has its own strength, beauty and uniqueness.

Time takes away my flowers, but it makes no difference, because all flowers (and I see this in all of life) go through cycles. There will always be another season. Today is important, but all of life can't happen in just one day. We must have patience. And love. "Flowers bloom where they are planted."

I love to garden. I find in my work in my garden not only my happiness, but also the joy that flowers create for others. The beauty of the flowers (and of other people) is a gift to be shared by all. I am involved, and the flower becomes part *of* me, not something *for* me.

Everyday Evidence

When I state, in the subtitle, that this book can guide you toward meaning and love, it's because I believe these stories can deliver the goods. In our cynical, sound-bite age, it is good to remember what the author of this brief piece so poignantly tells us. She is not making up nice-sounding phrases to place onto greeting cards; she is writing from the depth of her heart about what truly matters to her in life. She has learned, as most of us must learn, through pain and suffering. But, what pain and suffering have taught her is not cynicism and bitterness. Rather, they have taught her where to look for meaning and for love. Her map is one we all could follow.

—E. H.

God's presence means a great deal to me. I have learned to discover it in each day.

In order to make this discovery, I had to lose everything: my dream house (through fire); my lifestyle of charity balls, steeplechases and the ballet; my ability to dance (because of a badly broken ankle); and the loss of a baby.

Through all these losses, I discovered that things do not provide the basic joy in life. Joy is found in a sunset. I tell my children, "God painted that for you." Joy is found in music, a song of praise to God. Joy is found in the miracle of a hummingbird hovering briefly at your window, or in frost feathers in winter. Joy is found in your child's hug and smile. Being able to find joy and miracles in each day brings to you an attitude of gratitude. A gratefulness for your spouse's snoring in the night and your cat snuggled in your lap. Everyday evidence of God's presence in my life—and yours.

The Science Museum

I love this account, written by a scientist, of his brief theological discussion with his son. The "big questions" about life live on in us all, whether or not we believe in God. Sometimes, it takes a conversation with a child to prompt us to organize what we think. I love talking about the big issues—What happens after death? Where did we come from? Why are there bad guys?—with children. You don't have to worry about someone else's dogma; you can just explore the questions together with the child.

—E. H.

My son, Josh, is eleven years old. He is very bright, creative and intuitive. One day, while driving to the Boston Museum of Science, we heard an advertisement on the radio that started a discussion about the Trojan War. To my delight, Josh was well-versed in that subject and knew of Helen, the Trojan Horse and Achilles.

As we discussed Achilles, Josh asked if the story of him being dipped in the river while held by the heel was true. I told him it was a myth, and we ventured into a discussion of mythology, and the gods of the ancient world, as a means of explaining the unexplainable.

As the discussion unfolded, I explained that, sometimes, the concept of God was necessary to provide order and authority to leaders of men. I explained that, if God had not handed Moses the Ten Commandments to provide rules and order for the Hebrews after the flight from Egypt, Moses would have had to invent God to obtain the authority to enact this code of conduct.

Josh then asked if I, as a scientist, believed in God. I told him that, as a scientist, I could trace our origin back to the "Big Bang." But, I could not explain where the matter that came together to form the huge exploding fireball that created the universe came from originally. I explained that, to my mind, at the very beginning, God had to have started it all.

Josh listened intently, asking intelligent questions. Finally, as we walked down the corridor to enter the museum, he asked, "Dad, where did God come from?"

I felt a great joy and warmth as I looked down at him. "Josh, you have just hit the heart of the issue. If you accept the concept of God, then God, by definition, has always been." This was a great day, made unforgettable for me simply by thirty minutes of discussion with my son.

After My Husband Died

How does a wife deal with the death of her husband? Here, one woman, briefly, bravely and with great honesty, tells how she got through it.

This story, one of the briefest in this book, takes up a vast topic: how we react to a tragic, early death. The author of this piece could have written a book and, indeed, many books have been written about the experiences she and her children endured.

What I find extraordinary in this account is, in fact, its brevity. The author simply states what happened, explains with perfect honesty how she felt and what she did, poses the awful question her children naturally asked, answers the question and leaves it at that.

—E. H.

My two sons—Todd, now age sixteen, and Craig, now age fourteen—were four and two when their dad, my beloved, died of cancer. At that time, I said to another widow friend, in all seriousness, that I would just raise the kids, then

DIE. It made perfect sense, as my heart and mind could not grasp life without my "original connection," Sam, their dad. Thankfully, I have since decided that life is worth living. Mostly, that is because I don't want to miss one moment of my sons' lives. I want to be their source of unconditional positive regard. I want to be with them in quiet and in noise, in joy and in sadness, and in all the adventures one experiences in living. It is, in part, very true that they kept me alive by needing me, because they were so young and dependent. I did not have the luxury of giving up. I had to be strong for them when I really didn't feel strong myself. For that gift, I will always be grateful.

When the boys ask me why I believe in God, "When God took Daddy," I tell them, "My God did not take Daddy; cancer did. And God gave me other people so I knew that I wasn't alone, and God gave me you wonderful boys so I always have a connection to Daddy, even now that he is gone."

Beethoven

For some people, the most deeply felt moments of spiritual connection come via the arts. Music, literature, painting, dance, film, sculpture—all these can move us to "know" what we would not know otherwise, to become acquainted with what lies beyond words, on the other side of what can be proven or detected by our five senses. We use our senses to connect with art; then art, in turn, connects us to a world beyond our senses.

Because the artist—no matter what the medium, from words to paints to musical notes to dance steps—selects what to include and arranges it in a particular order, art has a great advantage over life. Art drives out the irrelevant. In great art, not one iota that is included is random. As the playwright Chekhov said, "If the audience sees a rifle hanging on the wall in the first act, it had better go off before the final curtain falls."

Since art can condense life down—or up?—to its essentials, art allows us a unique view. Day in and day out, even the most perceptive among us does not regularly perceive the depth and meaning of what is going on around him.

However, in a play, a poem, a painting, a novel, a movie or any other work of art, the artist lifts the veil of irrelevant and chance events that obscures what is really going on. The artist wrenches order out of chaos. The artist works against entropy—the law of thermodynamics that says all life tends toward a state of disorder—and chisels the statue out of the lump of stone.

The world we enter by means of art is a magical kingdom, conceived in imagination. Art brings us into worlds we could not reach by any other means. How do you ever get to the Land of Oz, except through art? How do you ever travel into the world of Hamlet, except through his words? How do you feel the impact of van Gogh except by looking at his paintings?

In the following essay, a man expresses his love for Beethoven. As you read it, you may find yourself thinking of some place in your own life where you find the inspiration and strength this man takes from Beethoven. Maybe it is through the works of a writer you love—or a painter or a filmmaker. Maybe it is in a song, or the works of one singer. If you are lucky, you find it in many places. Wherever you find such inspiration, when you go there, you are as close to life-without-chaos—which some would call beauty and others call truth—as a human can be.

I especially like how, in this man's description, Beethoven becomes human and accessible. In this account, Beethoven is not just a great genius, writing immortal masterpieces for us mere mortals. Here, Beethoven becomes one of us. And, through his art, this mere human lifts us all out of our mundane confines to a greater place.

—E. H.

I want to describe my connection to Ludwig van Beethoven, as I experience him through his music, particularly the vast choral works of his late period, the *Missa Solemnis* and the *Ninth Symphony*.

I can remember vividly the first time that I heard these works and the impact that they both had on me. It was difficult to fathom that these were human creations, for they seemed to soar to the very heavens and to express something transcendent.

Since my initiation to the *Missa* and the *Ninth*, I have heard them literally hundreds of times; when I am fatigued, cynical, disconsolate, disconnected, I turn to them for rejuvenation of mind, body and spirit. When I listen to them, with their integration of orchestra and voices, I am transported, transformed—taken to a higher level. At times, while listening, I have sensed the unity of all things.

I have traveled long distances to hear both works, and even have been known to go to the same concert twice. These performances, and participating in them in a public setting, are the closest I come to a religious experience. As the late Robert Shaw said, "Beethoven made a religion of music." This is where I derive a sense of transcendent meaning.

Inherent in both the *Missa* and the *Ninth* is a sense of struggle and of eventual resolution and overcoming. I am moved to tears consistently by these works when I think of, to use Nietzsche's term, "the human, all too human" person who created them, despite his own adversity and despair: his unrequited loves, his personal isolation, the abuse he suffered as a child, his own alcohol abuse and the deafness that shut him off from ever hearing either of these late masterpieces.

For me, Beethoven exemplifies what it is to be human: He was flawed, often unkind—even dishonest—yet he produced some of the greatest art this world has ever known. It is his perseverance in the face of crushing adversity, his refusal to capitulate, his integrity, his commitment to excellence that so moves me, along with the optimism and the victory that emerges in these works. He gives voice to what is the best of the human spirit, and celebrates what brings us together.

I often think of the premiere of the *Ninth*, when, after the audience broke into volcanic applause, one of the soloists had to turn Beethoven around, for he had heard none of it. I feel a connection to this man, with all his imperfections, as if I really knew him, albeit only through the music. There is a universal appeal, I think, to his art, which renders it the single most popular piece of music in Japan, and explains why we turn to him to mark momentous events, such as the fall of the Berlin Wall.

Three Peonies

As I read this and envisioned the three peonies, I thought of the author, not the peonies, and I felt the kind of admiration you feel for someone who has endured more than you think you could yourself, and has done so with grace and courage. At a lecture I gave, I met the woman who wrote this. She is, indeed, both graceful and courageous. She gives off a peaceful kind of aura. I don't mean to sound spooky, but, when I met this woman, I felt that she had a divine presence. In plain English, I felt that whatever or whoever God is, God was in this woman much more fully than in most of us.

If you let yourself, you can sense this presence of God in people that you meet. If you don't dismiss it as crazy or weird, if you allow yourself to go with the feeling, you might feel a kind of pull toward such people. Some of the people toward whom you feel such a pull will be frauds and charlatans, mere charismatic leaders, people who, in fact, do monumental damage by taking advantage of our frail, human need to believe. With good reason, we reflexively mistrust such people: They have destroyed billions of lives throughout history.

But, on the other hand, some of them really do carry God's word and love to a greater degree than you can find anywhere else on Earth. I hope you do not roll your eyes as you read this. I am not a kook. But I do know that some people possess an extraordinary power of loving-kindness and courage that I choose to call the presence of God. You can find such people anywhere. One, whom I was lucky enough to know well, was a janitor for years at a public school in Roslindale, Massachusetts. Another was my old teacher, Bill Alfred. Another is the author of this piece, whom I only met briefly, for a matter of minutes. But still, I felt the unmistakable power of her spirit, just by being in her presence for those few minutes.

The last sentence of this piece is the most succinct and simple way of stating what I hope for myself and for all people I know. It is what I hope you will get from reading this book. "Working in the garden," she writes, "a task I might once have found tedious, now gives me great joy."

Working in the garden. Living this thing called life. We might as well let it give us great joy.

—E. H.

My son died last year, three days before Mother's Day. He knew how much I loved flowers and bought me three peony plants as a Mother's Day gift. He even planted them for me. At the time he planted those peonies, his death—his suicide—was the furthest thought from my mind. Since his death, I have often wondered whether he was planning to end his own life as he planted those flowers.

Although I love flowers, I had never taken the time to garden. My busy life did not afford me that luxury, and it was always so much easier to get flowers from the florist. After the tremendous shock and pain of his death diminished a bit, I was able to try to seek connections to my son in some of the things he left behind. His many essays on life in general, his poetry, his music and his "things."

But, the greatest source of connection, for me, has been the garden I have been able to nurture around those three peonies, his last gift, his one last act of love. I have since planted many beautiful flowers, some purchased, some from friends—both my son's and my family's.

As winter turned into spring, I looked forward with excitement to see which flowers would bloom. My garden, with its array of flowers of various colors, textures and sizes, connects me in a real and special way to my son. He was a wonderful boy. In so many ways, my garden reminds me of him and keeps me connected to him. Working in the garden, a task I might once have found tedious, now gives me great joy.

CREATING
CONNECTIONS . . .

Invitation to reflect: How do you envision God?

Common obstacles to connection: Many people leave religion and spirituality out of their lives because they have been turned off by organized religion, and can't find an alternative they feel comfortable with. So, they sidestep the Big Questions, like what happens to us after we die, or why is there evil in the world. This is a mistake. You don't have to join an organized religion to develop a spiritual life. It is a mistake to avoid the Big Questions. You don't have to have the answers. As one man prayed, "Lord, help me always to seek for the truth, but spare me the company of those who have found it."

Possible steps to take:

Look into the eyes of a child.
Plant and tend a garden. Do it for at least a few years.
Listen to Beethoven or Louis Armstrong.
Walk the beach.
Visit the graveside of someone you love.
Turn fifty.
Hold a baby in your arms.

Fall in love.

Suffer injustice without simply blaming the bad guy.

Try to feel charitably toward one person you really dislike.

Keep asking the questions you can't answer.

Say good-bye to someone, knowing you'll never see that person again.

Swim underwater about five yards farther than you thought you could, then come up for air.

Win when you knew for sure you'd lose.

Lose when you knew for sure you'd win.

Talk to God, even if you have no idea what, or who, God is.

HUMAN MOMENTS
NEVER DIE

Just before I completed this book, an aunt of mine died. Her real name was Mary Francis McKey Hallowell, but I always called her Duckie, a name she acquired before I was born, back when the whole extended family lived on a farm. Mary Francis's hair was white, so someone imagined she looked like a duck, and the name stuck.

The week before she died, Sue and I drove down to Providence to visit her. We knew—and she knew—that she was dying. We sat and we talked about all kinds of things.

Dressed simply in her nightgown and robe, she still looked elegant, as she always did. She was frail, hard-of-hearing, and, at times, confused, but still, her eyes sparkled when Sue and I walked in for our visit of farewell.

I poured us some Scotch—her favorite drink—while Sue had a glass of wine, and I put out a little Canton china bowl filled with Pepperidge Farm goldfish. Duckie always had goldfish on hand, as well as Scotch.

In her small living room, we were surrounded by photographs, including one I also had on the wall in my house, a photograph of Duckie's father, the man I called Skipper.

At the beginning of this book, I wrote about Skipper and how he taught me to shake hands, so it seems fitting that I should turn to Skipper, and his daughter, Duckie, to shake hands and close up the book.

As I looked at Skipper's face in the photograph that night, and at Sue's face and Duckie's face (soon to be gone, only a photograph remaining), I sensed that the eternal ran through this room, from face to photograph to face, from past to present to future, all entwined. Was the Scotch getting to me? Maybe. But I sensed that I was in the presence of something that would never—*could never*—come to an end. It was too strong to disappear. Skipper had come before, then he did what we call "die"; Duckie, soon, would follow him; Sue and I would have more time, then go; and Lucy, Jack and Tucker would, as well. As much as I feared these dyings, I could almost hear Skipper's voice reassuring us: *Don't be afraid. It all works out.*

What was with us that night was not anything new, not even anything I hadn't always sensed, however dimly, as I lived my life. It had been present all along. It just became so vivid as to be unmistakable that night.

Whatever it is—the force that can never die—has been the subject of this book. It is the life force, and it appears most vividly in intense human moments.

Sue and Duckie and I talked for an hour or so, until Duckie, gradually, got tired. I asked her how she wanted me to remember her, and she said, looking off into the distance,

"Oh, you know, just as I always was, just as we always were. Just the truth."

In the human moment, that's all you need. Just the truth. It is more than enough to feed your soul, if you let it, if you feel in every human moment what Keats called "the holiness of the heart's affections."

Before we left, we helped Duckie into bed. I leaned down and gave her a kiss, as Sue adjusted her pillows. We both told Duckie that we loved her. She took our hands, Sue's and mine, and squeezed them hard, in the same firm grip her father, Skipper, had taught me years ago. She looked at each of us and said, using the Quaker terminology she always used for those close to her, "I love thee, and I love thee." She paused for a moment, then added, "Nighty-night." Those were her last words to us. But they were only her last words spoken out loud. I will hear her words in my mind and feel them in my heart forever.

Human moments never die.

An Invitation to Readers

First of all, let me thank you for taking the time to read this book. In today's world, time is a more precious commodity than ever; I am grateful you invested some of your time here. I hope what you found made the investment worthwhile. I would love to hear your comments and respond to any questions or suggestions you might have about future books in this series.

All the future books will be based on the idea of *human moments*. Each book will focus on one grouping of human moments—for example, human moments with children, or human moments at work, or human moments with grandparents. I would like to invite you to send me stories of human moments from your own life, regardless of what category they might belong to, stories that I could include in upcoming books in the *Human Moments* series.

After reading this book, I hope you have a pretty good idea of what I mean by a "human moment": those moments when we feel connected to someone or something outside of ourselves, and in the presence of what matters most to us.

If you have human moments you'd like to send me, I would love to receive them. I plan for each book in this series to follow the format of this book, and include stories both from my life and from the lives of others.

If you do send me a story, just write it from your heart and forget about spelling and grammar for now. Make it whatever length you want. The stories I will include in future books will average one thousand to three thousand words, but I would love to read whatever you send to me, regardless of length.

You may send your story to me via my Web site at:

www.DrHallowell.com

Or you may send it by regular mail to my office in Sudbury, Massachusetts. That address is:

The Hallowell Center
142 North Road
Sudbury, MA 01776

About the Author

DR Edward M. (Ned) Hallowell is an instructor at Harvard Medical School and the director of The Hallowell Center for Cognitive and Emotional Health in Sudbury, Massachusetts, a center serving children and adults.

Dr. Hallowell is the creator and editor of a monthly newsletter on mental well-being called *Mind Matters*, and he is the author of the bestsellers, *Connect: 12 Vital Ties That Open Your Heart, Lengthen Your Life, and Deepen Your Soul*; and *Worry: Controlling It, Using It Wisely*; and the coauthor of the bestseller, *Driven to Distraction*. In addition, he is an internationally acknowledged expert on ADD, has appeared several times as a guest expert on *Oprah*, and is frequently featured in *Prevention* magazine. He lives in Arlington, Massachusetts, with his wife Sue, a social worker, and their three children, Lucy, Jack and Tucker.

To contact Dr. Hallowell or learn more about his newsletter, books or The Hallowell Center, you may reach him via his Web site at:

www.DrHallowell.com.